ROSE CITY JUSTICE

Rose City JUSTICE

A Legal History of Portland, Oregon

Fred Leeson

Oregon Historical Society Press
Published in cooperation
with the Oregon State Bar

Cover photos, left to right:
Mark O. Hatfield United States Courthouse (BOORA Architects),
Portland Mayor Dorothy McCullough Lee (*The Oregonian*),
U.S. District Court Judge Matthew Deady (OHS CN002391),
Multnomah County Circuit Court Judge Ancer Haggerty (*The Oregonian*).
Since the photo was taken, Judge Haggerty has become a U.S. District Court judge.

Printed in the United States of America.

Designed and produced by the Oregon Historical Society Press.

The paper used in this publication meets the minimum requirements of American National Standard for Information Sciences—Permanence of Paper for Printed Library Materials, ANSI Z39.48-1984.

First Edition

Leeson, Fred
Rose City justice: a legal history of Portland, Oregon / Fred Leeson
288 p. cm.
Includes bibliographical references and index.
(ISBN 0-87595-269-0 (alk. paper)
1. Lawyers – Oregon – Portland – History. 2. Practice of law – Oregon – Portland – History. 3. Justice, Administration of – Oregon – Portland – History. 4. Portland (Ore.) – History. I. Title.
KF355.P67L44 1998
349.795'49 – dc21

98-40991
CIP

To those who taught me what's most important:
Barbara, Slade and Ben.

The Oregon Historical Society
and the Oregon State Bar
thank the following for
their support of this publication

Bullivant Houser Bailey, a Professional Corporation
Davis Wright Tremaine LLP
Pozzi Wilson Atchison LLP
Schwabe Williamson & Wyatt
Stoel Rives LLP

Maree Noble & Elizabeth Stumpf Memorial Foundation
Wentworth Foundation

John Arenz
Bowen Blair, Jr.
Jeanne T. Leeson
Susan M. Leeson
Mr. and Mrs. Robert W. McMenamin
William G. Wheatley

Table of Contents

Acknowledgements

History books have histories of their own. The story of this one could fill a chapter. The short version, however, is that *Rose City Justice* would have never occurred without the persistence of Robert W. McMenamin, a lawyer, author and past chairman of the Multnomah Bar Association's History Committee, who believed that his community deserved a history of its legal profession. When the first proposed publisher went into bankruptcy, McMenamin rescued the project by negotiating a joint effort with Chet Orloff, director of the Oregon Historical Society, and William G. Wheatley, chairman of the Oregon State Bar's Legal Heritage Committee. McMenamin then undertook the onerous job of raising money to meet publishing costs. Despite his dedication to the project, McMenamin never attempted to exert editorial influence over the manuscript, other than his oft-repeated encouragement to include humor wherever possible. An author couldn't ask for a better working relationship.

Many others lent helping hands along the way. Mary Oberst, of the Oregon State Bar staff, volunteered to edit the manuscript, a task she undertook with diligence and sensitivity. Cathy Ingram, also of the bar staff, designed the cover and layout. Marylee Lowry, as a member of the Multnomah Bar Association History Committee, collected material from Portland law firms that had traced their individual histories. Adair Law, publications director at the Oregon Historical Society, and Paul Nickell, editor of the Oregon State Bar *Bulletin*, coordinated production and offered many helpful suggestions. Jean Brownell compiled the index. The author also appreciated help from the staffs of the Multnomah County Library, Multnomah Law Library, Oregon Historical Society Library and the library of the Oregonian Publishing Co. The Oregon Historical Society and the Oregonian Publishing Co. graciously allowed use of photographs from their respective files. The author also wishes to thank many lawyers and judges who took time over several years to share reminiscences.

Finally, the author wishes to thank relatives who helped in a variety of ways. My wife, Barbara Coleman, assisted in research of the early chapters. My sister, the Honorable Susan M. Leeson, read several chapters and made helpful suggestions. My mother, Jeanne T. Leeson, cleaned up sloppy grammar. Special thanks also go to my sons, Slade and Benjamin Leeson, who proved that their father's prose could soar, if only briefly, by folding early drafts into paper airplanes.

Introduction

James Finch carried a revolver in his coat pocket and vengeance on his mind as he headed to the third floor of the Mohawk Building in downtown Portland. He walked into the law office of Ralph Fisher and paused briefly until Fisher's secretary waved him past.

Fisher had turned his chair from his desk and was gazing out the window into a late November afternoon. His view included a tangle of trolley-car wires and horse-drawn vehicles, mixed in with a few automobiles and gasoline trucks on the cobblestone streets below.

"Hello, Ralph," Finch said.[1] Fisher never had time to turn from the window before Finch shot him twice in the back of the head. The murder of Ralph Fisher on November 28, 1908, marked a tragic confluence of the best and worst elements of Portland's growing legal profession. Fisher had volunteered with the young Multnomah Bar Association to prosecute ethics violations. Finch was a lawyer with a history of ethics problems and alcohol abuse who had been disbarred as a result of Fisher's efforts. Finch was angry that Fisher wouldn't recommend his reinstatement to legal practice by the Oregon Supreme Court in less than one year. Of course, the possibility of reinstatement for Finch died with Fisher. Finch paid for his crime thirteen months later on the gallows at the Oregon State Penitentiary.

Criminal justice doesn't work as swiftly at the end of the same century, but some other aspects of the profession haven't changed, such as its continuing concern about its public image. Improving lawyers' standing in the community was among the reasons for creation of the voluntary Oregon Bar Association in 1892, the Multnomah Bar Association in 1906, and the Oregon State Bar in 1935. Founders of those organizations believed, as did Fisher, that vigilant policing of professional ethics would improve the profession's public standing.

By the end of the twentieth century, the Oregon State Bar could point to evidence suggesting that it was among the best in the nation for policing its members' conduct. Still, the profession waged long internal debates about lawyer advertising—a product of the 1970s—and whether such soliciting in telephone directories, television commercials, and letters to injury victims damaged the profession's reputation. Lawyers and judges wrote often in the Oregon State Bar Bulletin about insulting references to the profession that had taken on a generic name of their own: lawyer bashing. In retrospect, perhaps Ralph Fisher died in vain, but at least no other Portland lawyer since him has died at the hands of another lawyer.

Lawyers almost daily put their hands on tools of history as they use statutes and cases to evaluate and shape contemporary behavior. Unfortunately, the context and human drama of the underlying history is usually shorn away in the process. The profession has done little, with a few notable exceptions, to preserve its successes and occasional failings in an accessible form to a broader audience. Fortunately, that is changing. Some lawyers are using lengthy taped interviews to capture the personalities and tales of prominent lawyers and judges who are still living. Many of Portland's older law firms have been researching their histories for their own edification or for use in promotional materials. The inspiration for this volume began with a history committee of the Multnomah Bar Association in 1992. The Heritage Committee of the Oregon State Bar, created in 1996, decided to adopt the work-in-progress as a part of that committee's efforts to preserve state-wide legal history and artifacts.

The purpose of this volume is to recount many of the significant lawyers, judges, and cases that have highlighted more than 150 years in the history of Portland and the tiny, wooded village that preceded municipal incorporation. In many instances, Portland lawyers worked diligently to protect or to expand civil liberties in cases that affect all Americans. In some notable battles, lawyers have been pitted against their own profession. Beyond courtrooms and cases, however, Portland lawyers have made contributions to the physical development of Portland and to many institutions that help make the Rose City the special place that many of us believe it is. Even the city's nickname was advanced and promoted by a prominent lawyer whose avocation was roses.

Because history is no more tidy than the reality it is based upon, readers will find the tracks of some scoundrels here, as well. The author's purpose is neither to enshrine lawyers nor to attack them. As with any profession, lawyers come from differing personal backgrounds and bring to their work varying degrees of ethical commitment. From its earliest days to the present, Portland's legal community can claim outstanding models of professional virtue. Despite the profession's best efforts, however, it is unrealistic to think it can rid itself fully of members who succumb to temptations of greed, power, or shady practices.

At most, perhaps, this book is an outline. Several figures in the pages that follow, such as C. E. S. Wood, Gus Solomon, George H. Williams, Charles H. Carey, and John Hipple Mitchell to name a few, would be worthy of separate biographies. The collection of notables here is intended to be neither exclusive nor exhaustive. The author is reminded of William L. Prosser's note in the introduction to his massive *Law of Torts*: "A packrat is at best a collector… and the most that can be said for him is that he sometimes chooses well."[2] The packrat of this volume offers a couple special items. The appendix contains lists of judges and public lawyers, two of which—Multnomah County District Court and the old Portland Municipal Court—apparently have never been compiled before. The author also is pleased to restore Mercedes F. Deiz to her place as the first African-American woman lawyer in Oregon, a distinction that was erroneously bestowed on Beatrice Cannady in another local history book.

Readers may detect a preference in these pages for lawyers who have been involved in community activities. If so, it is because these attorneys have left more tracks in their community than those who confined themselves to their law offices. The civic activists also have been willing to give of themselves to improve their community. Love them or not, lawyers ought to be involved in their profession and in their city. That need will be just as great in the new century as at any time in Portland's history.

Fred Leeson, Portland, Oregon, October 1998.

Photo by Rick Keating

Mark O. Hatfield U.S. Courthouse.

CHAPTER ONE

Pioneer Days

Portland's skyline had seen nothing like it. Although not extraordinarily tall at 317 feet and sixteen stories, the building was an eye-catching blend of angular jigs and jags, wrapped in limestone and mirrored glass, accented with stainless steel, and topped by a graceful air-foil arch for a roof. An outdoor garden blossomed from the top of a lower section rising eight stories on the building's south side. At first glance, it wouldn't occur to a passerby that the unusual, playful-looking new tower was a government building, let alone the headquarters of the smallest, least-understood, and perhaps most conservative of the federal government's three branches. When the building's doors opened to the public in 1997, a passerby had to look to the small lettering to determine it was the Mark O. Hatfield United States Courthouse.

The new federal courthouse, the third such building in Portland's 146 years as a municipality, was a paragon of modern judicial design. Its labyrinthine interior had separate hallways for the public, for jurors, and for judges. A judge could park in the basement of the impressive new tower and proceed by elevator to his or her chambers without risk of unnecessary exposure to jurors, citizens, criminal defendants, litigants, or lawyers. Layouts for the fifteen new courtrooms had been tested long beforehand in a full-scale mock-up in a Portland warehouse to eliminate potential flaws in sight lines, roominess, and movement of people. Citizens leaving the sleek new courtrooms found themselves walking into stunning hallways with glass walls extending from floor to ceiling, offering panoramic views of the city from many angles. The light airiness of the architecture marked a new direction for federal courthouse construction in Portland, and in the nation. "This court has felt that federal courts shouldn't be so intimidating," said U.S. District Court Judge Malcolm Marsh, who worked with the architectural team of Bill Pederson, of New York City, and a Portland firm known as BOOR/A during the design stage.[1]

The absence of customary architectural trappings such as marble walls, Greek columns, and classical symmetry wasn't the only odd feature about the new courthouse. There also was the name. In his thirty years as a United States senator, Hatfield had reaped abundant federal funding for all sorts of projects in his state, including the new courthouse and its $128 million price tag. But Hatfield was neither a lawyer nor a judge. The name on the building very well could have gone to another veteran Oregon congressman and lawyer, just as it had more than twenty years earlier when Wendell Wyatt's name graced a new federal office building two blocks south of the Hatfield Courthouse. The most likely candidate would have been Bob Packwood, who had practiced law in Portland before being elected to the Senate in 1968, a mere two years after Hatfield's first election. However, by the time Congress named the courthouse in Hatfield's honor in 1996, Packwood was no longer in the Senate and out of the running for any honorific titles. A storm of controversy over his behavior toward women and other misconduct had forced him to resign in disgrace.

Startling as it was, Packwood's dénouement in the Senate wasn't the first time that a former Portland lawyer ended a long Senate career in disgrace. By selecting just the right angle from an upper corner of the new Hatfield Courthouse, a viewer could glimpse a portion of the site where Senator John Mitchell's Senate career came to an ignominious end in a federal criminal trial in 1905. The old U.S. Building, as it was called in Mitchell's era, nearly succumbed to disuse and demolition many years later.

However, a far-sighted campaign led to restoration of the city's first federal building, and Pioneer Courthouse with its quaint nineteenth-century cupola resumed playing a vital role in Portland's legal community.

While the view of Pioneer Courthouse was substantially blocked by other buildings, visitors could use the roof-top garden and the vast expanses of glass in the Hatfield Courthouse to peruse a rich legal landscape below. To the west, across a small green park graced with towering elms, stood the blocky Multnomah County Courthouse, the second to sit on the same block, where countless Portlanders dealt with such things as parking tickets, broken marriages, and the ugly criminal behavior of a major American city. Turning slightly to the south, a visitor could see the Gus Solomon U.S. Courthouse, the second home of Portland's federal trial courts, named after a judge who earned national recognition for his efforts for civil liberties, but whose demeanor struck terror into many lawyers who appeared before him. At the same angle, closer yet, stood Portland City Hall, another nineteenth century architectural antique, where lawyers and others thrashed out land-use plans that shaped the city. On the block immediately south of the new courthouse sat the Multnomah County Justice Center, a fourteen-story tower containing the largest county jail in Oregon plus the headquarters of the Portland Police Bureau and four courtrooms.

Looking in almost any direction, one could see other modern office towers. Nearly all of them contained law firms, a few tracing their roots back a century or more, where lawyers quietly went about the business of building fortunes for their corporate clients, and often for themselves. Perhaps the most historic view, however, was to the east, where the wide, gently curving waters of the Willamette River rolled northward to their eventual confluence with the Columbia River. If a person could stand on the top of the new courthouse and reel back the past 150 years or so—a mere two lifetimes placed end to end—a viewer could imagine how the scene looked to Portland's pioneers.

Verdant forests still sloped down to the muddy edge of the Willamette River when Asa Lovejoy and F. W. Pettygrove eased their small craft into that clearing on the river's west bank. It was early 1845 and the two pioneers had a dispute to settle on the wooded townsite to which they had staked a claim. Lovejoy, the first lawyer to practice in the Oregon Territory, had taken a half-interest in the claim with Pettygrove when he agreed in 1843 to file the papers and pay the twenty-five cent filing fee. Their proposed townsite, which at the time was only a small clearing about halfway on the river between Fort Vancouver and Dr. John McLoughlin's new settlement at Oregon City, did not have a name. Lovejoy, a graduate of Amherst College and a native of Groton, Massachusetts, suggested "Boston." Pettygrove, a native of Maine, wanted "Portland."

The two men agreed to settle their dispute by tossing an 1835 copper penny. It would be an efficient dispute-resolution technique: inexpensive and final. There would be no appeals. Pettygrove picked "tails," and won two-out-of-three flips. The township became known as Portland.

OHS OrHi 1432

Asa Lovejoy.

Within a couple of decades, the forest would be cleared and Portland would become the fastest-growing city on the West Coast. From the moment of Lovejoy's coin toss until the present, Portland lawyers would play major roles in the economic, physical, and political growth of the new city. Although Portland never would become Oregon's capital or the home of the state's appellate courts, the size and quality of its bar made it the legal nerve center of the lush and thriving new state.

On the legal front, Portland lawyers and judges quickly became involved in cases and issues that would set precedents across the United States. Aside from their legal pursuits, the city's attorneys would make lasting contributions to history and the arts, as well as creating and expanding the city's cultural organizations. Some would build powerful political machines, and others would tear them down. Some would reach heights of honorable ethical stands. Others would outrage their fellow citizens with their scandalous behavior.

Lovejoy, who was a member of the first wagon train that arrived in Oregon in 1842, didn't keep his Portland holding for long. He sold his share in November 1845 to Benjamin Stark, who a few years later also would study law and become a lawyer. Stark paid Lovejoy $1,215 for his half-interest in the Portland site and for fifty-five head of Lovejoy's cattle in the neighboring Tualatin valley. Given the value of the cattle, Lovejoy's twenty-five cent investment in Portland netted him a return of about $390.[2] Lovejoy took his profit and returned fifteen miles up the river to Oregon City, where he was elected mayor in 1846, and served as speaker of the House of Representatives in the Provisional Legislature of 1846.

Oregon City, with about seventy houses and a population of five hundred, became the seat of the provisional government in 1845, and later capital of the Oregon Territory when President James Polk encouraged Congress to establish the Oregon Territory in the waning days of his administration in 1848. Polk wanted to see the nation's boundaries extend from the Atlantic to the Pacific before his term ended. But even with its status as a territorial capital, the limits on Oregon City's growth already were obvious: rapids and sand bars blocked ocean-going vessels from navigating the full thirty miles up the Willamette River to its shores. Somewhere below

Oregon City, it stood to reason, there would be a townsite that could serve the growing shipping trade of the region and also be accessible to the fertile Tualatin valley to the west.

Another early Oregon lawyer, Peter H. Burnett, bet on Linnton, a townsite he named and tried to promote several miles north of Portland in 1845. Burnett, a Tennessee native, came to Oregon from Missouri in 1843 at age thirty-six. Like Lovejoy, he set up a law office at Oregon City. Burnett served as a legislator and judge under the provisional government, the origins of which stemmed from a probate problem arising in 1841. Ewing Young, a Willamette Valley cattleman, died without heirs and without a will. Settlers feared there would be violence by those interested in taking over Young's cattle unless there was a mechanism for handling his estate. Dr. Ira C. Babcock, a pioneer physician who was one of about two hundred fifty settlers in the region at the time, was appointed as a judge at a settlers' meeting in February 1841. Two years later, Dr. Babcock turned over proceeds from the estate to another meeting of settlers held at Champoeg, where settlers, by a fifty-two-to-fifty vote, decided they needed a formal government.

Burnett served as a judge on the provisional court, which kept no records. In 1848 he was appointed as one of the first three judges on the Oregon territorial supreme court, but he quickly resigned. Drawn by the lure of instant riches, Burnett and many young men like him rushed off to the California gold fields, leaving behind his townsite at Linnton, which, until several decades later when it became an industrial appendage to Portland, never amounted to more than a single shack. But Burnett was still young. He found both financial and political success in California, where he served as California's first American governor after Mexico ceded California to the United States and later as a member of the California Supreme Court. After resigning from the court, Burnett became president of the Pacific Bank of San Francisco, which he had helped establish.

Back in Portland, other entrepreneurs pinned their hopes on Milwaukie and Linn City, between Portland and Oregon City, and on St. Johns and St. Helens to the north, as potential sites for the major city of the Willamette valley. William W. Chapman, a lawyer and entrepreneur, poled the depths of the Willamette and bought a portion of the Portland townsite in 1849. Chapman was a native Virginian and former Iowa legislator and former U. S. Attorney for the Wisconsin Territory. He crossed the plains to Oregon in 1847 with his wife and seven children when he was thirty-nine years old. Like Burnett, Chapman rushed to the California gold fields in 1848. But apparently after meeting some success as a prospector, Chapman decided to stake his future on Oregon.

Based on his readings of the Willamette River, Chapman figured that ocean-going vessels could make it as far as Portland, but that sand bars and other obstacles would prevent any further southerly access. His hunch proved correct: there were fortunes to be made in Portland. They would be based not on the flashy gold-rush underpinnings of cities like Sacramento and San Francisco, but on steadier, lasting endeavors such as shipping, timber, farming, and real estate development. Chapman teamed up with two pioneer entrepreneurs, Stephen Coffin and Daniel Lownsdale. The trio sold off lots and actively promoted Portland. A tannery, a sawmill, and a shingle mill became the village's first

OHS CN000522

William W. Chapman.

factories. The little village was referred to by some as "Stump Town" because of forest obstacles still rooted in its primitive streets. Chapman built a log cabin for his family on the block that later would become the site of the Multnomah County Courthouse.

During a trip to San Francisco in 1849, Chapman recruited a newspaper editor, T. J. Dryer, to initiate a paper in Portland in 1850. The newspaper, although not the first in the territory, was considered a coup for the struggling little village as it tried to assert dominance in the region. Chapman suggested a name for Dryer's new weekly: *The Oregonian*. After more than a century of spirited journalism with several competitors, Dryer's publication would prevail as Portland's only daily newspaper. Chapman also recruited partners to invest in the *Gold Hunter*, a steamer that plied between Portland and San Francisco, helping to cement Portland's future as a seaport. He also helped promote and build the Great Plank Road, which linked his new village to the cattle and farming lands of the Tualatin valley. This vital early trade route generally followed the path now taken by the Sunset Highway and Canyon Road to Beaverton.

By 1850, the number of white settlers in the expansive Oregon Territory had climbed to some 9,000. But the territory still did not have a courthouse. Many early legal proceedings were held outdoors. A major exception was what might be called the territory's first high-profile trial— the 1850 murder trial of five Cayuse Indians accused of killing pioneer missionary Marcus Whitman. Whitman and his wife, Narcissa, and eleven other residents at the Whitman Mission located twenty miles east of Walla Walla (in what is now Washington) were killed by gunshots and hatchets during the incident on November 29, 1847. Some two-and-a-half years later, Cayuse tribal leaders turned over five tribal members to stand trial at the territorial seat in Oregon City.

A crowd of approximately three hundred settlers came to watch in May 1850 when Judge Orville C. Pratt convened the case in a hotel saloon on the east bank of the Willamette. Pratt, a native of Rushville, New York, passed the New York bar in 1840, after dropping out of the U.S. Military Academy at the end of two years. He also had practiced law in Illinois before being appointed as one of the first Oregon territorial judges by President Polk, along with Burnett and William P. Bryant. Amory Holbrook, appointed as U.S. attorney for the territory by President Polk, served as prosecutor. Pratt appointed Kintzing Pritchette secretary of the territory, and two nonlawyer members of the military to represent the Cayuse defendants. Pritchette had been trained as a lawyer in Pennsylvania and served as secretary for the Michigan Territory for two years before taking the equivalent appointment in Oregon.

Although the trial lasted over portions of four days, all testimony from prosecution and defense witnesses occurred in the equivalent of less than one day. Settlers of the era and historical accounts later portrayed the Whitman Massacre as a savage, unprovoked attack. Pritchette, however, presented some defense evidence indicating that the Cayuse were upset because many tribal members—sometimes five or six per day—had been dying of measles after being treated by Whitman's medicines. At least some of the Cayuse feared poisoning. Furthermore, trial evidence indicated that one defendant who was present during the attack was not armed. Nevertheless, the jury of twelve settlers returned a unanimous verdict of guilty after one juror held out briefly. The territory's lack of a prison made the sentencing all the easier for Judge Pratt: death by hanging. The five defendants were hanged in public view in Oregon City on June 6, 1850.[3]

Pratt's expeditious handling of the Cayuse trial and sentencing came as no surprise. He had a reputation as an aggressive businessman as well as a stern judge who acted quickly and, at times, impetuously. As a judge, Pratt frequently displayed a sharp temper. Chapman, the early Portland developer and lawyer, felt Pratt's wrath in October 1851, when Pratt held him in contempt for submitting an affidavit accusing Pratt of mistreating lawyers.

Pratt ordered Chapman to be disbarred and to be held by the sheriff for twenty days in Hillsboro. Hillsboro was the county seat of Tuality County, which then included the village of Portland. But Pratt's order was foiled when friends rescued Chapman from the sheriff and returned him to Portland. Chapman was rearrested and then rescued a second time before Chief Justice Thomas Nelson, a New York native who replaced Bryant on the Territorial Court in 1850, overruled Pratt's contempt order.

At a time when his annual judicial salary was $2,000, Pratt was said to have amassed more than $1 million as a trader of such goods as lumber, boots, and cook stoves during his seven years in Oregon. Pratt, whose judicial assignment covered the portion of the territory including Portland, a village of fewer than fifty people when he first arrived, was the leading figure among the three original territorial judges. None of them, however, left behind particularly enviable records. Burnett turned down his commission to pursue gold in California and never sat with the territorial court. The other original member, Bryant, served only six months and convened court on only a few dates between April and October of 1849. Bryant was born in Kentucky in 1806 and had served as a circuit court judge and as a state senator in Indiana before landing the territorial appointment. After expressing a distaste for travel in the territory, Bryant returned to Washington, D.C., where he lob-

OHS OrHi 45995

Territorial Judge Orville C. Pratt.

bied for passage of the Donation Land Law of 1850.

Until adoption of that act, there had been no formal means of perfecting legal title to land in the territory. Bryant's lobbying was motivated at least in part by flagrant self-interest. During his brief stay in Oregon, Bryant had bought from George Abernethy, Oregon's provisional governor, an interest in a critical Willamette River island at Oregon City to which both Abernethy and John McLoughlin claimed ownership. The island became the home of the state's first lumber mill, fueled by the raging waters near Willamette Falls. Bryant, still wearing the mantle of territorial judge even though he would never return to the Oregon Territory, successfully lobbied for the exclusion of McLoughlin's claim to the island in the Donation Land Law. Bryant at the time had sold his interest to Joseph Lane, the first territorial governor, but he still held $20,000 in notes when he lobbied for what became known as the McLoughlin Land Grab.[4] That law otherwise granted legal standing to the previously informal claims of other territorial pioneers. Ironically, a flood later wiped out Lane's profitable lumber mill, and the Oregon Legislature, five years after McLoughlin's death, tried to erase the injustice by restoring the island to his estate.

Although Pratt was clearly the hardest-working of the original territorial judges, his interest in law paled in comparison to his interest in politics. While a judge, he became leader of the territory's Democratic party and declared his desire to be elected to the U.S. House of Representatives by the territorial legislature. He was defeated, however, by fifty-three votes to six in 1855. The embarrassing defeat convinced Pratt that he had no political future in Oregon. In 1856, he moved to San Francisco, where he lived until his death in 1891. An indication of his success as a businessman and trader surfaced in 1875 when he settled a messy divorce with his first wife for $750,000, a sizable fortune for the time.[5]

Like other pioneers, Portland lawyers kept their eyes open for new opportunities. Chapman, for example, left Portland in 1853 for southern

Oregon. He held the federal post of surveyor general of Oregon from 1857 to 1861, when he quit because he had opposed the new Lincoln administration. Chapman returned to legal practice in Portland, where he became a major figure in the intense legal and political fighting over the coming of the railroads in the 1870s. When Chapman left Portland in 1853, the town was pulling ahead of its rivals on the river in population and importance.

The streets were still muddy and unpaved, but brick buildings were beginning to replace the clapboard structures on the streets closest to the river. Portland's population had grown to 700 in 1852, and by 1855 it had nearly doubled again, to 1,209 people, establishing Portland as the largest city in the territory. In 1854, the territorial legislature recognized the importance of the growing town on the banks of the Willamette. Legislators carved out a new county, the territory's smallest, to be called Multnomah County. Portland, soon to be the state's largest city, was designated the county seat.

Chapman's departure in 1853 coincided with the arrival of two more lawyers who would leave lasting marks on the new city, Matthew Deady and George H. Williams. Both men were appointed to the three-member Oregon territorial supreme court, joining Justice Cyrus Olney, a former circuit court judge in Iowa, who was appointed earlier the same year.

Williams and Deady brought entirely different backgrounds to the pioneer settlement. Williams, born in 1823 in New York, studied law and moved to Iowa, where he became a circuit judge while still in his twenties. During his Iowa years, he befriended Abraham Lincoln and served as a pallbearer at Lincoln's funeral. Williams made his first appearance in Oregon by appointment of President Franklin Pierce, whom Williams had supported as an elector from Iowa in the 1852 election. Over the next fifty years, Williams served as a territorial judge, United States Senator from Oregon from 1865 to 1871, and U.S. Attorney General under President Grant, who nominated Williams as Chief Justice of the United States Supreme Court in

1874. As senator, Williams helped draft the Fourteenth Amendment and write post-Civil War Reconstruction-era laws. Williams' lengthy service to Portland ended with a term as mayor from 1902 to 1905.

Deady came from humbler beginnings. The son of a Maryland teacher, he emigrated to Ohio, where he apprenticed as a blacksmith while studying to become a lawyer and teacher. Deady worked his way across the plains as a blacksmith, arriving in Lafayette, Oregon, in 1849. He practiced law, taught school, and served in the territorial legislature of 1850 before his appointment to the territorial court.

Members of the territorial supreme court traveled individually around the territory as trial judges and, with a quorum of two, heard appeals as well. The first judges heard few cases and established no mechanism for reporting opinions. The only written records were newspaper accounts of decisions. Furthermore, legal practice in early Portland and the rest of the territory was complicated by an absence of law books and confusion over the earliest laws.

The first territorial legislature, at Chapman's suggestion in 1849, adopted the revised statutes of Iowa of 1843 as territorial laws. This body of law came to be known as the "Chapman Code," or the "Big Blue Book." It was intended to replace the "Little Blue Book" of laws from Iowa adopted by the provisional government. But the Chapman Code wasn't published until 1853 because the territory had no equipment for publishing and binding books. And by then territorial judges were split by a legal technicality over which set of laws was in force. That difficulty was compounded by the fact there were no more than a few copies of either code in existence. A new code, based generally on New York state laws, was finished in 1853 and printed in New York, but a ship carrying two hundred copies of the new statues sank near the mouth of the Columbia River. New editions finally arrived in 1855.

Reuben P. Boise, a Massachusetts lawyer who emigrated to Oregon in 1850, found that the lack of reference materials didn't hamper the oral advocacy of the early-day lawyers. After arguing an early divorce case in Hillsboro, Boise recalled late in his life, "When the speeches of the learned counsel had been concluded, being much longer than I had been used to hearing in the courts of Massachusetts, I became impressed with the fact that the arguments of lawyers lengthened as the distance from the seats of legal learning increased."[6] Boise, who first settled on 640 acres near Dallas, was elected territorial district attorney in 1852, and later served a total of thirty-five years as a judge. His tenure began just before statehood by appointment of President Buchanan to the territorial supreme court in 1858. He served until 1870, then ran and was elected in 1875 for a total of four more years. Boise later served as a circuit court judge after the legislature established circuit courts in 1878.

Upon his arrival to the territorial court in 1853, Williams established a formal reporting system in which written decisions were bound into volumes, called Oregon Reports. Decisions of the provisional court sometimes had been printed in newspapers, but lawyers before Williams' time had no formal means of tracking court precedents. Williams and Deady tackled their new duties enthusiastically, often staying in private homes as travel necessitated. Court was held without benefit of courthouses or the customary trappings of courtrooms. Hearings occurred in private buildings and sometimes in taverns. Boise remembered

OHS CN 017808

Reuben P. Boise.

one case being heard at Eugene in 1854 "in the open air under a large oak tree, with a table and chair for the judge and some chairs and rude benches for the lawyers and other attendants, and when the court business got slack, we adjourned to the race track, which was nearby."[7]

While riding the circuit in 1854, Judge Deady wrote to a friend, "Logan has been here during the term. He has been beastly drunk and gambling since the first day. When I am not about he flourishes his revolver and says that he will shoot me on the bench, that he came out here to shoot me down himself."[8]

No such tragedy ever befell Deady, whose flaming red hair and blacksmith physique commanded respect. Deady was referring to Portland attorney David Logan. Logan was a Kentucky native who spent most of his youth in Springfield, Illinois, where his father, Stephen T. Logan, was a law partner of Abraham Lincoln. David Logan was admitted to the bar in Illinois in 1844 and practiced for a time with his father. The two did not always get along, however, ostensibly because of the son's penchant for liquor. Stephen Logan provided his son a wagon and provisions for a trip to Oregon in 1849.

After briefly operating a ferry on the Willamette River near Salem, Logan opened a law office in Lafayette. Like other pioneers, Logan knew there would be a great new city somewhere in Oregon. "I am living at this place

OHS OrHi 86816

David Logan.

and shall remain there until the point is discovered where the great city of the Pacific is to be, and to that place I shall go," he wrote to relatives late in 1850.[9] Within months, Logan moved to Portland and formed a law partnership with Chapman in 1851. Despite his proclivity for tippling, Logan quickly became the leading trial lawyer of his era. He entertained jurors with a biting and often sarcastic wit, which flourished a few years later when he joined Deady and Williams as delegates to the state constitutional convention of 1857. After Logan's death in 1874, an editorial in *The Oregonian* lauded him as being the state's best trial lawyer: "He had an intuitive perception of what point in his case would prove strongest before the jury, and no one knew better than he how to make the most of that strong point."[10]

As territorial judges, Deady and Williams ruled on many cases involving disputed land titles, as litigants jousted over how to perfect title under the laws of the provisional and territorial governments. The intensity of one such dispute led to Oregon's first murder case reported in the original volume of Williams' published cases. The homicide occurred in Benton County, where Nimrod O'Kelly fatally shot Jeremiah Mahoney over a dispute as to whether O'Kelly was entitled to 640 acres or only 320 acres under a donation land claim. O'Kelly had claimed 320 acres for himself and 320 acres for his wife. Mahoney had never seen O'Kelly with a wife, and he believed O'Kelly had illegally doubled his land claim.

A jury, at the urging of prosecutor Reuben P. Boise, convicted O'Kelly of murder in 1852. Williams and Deady heard O'Kelly's appeal of the conviction and death sentence. It was filed and argued by attorney James K. Kelly, who twenty years later would represent Oregon in the United States Senate. Kelly raised nine technical objections, such as the setting of the court term, impaneling of grand and petit juries, and wording of the indictment. Williams and Deady were not impressed by the technicalities. In what he referred to as olden days, Williams wrote, "courts tried to make technicalities the means of justice... The awful import of these views to [O'Kelly] is not forgotten; but criminal laws were made to prevent crime, and their firm enforcement by courts is a duty as plain as it is painful," he concluded, affirming the death sentence.[11]

However, O'Kelly won an unusual reprieve. Before the order to hang him could be carried out, O'Kelly's son arrived by wagon train. It thus became apparent that O'Kelly had been truthful about having a wife. Imposition of the death sentence was delayed, and O'Kelly ultimately won a pardon from the governor.

Of the various land disputes heard by the territorial court, none would have as much impact on their young city as a dispute first brought in 1850 when Josiah Parrish, an early investor on Water Street (now Naito Parkway) next to the river, filed suit to stop the construction of a building on the river bank that would interfere with shipping. When Pettygrove and Lovejoy laid out the town in 1845, they appeared to have left no provision for a narrow strip between Water Street and the river. Was it public ground or private property? Deady and Williams came to different conclusions. Deady's view ultimately prevailed.

The case reached the three-judge territorial court in 1853. "It is quite as important to the town proprietors as to the individual lot holders and citizens, that the loading and unloading of vessels, which confers upon the town its principal importance, should not be embarrassed by the caprice and avarice of private persons who might own land adjacent to the water," wrote Justice Cyrus Olney, the court's third member. "That this street was intended to adjoin the river to form the connecting link between all the highways of the town and the great highway of water, upon which the town is dependent, is, therefore, both reasonable in itself and apparent from the face of the plat." Williams agreed. "Public levees are almost as necessary in such towns as public streets," he wrote. Deady dissented. His reasons were not published.[12]

The territorial court's ruling was appealed to the United States Supreme

Court, the first case from Portland to reach the nation's highest court. Associate Justice John Catron in 1858 suggested that, given the technicalities of provisional and territorial property laws, perhaps none of the parties had any interest in the land. Regardless, the Supreme Court dismissed the appeal on the ground that it raised no federal or constitutional issues.[13]

That wasn't the end of the matter, however. James Lownsdale, son of Daniel H. Lownsdale, Chapman's early-day business partner, claimed that the strip of land was his and began erecting wharves. The city government, which had been established in 1851, threatened to demolish them. Lownsdale sued the City of Portland in federal court, where Matthew Deady had been elevated to the bench after statehood in 1859.

Deady, deciding the case in 1861, noted that Daniel Lownsdale was out of town when the Parrish suit was in court. "He came home soon after and said to Chapman, who had been acting as his agent in his absence, that he had not intended to have that piece of ground built upon, but intended it for wharves . . . ," Deady wrote. "The words plainly imply a private ownership on the part of D. H. L., and an intention to have it used in a special manner, which he could not do if he dedicated it to the public." Deady also rejected the city's claim that Parrish represented the city's interest in the earlier case. Although the city was not yet a legal entity when Parrish filed suit in 1850, Deady said that the city could have joined the suit after its 1851 incorporation and before the case was decided. Deady halted the city's proposed demolition.[14]

The lawyer on the losing end, representing Portland, was George H. Williams, who had resigned from the territorial court in 1858 a few months before statehood to enter practice with Addison C. Gibbs. Deady's decision killed public docks in Portland for more than fifty years. However, the notion of the importance of public docks didn't die. As Portland grew in stature among ports of the world, a later Portland lawyer, Joseph N. Teal, would help bring public docks to fruition.

While the dock case percolated in the courts, sentiment grew in the territory for statehood. Sixty delegates, including Deady, Williams, and Logan from Portland, gathered in 1857 to draw up a proposed state constitution. Deady, only thirty-two years old, was elected convention president. Williams chaired the judiciary committee.

The delegates included thirty-three farmers and eighteen lawyers. "Truth, however, justifies the statement that the lawyers monopolized most of the time and the farmers the least," noted one of the lawyers, John R. McBride, who was elected from Yamhill County.[15] The lawyers, according to McBride, frequently engaged in flowery oratory. Their speechifying often was cut short, however, by David Logan, who "with his sarcastic tongue, made many a member subside in silence to his seat," McBride recalled years later.[16] Logan was a Whig whose party was heavily outnumbered by Democrats. Frustrated by steady losses in convention votes, he once proposed that "the legislature shall meet only once every 10 years, and then solely for the purpose of repealing laws passed at the previous session."[17] Once again, Logan lost.

One major issue of the convention was whether Oregon, if it became a state, should allow slavery. The views of Portland's jurists, Williams and Deady, were split. Deady believed that slavery was the law of the land; as a judicial enforcer of the law, Deady supported it. Williams opposed it. The issue was framed at the time not as one of human rights, but more as a matter of legal tradition. Because most Oregonians had emigrated from New England and from the Midwest, the majority of delegates believed that Oregon had little in common with slavery's Southern roots. Ever a pragmatist, Williams offered an unusual reason for opposing slavery: he contended that it would be cheaper in the long run for farmers to hire labor than to maintain slaves.

Williams' economic reasoning led some later critics to question his dedication to racial equality. But in two racially oriented cases that came before

Williams as a territorial judge, he sided both times against racial bias. In one of his first decisions after reaching Oregon, Williams, sitting as a trial judge, declared that the children of a freed slave should be returned to their natural father and removed from the custody of the father's former owner. The decision in the 1853 case, *Holmes v. Ford*, preceded the formal publication of court opinions but was printed in the Oregon City newspaper.[18] It was the only attempt to enforce slavery in Oregon. A year later, Williams and the territorial court rejected a claim contending that a white settler who married an Indian woman should give up half his land claim. The donation land act allowed white settlers 320 acres, and doubled that amount if the settler was married. The statute was silent about whether the wife had to be white. "Now, is not a man legally married to an Indian woman as much a married man, to all intents and purposes, as though his wife were the fairest of the fair?" Williams wrote. "If two women are married in the same way to the same sort of men, can it be said that one is a wife because she is white, and the other is not a wife because she is copper-colored?"[19]

OHS CN018333

George H. Williams.

As the constitutional convention progressed, Judge Williams saw no need for establishing a bill of rights to accompany the state constitution. But in the end, delegates eventually adopted thirty separate rights and placed them at the front of the new constitution. Their significance lay unappreciated for many years, but the

Oregon Supreme Court more than a century later relied on them to establish greater rights for criminal defendants, for free speech, and for bearing arms than have been recognized under the United States Constitution.

Convention delegates proposed to ban slavery but they wanted voters to consider the question at the polls when they voted whether to adopt the state charter. Oregon voters approved the new constitution in 1858 by 7,195 votes to 3,215. The count in favor of banning slavery was 7,727 to 2,645, but a companion measure excluding Negroes passed 8,640 to 1,081. After debate by Congress, Oregon became a state on February 14, 1859.

Deady's leadership at the constitutional convention was only one of his many contributions to Oregon law. He prepared for publication laws enacted by the territorial legislature in 1849-50, and in 1862 drafted state civil procedure laws adopted by the legislature. He later drafted state criminal laws which, with amendments, stayed in effect until the criminal code was revised in 1971. He also wrote pioneering incorporation laws that allowed any three individuals to form a corporation without a grant of authority from the legislature. As his fellow judge, Williams, put it, "No hand has been so strongly and deeply impressed upon the legislative and judicial history of Oregon as that of Judge Deady."[20]

Oregon's court system changed little upon statehood. Each of the three members of the Oregon Supreme Court served as a trial judge in the judicial districts and sat together as the appeals court. Judge Deady was elected to the first state supreme court, along with Reuben P. Boise and Aaron E. Wait, a pioneer Oregon City lawyer who helped create the region's first newspaper, *The Spectator*, which started appearing fortnightly in Oregon City in 1846. It was the first newspaper published on the Pacific Coast.

Deady never sat with the new state court, however. President James Buchanan appointed him as Oregon's first federal judge on March 3, 1859. Paine Paige Prim, a Jackson County lawyer, was appointed to take Deady's place on the state court. Justice Wait, who as a youth had been apprenticed as a broom maker, was assigned to hear cases in Portland during 1859 and 1860. He was followed in 1862 by William W. Page, who at the age of twenty-five was appointed by Oregon's first governor under statehood, John Whiteaker, to fill a vacancy when Wait resigned to make an unsuccessful run for Congress. Page, whose term lasted but six months, was the youngest

OHS CN002391

United States District Judge Matthew Deady.

Oregon Supreme Court justice ever. He returned to Portland, where he practiced law until his death in 1897.

Salem was designated as the home of the new U.S. District Court but, after working there only one year, Deady successfully lobbied to have the headquarters changed to Portland. Portland's population had soared to 3,000. City officials were talking about paving some streets with cobblestones. Deady knew that Portland would be the state's commercial and legal headquarters. Still, the young city had no home for a sitting judge. Deady arranged to rent a third-floor room with an adjoining office from Benjamin Stark at 63 Front Street, since renamed from Water Street.

By 1864, Portland's population had climbed to 5,000. That year, Deady and a committee of citizens, including Oregon Supreme Court Justice Erasmus D. Shattuck, established the Library Association of Portland. Shattuck, like Deady, was a continual supporter of education. He had taught school at Oregon City and at Pacific University in Forest Grove before establishing a law partnership with David Logan in Portland in 1859. Shattuck was an early member of the Portland School Board and the Portland City Council. He served as Oregon's second United States attorney in 1862 by appointment of President Abraham Lincoln, but he resigned that post when he was elected to the Oregon Supreme Court, where he served from 1862 to 1867. Shattuck also served a second stint on the supreme court from 1874 to 1878. During both those spans, Judge Shattuck was assigned to preside over trials in Portland.

Although Deady wasn't elected to the initial board of library directors, he served as president for twenty-one years before his death in 1893. Early fund-raising for the library took longer than expected. After operating in rented space for several years, the subscription library built its first permanent home the year that Deady died. "It is hard to think of the early library days without Judge Deady," a library historian wrote decades later. "With only common school education he became a scholar and a remarkable judge

OHS CN002801

Oregon Supreme Court Justice Ersamus D. Shattuck.

through much hard reading and a retentive memory. In consequence he believed in the value of good books for others and with that faith he became the most ardent and persistent advocate of the library cause."[21]

County officials in 1864 commissioned construction of the first Multnomah County Courthouse, completed in 1866. The site originally had been owned by William Chapman, the early lawyer and city promoter, who had built a residence on the lot in 1853. Portland architects William W. Piper and Elwood M. Burton designed a two-story Italianate structure with tall, narrow windows and a small dome with windows that perched 106 feet above the ground, affording perhaps the best view of the city growing up around it. A likeness of Abraham Lincoln was carved into the large keystone over the main entrance. The basement was used for the jail. Judge Deady, who wrote articles for a San Francisco newspaper, said that the view from the dome showed "the green semi-circle of irregular shaped fir clad hills, on the west and south, and the water of the bright Willamette curving outwardly from the north to the south."[22] Editors of *The Oregonian* advised citizens that they would find the view all the more beautiful "remembering that what you see before you is all paid for."[23] The price tag had been $65,000.

The new courthouse was Portland's first public building. Municipal and federal officials, including Deady, still worked in rented quarters. Among its many uses, the new courthouse became the scene of hangings for murder convicts. Approximately a dozen killers met their deaths in the courthouse yard before the state legislature in 1903 declared that all future executions would occur at the state prison.

At least two hangings were held before public crowds, but in most cases the county official erected temporary, high wooden fences to shield the proceedings. One defendant, Alfred Anderson, who was convicted of killing

OHS OrHi 24375

First Multnomah County Courthouse.

and robbing his brother in 1883, made a speech on the scaffold lasting one hour and twenty minutes. Anderson's oratorical flurry was inspired by the mistaken belief that he could not be executed if he stalled beyond the hour specified for his hanging.

County officials added a major wing on the Salmon Street side of the courthouse in 1885, and by the early 1890s there was talk that the first courthouse had been outgrown. Plans were discussed for a new, $3 million courthouse in 1893, but a financial panic that swept in from the East Coast killed those plans. The county continued to expand and modify the original courthouse until it was replaced over a period of years beginning in 1912.

A few blocks away from the Multnomah County Courthouse, construction began in 1869 on the United States Building, which was designed to house the U.S. District Court, the federal customs office, and the post office. The city's population had blossomed to nearly 9,000, but most of the commercial activity was still concentrated on the blocks closest to the Willamette River. A cow roamed the streets while construction workers toiled on the U.S. Building between 5th and 6th avenues. It was the first major federal building anywhere in the Pacific Northwest. Architect A. B. Mullett, who had designed many federal buildings from Washington, D.C., to San Francisco, designed a rectangular plan with classical pilasters and pediments, and Italianate window decorations. Although the exterior was not ornate for its era, the interior was finished elegantly with oak and ash, and the two-story courtroom featured a decorated baroque ceiling. The pace of work was slow. Deady's new courtroom and chambers weren't finished until 1875.

"Moved from old quarters to the U.S. Building," he noted in his diary. "For near 16 years I have gone in and out of those old rooms, daily, administering justice between man and man as best I could. It is a long time in one place. My new chambers are very fine compared with the old and I may consider myself well fixed."[24] The building, later known as the Pioneer Post

Office and then as the Pioneer Courthouse, housed Portland's federal court until 1933.

As the young city grew, its lawyers continued to play major political roles. Lansing Stout, a New York native who arrived in Portland in 1857 after being attracted by the California gold rush, became Portland's first national legislator following Oregon statehood. He was elected to one term in Congress from 1859 to 1861, having beaten David Logan in the race by a mere sixteen votes out of more than 11,000 cast. The first news to arrive in Springfield, Illinois, Logan's native city, indicated that Logan had won. The final result arrived later. "It is a matter of much regret here that Logan failed to his election," Abraham Lincoln wrote to a friend in Oregon. "He grew up and studied law in this place, and his parents and sisters still reside here."[25] Congressman Stout helped secure overland mail service between Portland and Sacramento. Pioneer Benjamin Stark became Portland's first member of the United States Senate when he was appointed late in 1861 to

OHS OrHi 7122-9

Construction of the United States Building, later known as Pioneer Courthouse. Note the ghostly cow grazing.

succeed Col. Edward D. Baker, who was killed at the Battle of Ball's Bluff, Virginia, during the Civil War. Stark served for just under one year, and by 1864 had returned to Connecticut, where he spent most of the rest of his life. David Logan, rebuffed in three different races for the U. S. House of Representatives and one for the Senate, won a term as Portland mayor in 1863-64. As mayor, he received the city's first telegram, signaling a technological advance that speeded communication between Portland and other major commercial centers. The wires were extended first from St. Louis to San Francisco, and then north to Portland.

Logan's intemperance remained unchanged. Three years before Logan's death in 1874, Judge Deady noted in his diary, "Logan called this afternoon. Looks as well as I ever saw. Has just recovered from a long drunk. I believe a few months drunk once in three or four years does him good. It renews his youth and strength, but how depraved he becomes."[26] That was Logan's last year practicing law, however. He retired to Lafayette in 1871. After Logan's death, *The Oregonian* noted his brilliance as a trail lawyer but said nothing about his tenure as mayor. The newspaper said that Logan had vast political ambitions "but he was not a skillful politician in the matter of managing men for his own ends."[27]

George Williams' law partner, Addison C. Gibbs, was elected governor in 1862, becoming the state's second chief executive after statehood. Gibbs had emigrated west from New York to the California gold mines in 1849, but he disliked mining conditions and settled in southern Oregon in 1850. He served in the first state legislature from Umpqua (now Douglas) County, and later moved to Portland, where he became partner with Williams in 1858. Gibbs ran for governor on a Union platform and helped keep Oregon as a member of the United States during the Civil War. During his term, Gibbs raised troops to protect Oregon and Washington from Indian raids during the war.

Gibbs returned to Portland after his term as governor, and served as

Multnomah County district attorney from 1868 to 1872, as United States Attorney for Oregon from 1872 to 1873, and as Portland city attorney in 1875. He is the only person ever to hold all three of those public-law posts. Another versatile pioneer was Marion F. Mulkey, a Missouri native whose family emigrated to Oregon in 1846 when he was ten years old. After attending frontier schools, Mulkey did his undergraduate work at Yale College from 1858 to 1862, and then studied law in Portland under Judge Erasmus Shattuck. Mulkey practiced with W. Lair Hill in Portland before being elected Multnomah County district attorney in 1866.

Mulkey held that post for a single two-year term. In 1867, he won election to the Portland City Council and served as Portland city attorney in 1874-75. Mulkey then formed a partnership with John F. Caples, who won an unprecedented three terms as district attorney from 1878 to 1884. Mulkey returned to the courthouse to serve as Caples' deputy. Caples and Mulkey represented the state in many of the death penalty cases of the era. Mulkey's son, Frederick W. Mulkey, carried on his father's interest in both law and politics. He represented Oregon in the United States Senate for brief terms in 1907 and 1918. Caples, meanwhile, left Portland from 1897 to 1901 to serve as U. S. consul in Chile by appointment of President William McKinley.

George H. Williams ran for the U.S. Senate in 1865 and was elected by state legislators, who, until adoption of the Seventeenth Amendment in 1913, decided senatorial races. During his six-year term, Williams worked on Reconstruction-era legislation and helped manage impeachment proceedings against President Andrew Johnson. But a few years later, a confrontation with his old law partner, Gibbs, would mark a dramatic turn in Williams' public career.

Between 1851 and statehood in 1859, the Oregon territorial court admitted fifty-two lawyers to practice. Fewer than twenty of them had settled in Portland by 1862; by 1868, however, their ranks had more than doubled to forty-one. Oregon did not yet have a law school. The Oregon Supreme Court in 1865 adopted a rule formalizing an examination for prospective lawyers, who would be tested on the subjects of pleadings, evidence, contracts, real property, and equity. The rules required each applicant to "be prepared for examination in the following books, viz: Chitty, on *Pleadings*, Wharton's *Criminal Law*, Greenleaf on *Evidence*, Blackstone's *Commentaries*, Kent's *Commentaries*, Story's *Equity Jurisprudence* or Willard's *Equity Jurisprudence*."[28]

As Portland's small legal community began to grow, two newcomers arrived in the early 1860s who would play prominent legal and political roles for decades, Joseph N. Dolph and John H. Mitchell. They became law partners and built the most politically influential law firm in the young city. Eventually, both of them would serve as U.S. Senators. But their careers ended decades later on dramatically different notes.

Mitchell was born in 1836 in Pennsylvania as John Mitchell Hipple. He reversed his middle and last names when he came to Portland in 1860, probably hoping to camouflage himself from domestic turmoil that had begun in Pennsylvania and continued later in California. As his political opponents later learned, Hipple, at age twenty-one, had married a fifteen-year-old Pennsylvania girl, Sara Hoon, who was pregnant at the time with his child. Hoon had two more children, but Hipple then took up with a school teacher, identified as one Mary J., who lived in the Hipple residence with Hoon. Four years after marrying Hoon, Hipple departed suddenly from Butler, Pennsylvania, with Mary and his oldest child, leaving behind his wife and a $4,000 debt owed to his Pennsylvania law partner, John M. Thompson. After one year in the San Luis Obispo, California, area, Hipple showed up in Portland for the first time with his daughter, calling himself John H. Mitchell. What became of Mary is not known, but she did not come to Portland with Mitchell.

Mitchell's move to Portland did not end his turbulent domestic life. In

1862, he married Portland resident Mattie Price, although he was legally still married to Hoon. Over time, however, he fell in love with Mattie's sister, Carrie. By the end of Mitchell's tumultuous life in 1905, Mattie had left him, but Carrie Price had not.

Details of Mitchell's name-change, his marriage to Hoon, and other facts about his early life didn't surface in Portland until Mitchell had established himself as a prominent lawyer and political powerhouse. A man of great charm, he began representing Portland's municipal government within a year of his arrival. After a mere six years, he came within one vote in the legislature of being sent to Washington as a U.S. Senator. He ran six more Senate races during his career, and eventually won four of them. They all occurred in the era when senators were chosen by the legislature, and they were among the most bitter contests in the state's history. The Mitchell & Dolph firm, and its successors, eventually sent four of its members to the U.S. Senate for a combined total of forty-two years.

Dolph, a native of rural New York, had read early adventure stories about the Oregon Trail and was smitten by them long before he joined the New York bar in 1861. He made his way west by joining the Oregon Escort, a military force raised by Congress to protect immigrants on the Oregon Trail from Indian attacks. He formed a law partnership with Mitchell in 1863, which lasted until Mitchell won his first U.S. Senate term in 1872. Dolph's early years included service as Portland city attorney in 1864 and as U.S. Attorney for Oregon in 1865. He was joined a few years later by his brother, Cyrus Dolph, who, while less politically involved than Joseph, also became a leading lawyer. Like his brother and Mitchell before him, Cyrus Dolph also served as a Portland city attorney. The law partnership first created by Joseph Dolph continued for more than 110 years in Portland, until the death of the last surviving partner, Edgar Freed, in 1976.

The impressive credentials of the Mitchell & Dolph firm attracted as a client Ben Holladay, a wealthy stagecoach magnate from San Francisco who ventured to Portland in 1868 seeking more riches in the transportation field. This time Holladay's business was railroads. As the flashy Holladay arrived with his heavy gold watch chains and quartz-studded walking stick, Portlanders and their young legal community stood on the cusp of a new chapter in the growth of the city that Matthew Deady called "Portland on-the-Walamet."

CHAPTER TWO

Building Legal Institutions

Since early territorial days, Oregonians had dreamed of railroad connections to the East, not so much for moving people but for mail and for transporting goods and agricultural products to markets. The Willamette River remained Portland's primary artery for commerce but the river wasn't accessible to many farmers in the lush western Oregon valleys. The rain that made the region so fertile also made wagon roads impassable during many months of the year.

Congress in 1864 approved land-grant legislation authorizing the Northern Pacific Railroad to build a line above the forty-fifth parallel from Lake Superior to the Puget Sound or to Portland. The Civil War and financing difficulties slowed Northern Pacific's construction. In 1866, Congress made a similar land grant for railroad construction from Portland south to the California border.

Two competing private companies hurriedly started construction from Portland, hoping to cash in on the land grants. One headed south on the west side of the Willamette River and the other on the east side. Both were running low on cash when the fast-talking, big-spending Ben Holladay arrived in Portland in September 1868, flush with $1.5 million from the sale of his stagecoach lines to Wells Fargo. Represented by Portland's most prominent law firm, Mitchell & Dolph, Holladay infused money into the east-side line, fought the west-side company in the Oregon Legislature, and finally bought out his beaten competitors in 1870. Holladay reorganized his properties under the name Oregon & California Railroad Company, and sold bonds in European markets to finance the line toward California.

As in other states, the arrival of railroads came wrapped in court litigation over financing, route alignments, land condemnation, terminal locations, and disputes over federal land grants. Mitchell & Dolph became Oregon's leading railroad-law firm. The flamboyant Holladay and the politically ambitious Mitchell developed a close friendship, and Mitchell became Holladay's personal lawyer. With Holladay's backing, Mitchell won his dream in 1872 of being elected by the legislature to the U.S. Senate. That was the year that Holladay and a partner also built Portland's first street railroad, a horse-drawn car that carried passengers along First Avenue from Northwest Glisan to Southwest Sherman streets.

While early railroad development unfolded in Oregon, U.S. Senator George H. Williams became the first Oregonian to be appointed to a federal cabinet position. President Ulysses S. Grant named Williams as United States Attorney General in 1871. Grant's respect for Williams' abilities became evident two years later when he nominated Williams for the position of Chief Justice of the United States Supreme Court, following the death of Chief Justice Salmon P. Chase.

Williams ultimately was denied that loftiest of American legal posts, however, by a convergence of unusual circumstances. Eastern traditionalists questioned whether his five years on the Oregon territorial court was sufficient experience for a chief justice. Meanwhile, Williams' wife, Kate, made social enemies in Washington by airs she affected as wife of a cabinet member, and by her exultant reaction to her husband's nomination as chief justice. The fact that she rode around Washington in a horse-drawn landaulet provided to Williams by the federal government prompted an investigation into Williams' spending. Although the investigation ultimately found no improprieties, Williams' political opponents labeled him with the sneering nickname "Landaulet Williams," an appellation that stayed with him the rest of his life.[1] Back in Oregon, a political dispute involving his old law partner, Addison C. Gibbs, undercut Williams' home-state support.

That dispute arose from an 1873 congressional election, in which a Republican nominee supported by Senator John H. Mitchell was defeated by his Democratic opponent. Mitchell, whose recently disclosed domestic and marital problems were a primary topic in the campaign, was thought by some to have engaged in voter fraud in Portland during that race. Former Governor Gibbs, then serving as United States Attorney for Oregon, presented evidence to a federal grand jury, which refused to issue indictments. Gibbs sensed chicanery in the selection of the federal grand jurors and convinced Judge Deady to select a new panel at random. At Mitchell's request, Williams ordered Gibbs to halt the investigation or be replaced. Gibbs refused to back down. So Williams fired his old partner and replaced him with Rufus Mallory, who subsequently became a leading corporate lawyer. The outcry over Gibbs' removal helped convince Williams that he lacked the political support to be confirmed as chief justice. Rather than face that humiliation, he told President Grant to remove his name from consideration. Mallory, after seven years as U.S. attorney, was elected to one term in Congress to represent Oregon, from 1867 to 1869.

OHS CN011542

Addison Gibbs

Although George H. Williams remained in the East until 1881, he deepened his

Portland ties in 1872 while serving in the Grant administration. Williams and Edwin Russell, a Portland banker, bought an interest in a small township just across the Willamette River from Portland. They named the township Albina, for the wife of the prior owner. Albina grew quickly after the original Morrison and Steel bridges (both later replaced) linked the east and west sides of the river in 1887 and 1888, respectively. Albina's western edge became the home of a major railroad freight and repair yard. Albina's commercial center, which was the intersection of Russell Street and Williams Avenue, was the heart of a thriving community that officially merged with Portland in 1891.

After John H. Mitchell's departure from the Dolph law firm in 1872, Joseph Dolph added a new partner, Joseph Simon. Like Mitchell and Dolph, Simon held a deep interest in politics as well as law. A native of Germany, Simon had come to Portland as a child with his merchant father in 1857. He won election to the Portland City Council at the tender age of twenty, and later served eight terms as a state senator, including five sessions as senate president. For nearly forty years, Simon played a leading and often controversial role in Republican politics, and late in his career won terms in the U.S. Senate and as Portland mayor. Ironically, Dolph's new partner, Simon, and former partner, Mitchell, became staunch rivals, and their warring Republican factions engaged in some of the most bitter fights in Oregon political history.

Ben Holladay's railroad construction crews continued working south toward California in the early 1870s, but many Portland residents had become discouraged with the Northern Pacific's slow progress toward the West Coast. One of them was lawyer William W. Chapman, the early promoter of the Portland townsite and a backer of the railroad company that lost out to Holladay in the bid to build a line through the Willamette Valley to California. Chapman envisioned a rail line from Portland along the southern bank of the Columbia River to The Dalles, and from The Dalles to

Salt Lake City, where it would meet the Union Pacific.

Chapman organized three separate companies between 1870 and 1876 in hopes of carrying out his plan. He spent money on surveys, courted financial backers, lobbied Congress, and filed lawsuits trying to win access to key points held by steamship operators along the Columbia River. His efforts failed, even though he counted Senator Mitchell among his supporters. A few years after Chapman gave up, his exploratory work helped another railroad entrepreneur with sweeping vision, Henry Villard.

Villard entered the picture in 1874, the year after a national financial panic wiped out Ben Holladay and his Oregon & California Railroad, which had built 200 miles of track as far south as Roseburg. Villard was a German native who represented some of Holladay's European bondholders. He visited Portland and quickly dreamed of a more expansive transportation network. Represented by the law firm of Dolph, Bronaugh, Dolph & Simon, Villard took over Holladay's railroad, and then purchased the Columbia River's major steamship line. Capitalizing on some of Chapman's planning, Villard planned to build a rail line along the Columbia River's south shore. After the Northern Pacific announced plans to build on the Columbia's north shore, Villard and the investors who he quietly recruited bought up control of the Northern Pacific in 1881. In September 1883, Villard's new line brought Portland its first transcontinental train. The celebration was "the greatest display ever witnessed in this city,"[2] *The Oregonian* reported. But the glory didn't last long for Villard. Like Holladay before him, Villard's financial empire crashed suddenly, only months after its greatest success. Investors discovered that the finished rail lines, because of the immense distances they covered, offered slim possibilities for profits. By the end of the 1880s, Southern Pacific took control of the Oregon & California Railroad, and the Northern Pacific freed itself from Villard's corporate umbrella.

The 1870s and 1880s brought spectacular growth to Portland. Portland's population jumped to 21,500 by 1880, far ahead of Oregon's second largest city, Salem, with a population of just 4,100. East Portland, not yet merged into Portland, was the state's third largest city with 3,918 residents. By 1891, the year of the three-way merger of Portland, East Portland, and Albina, Portland had more than doubled again to 50,560 residents.

The city's legal community grew as well. Between 1880 and 1890, the listings of Portland lawyers soared from 67[3] to 172.[4] Most of those lawyers practiced in small offices by themselves as general practitioners. An exception, however, was Cornelius Beal, who concentrated on domestic relations cases. Beal handled more than five hundred divorces between 1880 and his retirement in 1905. Perhaps as a result of this legal experience, Beal was one of the early supporters of Oregon's temperance movement, which eventually made the state a national leader in the prohibition movement. Beal's professional success allowed him to purchase forty acres at the top of Council Crest. Although the land was almost impenetrable because of its heavy forests and steep slopes, Beal predicted that his mountaintop aerie would be worthy someday of becoming a public park. Ultimately he was correct, but the property first became a commercial amusement park before it came into public ownership as Council Crest Park.

Besides mere growth, the 1870s and 1880s brought important changes in the city's legal community. City officials in 1870 established the Portland Police Court, later to be known as Portland Municipal Court. Since the city's incorporation in 1851, minor criminal matters and city ordinance violations had been adjudicated by the municipal recorder. The Portland jail, a two-story structure with arched windows and a decorative cast-iron entry porch, included a courtroom. Built in 1873, the jail, with its police court and police headquarters, was the city's first municipal building. In 1912, municipal court moved into the new police headquarters at 209 Southwest Oak Street, which replaced the older jail. The city courts remained there until merging with Multnomah County District Court in 1971. After the arrival of automobiles, traffic court became a major part of the municipal court dockets. Throughout its century-long lifetime, municipal court was noted for its spirited litigation and colorful personalities. It also served as a training ground for many judges who rose higher in Oregon's judicial ranks.

The early 1870s marked the start of legal partnerships that would mature into some of Portland's major law firms more than a century later. George H. Durham, an Illinois native whose parents came to Oregon when he was three years old, formed a partnership with C.A. Ball in 1870, and then with H.Y. Thompson in 1872, the same year that Durham began a four-year term as Multnomah County district attorney. W. Lair Hill, a

OHS OrHi 5626

The Portland Jail, the city's first municipal building, was the home of the Portland Municipal Court.

notable trial lawyer and codifier of Oregon statutes, joined the firm in 1877, followed by former United States Attorney General George H. Williams, who returned to Portland in 1881 to form Williams, Hill, Durham, Thompson & Mays.

Durham left the partnership in 1887, the same year that it was joined by the man who would become its most famous partner, Charles Erskine Scott Wood. Wood was a Pennsylvania native who had earned a footnote in U.S. military history long before his arrival in Portland at age thirty-five. As a graduate of West Point, Wood served as a lieutenant to General O. O. Howard in the Nez Perce war of 1878, in which Chief Joseph led the U.S. Army on a chase of more than 1,400 miles through Oregon, Idaho, and Montana before finally surrendering in the Bear Paw Mountains in eastern Montana. Chief Joseph's leadership later came to be recognized as a marvel of military tactics and planning. Wood was among the first to sense Joseph's greatness. "No one suggested that Joseph's surrender speech be taken down," Wood recalled later, "but I felt it was an important occasion and I knew the simple eloquence of the Indian. So I prepared my pencil and pad ready to record what Joseph said."[5] Chief Joseph spoke but seventeen terse sentences, describing the impact of the war on his tribe and his relatives. He finished with the memorable lines, "Hear me, my chiefs, I am tired; my heart is sick and sad. From where the sun now stands I will fight no more forever."[6] Wood later returned to West Point as adjutant of the military academy. During his spare time, he studied law at Columbia University. After his arrival in Portland in 1884, Wood quickly became a leading corporate lawyer, as well as a noted free-thinker, civil libertarian, artist, poet, and satirist. His son, Erskine Wood, and a grandson, Erskine B. Wood, later practiced in the firm that became known as Wood, Tatum, Wonacott & Landis.

Wood quickly made a lasting impression on his new city. About a year before Wood's arrival, pioneer Portland druggist, volunteer fireman, and city council member Stephen G. Skidmore had died, bequeathing $5,000 to the city to build a public fountain. Drawings of the proposed fountain were being circulated when Wood arrived, and Wood thought the proposals were unworthy. He met with the fountain planning committee, the members of which agreed to let Wood seek an artist willing to suggest a different scheme. Wood eventually prevailed on Olin Warner, a Connecticut-born sculptor who had spent several years studying in Paris before opening a studio in New York City. Warner was considered one of the nation's leading classical sculptors when he agreed, at Wood's request, to sculpt what would become the Skidmore Fountain, located near Southwest First Avenue and Ankeny Street.

Warner's design featured two classically styled women holding a circular basin, standing above an octagonal pool of polished marble. The beautiful fountain ended up costing $18,000 instead of the $5,000 left by Skidmore, but the planning committee quietly found contributors to make up the difference. Wood, whose name is engraved on the base of the statue as one of the planning committee members, was charged with writing the inscriptions. "Good citizens are the riches of a city," one of them says. It was the theme that Wood touched upon in the opening ceremonies. "There is no nobler ambition than to live in memory as the giver of good gifts," he told the multitude that assembled to view the city's beautiful new adornment in 1888. "This path is open to all, and, alas, is never crowded."[7]

Another long-lasting law firm whose roots began in the early railroad era started in 1873 when two relative newcomers to Portland, Henry H. Northrup and William B. Gilbert, formed the first of two partnerships. Northrup, a Massachusetts native, had fought in the Civil War and worked as a school teacher before coming to Portland in 1871 after studying law in Washington, D.C. Gilbert, a Virginian whose adventurist spirit made him an early explorer of the Amazon region in South America, arrived a year later after having studied law at the University of Michigan. In addition to his own law practice, Northrup worked part-time as the Registrar in Bankruptcy.

Northrup & Gilbert dissolved in 1876, and Gilbert became a partner with former governor Addison C. Gibbs. That partnership ended in 1877, when Gilbert and Northrup reunited for another seven years. Both men eventually went on to serve as judges. Northrup was elected in 1894 to the Multnomah County Circuit Court, where he served for six years. At the end of his term, Northrup returned to private practice for another nineteen years before his retirement in 1919. When Congress created the U.S. Circuit Courts of Appeal in 1891, Gilbert was nominated by President Benjamin Harrison to serve on the new Ninth Circuit, a position that he held until his death in 1931. A hundred years after Gilbert left his old firm, it had grown into Miller, Nash, Wiener, Hager & Carlsen LLP.

The late 1870s also brought significant political and judicial changes in Portland's legal landscape. Senator Mitchell, whose stormy domestic relations had become well known, was defeated in his bid for reelection in 1878 by James H. Slater of eastern Oregon. Never a quitter, Mitchell ran for the state's other Senate seat in 1882, but he found himself stalemated by his political opponents. Mitchell ultimately threw his support to his former law partner, Joseph Dolph, who won the Senate seat on the eighty-fifth ballot by the legislature. Dolph quit practicing law when he went to Washington, D.C., setting an ethical standard that Mitchell, to his detriment, did not follow later in his political career.

Mitchell's defeat in 1878 coincided with the election of Portland lawyer William W. Thayer as Oregon's sixth governor. Thayer, a native of rural New York who began practicing in the Empire State in 1851, crossed the plains in 1863 at the suggestion of his older brother, Andrew J. Thayer, who had settled on a farm near Corvallis ten years earlier. William Thayer moved to the Idaho Territory in 1863, but returned to Portland and opened a law office in 1867. The brothers were proficient lawyers. Andrew Thayer, who served for nearly three years as Oregon's first United States attorney after statehood, won a term on the Oregon Supreme Court in 1870, but died three years later. As governor, William Thayer supported construction of Oregon's first state hospital and strengthened government accounting procedures and management of state lands. Like his older brother Andrew, William Thayer also served on the Oregon Supreme Court. He won a six-year term in 1884 and served as chief justice during his final two years, 1888 to 1890. He is the only Oregonian ever to serve as both governor and Oregon Chief Justice.

During his tenure on the supreme court bench, Justice William Thayer wrote the lead opinion in *Holladay v. Holladay*, which concluded a venomous court battle between the early railroad entrepreneur, Ben Holladay, and his older brother, Joseph. The brothers had maintained a close relationship for many years before Ben Holladay filed suit in 1883. Their litigation over personal financial dealings dragged on at length in Multnomah County Circuit Court and attracted widespread public attention to the convoluted financial dealings of the colorful Ben Holladay. Thayer's appellate ruling briefly contrasted the two men. Ben Holladay, he said, "has raised a family, has during a great portion of his life been actively engaged in financial enterprises of great magnitude, has acquired and lost large property interests and been accustomed to luxurious habits of living. His gains and profits have been immense; and his generosity and liberality bordered upon profligacy." Joseph Holladay was a bachelor. "He has confined his financial operations to a limited business, and pursued a cautious and frugal course; and while his brother has been endeavoring by shifts, devices, and speculations to make a great fortune, he has by prudence and economy succeeded in saving a very good competency. The career of one has alternated between munificence and distress, and that of the other been attended by gradual and constant thrift."

The battle stemmed over a $163,000 promissory note signed in favor of Joseph Holladay in 1876, and Ben Holladay's conveyance of real property, stock, and personal goods to his brother at approximately the same time.

Ben Holladay, who had left Portland in 1876, returned in 1883 and offered to pay off the debt to his brother. In return, he wanted his property back. Joseph Holladay, who had prospered while living in his brother's house and managing an ocean resort formerly held by Ben Holladay, contended that the property had been conveyed to him permanently. The bitter trial even included a demand that Joseph Holladay repay $100 worth of the $6,000 supply of fine wines and liquors depleted in the personal residence that Ben Holladay had deeded to him.

Thayer and the supreme court sided with Ben Holladay, ruling that payment of the $163,000 note and 12 percent interest required Joseph Holladay to return the real property and stock. "He is quite an old man," Thayer wrote of Joseph Holladay, "and probably inclined to be churlish, and it is very likely that the whole difficulty has arisen out of some supposed affront." However, the court stopped short of making Joseph Holladay pay his brother for the modest amount of liquor that Joseph had consumed over the seven years in Ben Holladay's house. "A person who has husbanded that amount of wines and liquors so faithfully as that should not be compelled to pay for the small portion used," Thayer said.[8]

State legislators in 1878 realized that Portland and some other parts of Oregon were growing too quickly for the supreme court to retain both trial and appellate jurisdiction. As a result, the legislature reorganized the state judicial system by creating circuit courts. The first Oregon Chief Justice under the new system was James K. Kelly, whose roots and influence in Oregon stretched back to Portland's earliest days. Kelly was born and reared on a Pennsylvania farm, but his intellectual abilities led him to Princeton University, where he graduated in 1839. Two years later he finished law studies at Dickinson College and was admitted to the Pennsylvania bar. The lure of gold pulled Kelly to California in 1849, and in 1851 he settled in Oregon City where he became a law partner of pioneer lawyer Asa Lovejoy. Partly as a result of Lovejoy's influence in the territorial legislature, Kelly was chosen as one of the three lawyers to draft a new territorial code in 1853, along with Reuben Boise of Polk County and Daniel Bigelow of Thurston County, the latter being a portion of the territory that later became part of Washington state. Kelly later served as a member of the state constitutional convention, and then opened a law office in The Dalles, where he practiced from 1862 to 1869. He served as a state senator from 1860 to 1864, and turned down a proposed appointment as U.S. Attorney for Oregon to continue his political career. Kelly was defeated, however, in statewide races for Congress in 1864 and for governor two years later. Kelly practiced law in Portland from 1869 until his election to the U.S. Senate, where he served from 1871 to 1877. Upon his return, Kelly served as Chief Justice of the Oregon Supreme Court from 1878 to 1880, by appointment of Governor Thayer. He resumed practice in 1882 in Portland until moving to Washington, D.C., in 1890, where he spent his final ten years.

Charles Bellinger, who served as clerk of the Oregon Supreme Court from 1874 to 1878, was appointed the first judge of Multnomah County Circuit Court. Bellinger's parents, who were farmers, had come across the plains from Illinois when he was eight years old to settle near Salem. Bellinger was admitted to the bar in 1863 at age twenty-four, but he spent his early years editing a newspaper in Salem. He practiced law in Albany and Portland before accept-

OHS CN021178

U.S. District Judge Charles Bellinger.

ing the supreme court clerkship. After two years as Multnomah County Circuit Court judge, Bellinger lost the election to retain his seat and returned to private practice. He joined the old Dolph firm in 1883, creating Dolph, Bellinger, Mallory & Simon. He remained there ten years, when, after the death of U.S. District Court Judge Matthew P. Deady in 1893, he was nominated by President Grover Cleveland and confirmed as Oregon's second federal judge. Bellinger held that post until his death in 1905. Bellinger also served as the second president of the Oregon Historical Society, from 1901 to 1905.

Having worked in farming, journalism, and a small store before becoming a lawyer, Bellinger at times expressed displeasure with the pace of court proceedings before him. "He had not that perfect patience which in a Judge is so comforting to those before him," C. E. S. Wood noted after Bellinger's death. "Judge Bellinger was by nature an advocate: ardent, quick, versatile, powerful. . . . He comprehended a situation instantly and seemed to proceed to the end by intuition rather than by slow stages." At times, Wood recalled, Judge Bellinger "would break in with some interruption, reproof or ruling like a shot from a gun," and then politely try to restrain himself in silence as the lawyers went about their work.[9]

The new circuit court judgeships established around the state in 1878 apparently compared favorably with service on the supreme court. Reuben P. Boise, one of the original supreme court justices after statehood, opted to become a circuit court judge in Marion County, where he ended his lengthy judicial career after the turn of the twentieth century. Likewise, former Portland lawyer Erasmus Shattuck, who had served on the supreme court from 1862 to 1867 and again from 1874 to 1878, later served twelve years as a judge in Multnomah County Circuit Court, beginning in 1886. The bookish Shattuck briefly had been a partner with hard-drinking David Logan in the late 1850s. Logan, whose oratorical skills surpassed his interest in legal research, once described their partnership this way: "Nobody expects me to work in the office and no one expects him to appear in court."[10]

The pioneer lawyers like Boise and Shattuck, who had helped build Portland's legal and cultural institutions from the forest wilderness, felt a special kinship as the nineteenth century faded. George H. Williams, speaking at a dinner honoring Shattuck in 1900, could have been speaking as well for himself when he said, "When you came to Oregon, civilization had just commenced to make inroads upon the wilderness, and our political, education, judicial and civic institutions were in their embryo state. All of these bear the impress of your ability and influence in their growth and development."[11]

Portland's rapid population growth in the 1870s and 1880s prompted hefty increases in real estate values. Soaring value appears to have been an underlying factor in a Portland lawsuit filed in 1874 that became one of the most famous in the history of the United States Supreme Court. It pitted an uneducated pioneer against Sylvester Pennoyer, a Harvard-trained lawyer and successful Portland lumberman.

Marcus Neff, an unmarried and apparently illiterate pioneer, in 1850 staked a claim to 320 acres in the hills of what became Northwest Portland. In 1866 he hired John H. Mitchell to perform some legal work, but he moved to California without paying Mitchell's $294.98 bill. Mitchell filed suit to collect his fees and tried to notify Neff by advertising the lawsuit in a newspaper. Mitchell obtained a default judgement for his fees in 1866, and Pennoyer bought Neff's land for $341.60 at a sheriff's sale. Neff was not pleased when he returned to Portland in 1874. He filed suit in U.S. District Court seeking to win back his land. Judge Deady ruled in Neff's favor, saying that Mitchell had not complied with technicalities for summoning an out-of-state defendant. Pennoyer appealed to the U.S. Supreme Court. He wanted to hold on to the valuable real estate, which by then was worth $15,000.

In 1877, the nation's highest court issued its famous *Pennoyer v. Neff* ruling.[12] Justice Stephen E. Field, a personal friend of Judge Deady's, affirmed

Deady's ruling but on a different legal ground. The Court ruled that, because Neff's land itself was not the issue in Mitchell's personal judgment against Neff, Neff's property could be used only to satisfy the amount of the judgment, not more. The case became a landmark in determining legal jurisdiction over citizens in differing states. It has been cited in literally thousands of appellate cases since 1877 and it continues to bedevil first-year law students with its complexity.

Neff wasn't finished in court. He wanted $4,600 in damages, claiming that Pennoyer had cut timber and destroyed a log cabin on the site. But Deady wasn't so inclined. He ruled that "the clearing of a portion of the land for pasture was and is a benefit to the premises, but it does not appear that the cabin is any benefit to the property, or what the present value is."[13] Neff's property eventually became part of Willamette Heights, one of Portland's most elegant residential neighborhoods.

OHS CN 014004

Governor Sylvester Pennoyer.

Pennoyer's fame did not end with the Supreme Court case. The outspoken lawyer-businessman served as Oregon governor from 1886 to 1895, and as Portland mayor for the following two years. He was an outspoken and relentlessly independent public official. As governor, he proclaimed that the Oregon Supreme Court had no right to declare legislative acts unconstitutional. When President Grover Cleveland's secretary of state wired Pennoyer that violence might occur after passage of a federal law in 1893 halting Chinese immigration, Pennoyer wired back, "I will attend to my business. Let the President attend to his."[14] The following year, Pennoyer proclaimed Thanksgiving in Oregon to be one week later than the national holiday. Judge Deady, who enjoyed playing with words in his private diary, came up with his own nickname for the governor: "Sylpester Annoyer."[15]

One of Pennoyer's notable achievements as governor was his appointment of George E. Chamberlain as Oregon's first attorney general after legislators created that position in 1891. Chamberlain, a Mississippi native who had come to Oregon in 1876 at age twenty-two, became one of the state's most popular elected officials during a political career that spanned forty years. After settling in Albany, Chamberlain was elected a state representative in 1880, and soon thereafter district attorney of Marion County in 1884. After winning a full term as attorney general, Chamberlain in 1895 moved to Portland and engaged in private practice until being elected Multnomah County District Attorney in 1900.

A Democrat in a state that was then heavily Republican, Chamberlain won the governorship in 1902 when the Republicans were badly split. He proved popular, however, and easily won a second term in 1906. As governor, Chamberlain pushed for more equitable property tax assessments among counties and held out for better prices when public lands were sold for the benefit of public schools. Some of the ideas he favored, including an employer's liability law and a state engineering department for water reclamation and irrigation, were adopted after he left Salem in 1908 for the United States Senate.

As a Senator, Chamberlain chaired the Senate Military Affairs Committee during World War I and helped sponsor war legislation. He won a second term in 1914 when Republicans outnumbered Democrats by a three-to-one margin, but his luck ran out in 1920 when he was defeated, for the first time in his career, by Robert N. Stanfield of eastern Oregon. President Harding then appointed Chamberlain to the United States

Shipping Board, a forerunner of the Federal Maritime Commission. Chamberlain served for two years before ending his career as a private lawyer in Washington, D.C., where he died in 1928.

Despite Portland's fast growth in the early 1880s, the state's largest city was not yet a seat of formal legal education. Willamette University, fifty miles to the south, opened the state's first law school in 1883. Judge Deady proposed the creation of a state-run law school the same year. Deady was an early advocate of a state university and became a member of the original University of Oregon Board of Regents, formed in 1872. The first building on the university campus, located in Eugene City, was named for him in 1876. When Deady proposed adding a law school, he already had in mind a person to run it. Richard Hopwood Thornton was an English scholar and educator who was practicing law in Philadelphia. Thornton had sent Deady several proposals for starting a law school.

Deady's fellow regents apparently expressed reluctance, but in 1884 they accepted his idea to create a law department in Portland, which was more than 100 miles away from the young university campus in Eugene City. University regents apparently recognized what was obvious to Deady: that as the business and legal center of the state, Portland was the logical place for the state's law school. Thornton accepted an appointment as the first law professor without a salary. He agreed to collect tuition, pay bills, and retain any profits for himself. Thornton rented space in a downtown building and opened his doors for business. Classes were held at night so that students could work during the day and so that lawyers and judges, such as Deady, could give lectures. Seven students enrolled the first year, but three of them later dropped out. Thornton's net income at the end of the year was a meager $125.

Thornton was disappointed with his income that first year, but not with the prospects for his new department. He confidently predicted increased enrollments, and university regents in the second year began providing budget allocations. But Thornton was still paid from net profits. "Insomuch as my income from the Law School for the first two years has amounted to less than a thousand dollars—the actual sum being $977—I would ask whether you think that the Board might be disposed to make me an allowance of (say) $500 in respect thereof," he wrote in 1887. "This matter is not put forward as a claim, because I voluntarily took my chance on the first year, but merely as a suggestion to your kindness."[16]

The law school remained in Portland until 1915, when university officials relocated it to the Eugene campus and turned it into the University of Oregon Law School. But that wasn't the end of formal legal education in Portland. The law dean at the time, Multnomah County Circuit Court Judge Calvin U. Gantenbein, refused to leave when the school moved to Eugene. Judge Gantenbein had moved law classes into the Multnomah County Courthouse, and he decided to continue. He paid the state for the few assets of the law department and opened his own night law school, which he named Northwestern College of Law. Northwestern remained downtown for another fifty years.

All of Dean Thornton's students were men, as were all lawyers admitted to practice in Oregon. Indeed, state statutes excluded women as potential lawyers. But Mary Gysin Leonard changed that. Perhaps no lawyer ever had to work harder than she to be admitted to Oregon practice.

Mary Gysin, an immigrant from Switzerland, arrived in Portland in the early 1870s, where in 1875 she married Daniel G. Leonard, who operated an inn and a ferry on the Oregon Trail, east of The Dalles. The marriage was not a happy one. Divorce papers with nasty accusations offered by both spouses had been filed about a month before Daniel Leonard was found one morning in his bed in 1878, shot once in the head. Mary Leonard was charged with murder. She was held in custody for eleven months until her trial. W. Lair Hill, a prominent Portland lawyer who had moved to eastern Oregon for health reasons, defended her and won an acquittal. Leonard returned to Portland and operated boardinghouses until 1883, when she moved to Seattle and studied law with a prominent firm. She was admitted to practice in the Washington Territory in 1885.

Leonard promptly returned to Portland, where Judge Deady admitted her to federal practice in Oregon. However, the Oregon Supreme Court, noting that state laws regulating lawyer admission referred only to the masculine gender, reluctantly refused Mary Leonard's petition for admission. "The question is not free from embarrassment, and the court would gladly avoid the responsibility of determining it," the court said in an unsigned opinion. But the three justices said it would be "highly improper for the courts of the State to take the initiative in so important a movement."[17]

Fortunately for Mary Leonard, the Oregon Legislature met in a special session in the fall of 1885. Legislators passed a bill (Senate Bill 50, 1885) providing that "Here-after women shall be admitted to the practice of law as attorneys...upon the same terms and conditions as men."

OHS OrHi 72693

Mary Gysin Leonard.

Even so, victory was not yet hers. A newly published rule required out-of-state lawyers to reside in Oregon for one year before admission. Leonard returned again to the state supreme court, where she noted the rule had not been applied to any men. "I may not be a free man, but since I do belong to the protected sex, or oppressed sex, whichever you please," she argued, "and since the legislature with almost unanimous voice has agreed to relieve me from the cruel shackles placed upon my wrists, I stand before this court a woman thrown upon her own resources, and beseechingly I reach out my imprisoned hands and ask to have these shackles removed."[18]

Mary Leonard was admitted to practice in January 1886. She was Oregon's sole woman lawyer for a decade, and one of only seven admitted to practice before the turn of the century. The better part of another century would pass before women were admitted to the bar almost as frequently as men. Leonard remained in Portland and practiced law, mostly in municipal court, until shortly before her death in 1912. Her practice was not lucrative, and she died in poverty.

While Leonard was beginning her quest for admittance, more legal partnerships were formed in Portland that would have lasting consequences. Milton W. Smith, a Marion County native who was admitted to practice in 1881, formed a partnership in 1885 with Joseph N. Teal, the son of a pioneer steamship operator and son-in-law of early Portland mayor David P. Thompson. Teal became deeply involved in water transportation law and later became the leading advocate for the establishment of public docks in Portland. Teal remained with the firm until his death in 1929. Another early member of the firm, Wirt Minor, was an avid golfer who helped found the Waverley Country Club. Office pressures in the 1890s apparently were less demanding than in the decades to come; Minor often golfed as many as thirty-six holes per day. The partnership originally created by Teal, Teal, Minor & Winfree at times ranked among the biggest in the city. In the 1980s and 1990s, however, it splintered into several smaller firms.

A year after Smith and Teal opened their office, two brothers established a firm under the name of Cake & Cake. Harry and William Cake, both born in Fostoria, Ohio, arrived in Portland in 1885 and 1886, respectively, after they both had graduated from Oberlin College and Cincinnati

Law School. At the time, a law school education was still rare in Portland. Most lawyers "read the law" while working for law firms and took the bar examination when they thought they were ready. The Cakes practiced primarily business law, with Harry Cake handling trial work and William Cake taking charge of office duties. Harry Cake practiced until retiring in 1913 to form the Commerce Mortgage Securities Company, while his younger brother continued in the firm for more than fifty years. Ralph Cake, William's son, took the firm into a second generation, continuing the emphasis on business practice. The firm evolved and grew into the firm of McEwen, Gisvold, Rankin, Carter & Streinz more than one hundred years after its founding.

The early- and mid-1880s also marked the arrival in Portland of two more lawyers who would establish the foundations of the city's largest law firms one hundred years later. Charles H. Carey, a slender Cincinnati native, whose interests included history and politics as well as law, formed the first of several partnerships in 1883. When he retired fifty years later, he was the patriarch of Oregon's largest law firm, Carey, Hart, Spencer & McCulloch. Carey served as a Portland Municipal Court judge from 1891 to 1894, thus earning the title of "Judge Carey" that stayed with him the rest of his career. Carey's firm evolved into Stoel Rives LLP, the

OHS OrHi CN000935

Charles Carey.

largest law partnership in Oregon.

As a historian, Carey published a *General History of Oregon* in 1922, which is one of the most complete volumes on the state's earliest years. In 1926, he issued *A History of the Oregon Constitution* based on newspaper accounts and other historical materials surviving from the constitutional convention over which Judge Deady presided in 1857. Because no official minutes were kept at the convention, Carey's book became—and remains—one of the most authoritative sources used by lawyers who try to analyze the history of the Oregon Constitution.

Politics was another vital interest of Carey's. Soon after his arrival in Portland, Carey became a strong supporter of John H. Mitchell and a leader in Mitchell's faction of the deeply split Republican party. The intra-party feud pitted Joseph Simon, who controlled Portland Republicans, against Mitchell, who led the rural faction. At stake was control of the dominant political party in the state, which Mitchell, damaged as he was by the revelations about his personal life, wasn't willing to cede. Later, the struggle focused on differences about the American monetary system, with Mitchell favoring free coinage of silver money while Simon supported the gold standard.

Simon's forces and Mitchell battled to a stalemate at the 1885 legislature, where Mitchell sought a new term in the United States Senate against Simon's candidate, merchant Solomon Hirsch. Legislators cast sixty-nine ballots in the regular session but left Salem without having elected a senator. They returned in the fall for a special session, where Mitchell, having lined up unexpected help from Democrats, won the Senate seat by a single vote. It was an extraordinary feat by Mitchell, in the view of Joseph Gaston, a lawyer and historian who lived through the era. "When Republicans rebelled at his leadership and repudiated his acts, he called in Democrats and beat down his own party leaders with the club of their political opponents," Gaston wrote.[19] Accusations of bribery, common in politics of the era, were hurled frequently in the newspapers, but formal charges were seldom prosecuted. The year 1885 also marked the arrival in Portland of William D. Fenton, a Missouri native whose family had crossed the plains to Yamhill County when he was a youth. Fenton was admitted to the Oregon bar in 1875, and handled several trials for the Southern Pacific Railroad before moving his office to Portland.

In 1891, Fenton became Southern Pacific's Oregon counsel. Fenton practiced in three partnerships in Portland between 1897 and 1900, but mostly he preferred to manage his own firm without entering partnership agreements. He occasionally also worked with his younger brother, James E. Fenton, who at various times practiced law in Eugene, Spokane, San Francisco, Seattle, and Portland. The two Fentons worked together on litigation that spanned seventeen years involving the three-million-acre land grant awarded to Southern Pacific's predecessor, the Oregon & California Railroad Company. The case arose after the federal government accused Southern Pacific of failing to honor land-grant rules of 1866, and the case made two trips to the United States Supreme Court. Southern Pacific ultimately was paid $4 million by Congress to settle the claims, and much of the remaining land was returned to public ownership.

Late in his career, Fenton joined with other lawyers, including his son, Kenneth Fenton, who subsequently was killed in an accident in 1917, to form a firm that evolved into the modern firm of Lane Powell Spears Lubersky LLP. More than one hundred years after Fenton's first links with Southern Pacific, the railroad continued to be a major client of the same office.

Besides new partnerships that proved to be long-lasting, the 1880s also ushered in technological changes. Portland lawyer Frederick V. Holman incorporated the United States Electric Lighting & Power Company in 1884 with entrepreneurs P. F. Morey and George Weidler. The firm was the predecessor of Portland General Electric Company, which Holman helped to incorporate in 1892. Holman, who was a leading utility lawyer for more than twenty years, had been born in 1852 in the hamlet of Pacific City. After coming to Portland as a young man, Holman worked at the *Daily Herald* newspaper for four years before heading off to undergraduate studies at the University of California. After graduating in 1875, Holman studied law in Portland and passed the bar in 1879.

As a fringe benefit of his utility work, Holman's law office in the Union Block in 1885 became the first in Portland to be outfitted with incandescent lights. Besides his utility work, Holman was a devoted rose enthusiast and Oregon historian. He wrote three history books and maintained an impressive personal library of rare historical books. He served as president of the Oregon Historical Society from 1907 until 1926, and died in 1927. Holman also was a member of the University of Oregon's board of regents from 1903 to 1915. Holman's successor as Oregon Historical Society president was Charles H. Carey, who headed the society for the next decade.

As Portland entered the 1890s, its growing community of lawyers helped create two new institutions designed to help meet the changing needs of the profession. Charles Carey joined two other prominent lawyers, Rufus Mallory and Alfred F. Sears, Jr., to form the Multnomah Law Library in October 1890. Mallory was the former U.S. attorney and congressman who had joined the Dolph firm. Sears, who later served as Multnomah County Circuit Court judge from 1896 to 1907, was then in partnership with Nate Simon, the brother of Joseph Simon. Carey, Sears, and Mallory formed a stock corporation and recruited one hundred Portland lawyers, each of whom pledged $100, to fund the new library. Julius C. Moreland, a former city attorney and then a county judge, pledged free rent and heat for the library in the Multnomah County Courthouse. As envisioned by its founders, the library would be open only to lawyers who paid annual dues.

The early years of the new library were bumpy ones. It opened shortly before one of the financial panics that swept Portland about every ten years during the latter decades of the nineteenth century. In 1893, Carey mailed out a notice warning that many of the one hundred lawyers who had made pledges had not paid them, and he added that "a large number of attorneys who are able to pay for their shares and should be interested in the success of the institution have failed to subscribe."[20] Another sign of financial stress occurred soon thereafter when the library sliced the monthly salary of its librarian from $40 to $25 per month.

The law library went through more financial upheavals as the years passed. Carey's commitment to the library, however, was unwavering. In 1907, he successfully lobbied for a state law allowing a portion of civil filing fees to be paid to the library in return for free library use by judges and district attorneys. Other lawyers were still required to pay dues. Carey remained on the library's board of directors until his death in 1941. Seventy years after Carey created the stock corporation, it became the target of an intense proxy fight that eventually led to the emergence of a comprehensive, modern legal research facility.

One year after the library was formed, seventy charter members, mostly from Portland's legal community, formed the Oregon Bar Association. Lawyers had to be admitted to practice by the Oregon Supreme Court for at least one year before they could become members of the voluntary association. Its founders envisioned the new association as a means of studying problems in the profession and for making recommendations about legal education and bar admissions.

In October 1891, the association's first president, Cyrus Dolph, addressed the charter members in Deady's ornate courtroom in the heart of a thriving city of 50,000 residents. It was a poignant moment for Dolph, who had arrived in Portland with his brother, Joseph, when the city was little more than a frontier village. Mansions of successful early-day bankers, lumbermen, and merchants were rising on blocks that had been virgin forest when Dolph arrived, and successful confectioner Frank Dekum was busy erecting a nine-story office and commercial building a few blocks away from the U.S. Building.

"Here, where within the memory of some of us dwelt only uncivilized Indians, without so much as a form of government, dwells now a civilization protected by law, in the enjoyment of domestic life, civil and religious liberty and the undisturbed possession of private property," he said. "In this flourishing city, animate with the activities of industry, we meet in a building appropriated to the convenient administration of justice, which compares favorably with those of the oldest of the States."[21]

The bar association grew to 132 members in its second year. Topics of discussion in the early years included many that would echo through the profession for decades to come: professional ethics and grievances, fees, and what to do about a lawyer who advertised his services in the newspaper. The Oregon Bar Association remained a voluntary association until 1935, when legislators created the Oregon State Bar as an "integrated" bar that all practicing lawyers were required to join.

The early 1890s also marked the beginning of another law office that would grow into one of Portland's largest. A Vermont native who had just completed his law degree at Boston University, Ralph W. Wilbur, arrived in Portland in 1891 at the urging of his brother, Earl, who was a pastor at Portland's Unitarian Church. Ralph Wilbur practiced law for nearly eighteen years by himself, primarily defending civil claims for insurance companies, before adding his first partner, Schuyler C. Spencer, in 1909. The firm grew through the years to become Portland's second largest, Schwabe Williamson & Wyatt. A century after its founding, the firm still maintains insurance defense as a major practice area.

Oregon and Portland politics were dominated in the 1890s by power struggles between the two Republican factions, led by lawyers John H. Mitchell and Joseph Simon. Never was the heat more intense than at the 1894 legislature, where the factions staged an unparalleled "holdup" session in which no work was conducted for the entire forty-day term.

Mitchell, who had been reelected to the United States Senate with little fuss in 1891, hoped to win another Senate term. The issue that caused the unprecedented rift in the state Republican party was money. Mitchell had been an avid supporter of silver money, while the Simon faction backed gold. The Republican national platform in 1897 adopted a gold plank, and Mitchell announced his support for the platform without repudiating his early stand for silver. His decision outraged Jonathan Bourne, the son of a Massachusetts whaling-vessel owner who had come to Portland after being shipwrecked near Formosa as a young man. Bourne studied law in Portland and passed the bar examination in 1881. Bourne also was involved in mining, but his foremost interest was politics. "He had a facility for forming and

OHS OrHi 26849

John H. Mitchell. Photo by Stohmeyer and Wyman.

preserving friendships; inherited much wealth which he was delighted to squander but, always, when his bank account slid low, some rich and kindly relative died and shifted it back to high," recalled Oswald West, a political reformer who later became governor.[22]

Bourne, a prominent state legislator who had been a fervent Mitchell supporter, suddenly shifted his support to Simon. Meanwhile, attorney William S. U'Ren, a leader of the minority Populist delegation, negotiated Simon's backing for U'Ren's proposed state constitutional amendment that would allow voters to act directly on state legislation by initiative and referendum. Bourne and Simon devised a simple plan to beat Mitchell: Mitchell couldn't be elected if a quorum of forty state representatives never showed up to conduct business. U'Ren joined the scheme after Simon promised to back the initiative and referendum proposal.

Bourne provided room and board at a Salem hotel for the legislators who didn't attend sessions. As Oswald West recalled many years later, "There the hungry could find food, the thirsty, drink, and the lonely, male or female companionship. There appeared to be no lack of funds for the relief of the legislative needy."[23]

The anti-Mitchell plan worked. Legislators went home after forty days, never having established a quorum to begin the session. Mitchell's Senate seat officially fell vacant. Governor William P. Lord appointed Portland businessman Henry Corbett to replace Mitchell. But that didn't end the controversy. The U.S. Senate, not pleased with Oregon's handling of the election, refused to seat Corbett. The vacancy remained until 1898, when a special session of the Oregon Legislature elected Mitchell's rival, Joseph Simon, to the seat. Simon thus became the third member of the Dolph law firm to reach the U.S. Senate.

The final years of the century also marked the start of the legal career of George Black, a native of Scotland who emigrated to the United States in 1889 and to Portland in 1890. Black graduated from the University of

Oregon law department in 1898 and opened an office in Portland. Black spent the bulk of his career in the accounting and investment business, George Black & Company, but he practiced law briefly with one of his two sons, Harvey N. Black. Harvey Black later opened his own office, which continues into the 1990s as Black Helterline.

A second son of George Black, George Black, Jr., also became a prominent Portland business lawyer. His firm, earlier known as Black, Kendall & Tremaine, later merged with two other Portland firms and a Seattle firm to create the Portland office of Davis Wright Tremaine LLP.

As the nineteenth century drew to a close, Portland continued on its fast growth. The city's population approached 100,000 and the electrification of privately run street railways opened the door for residential development of neighborhoods in Northeast and Southeast Portland, which had once been considered out in the country. The city's list of practicing lawyers had grown from 172 in 1890 to 300 as the new century beckoned.

CHAPTER THREE

The Progressive Era

Changes loomed on every horizon as Portland greeted the twentieth century. Inspired by lawyer L.B. Cox, a partner of Joseph N. Teal, civic boosters began laying plans for the 1905 Lewis and Clark Centennial Exposition that would transform marshes at the edge of the Willamette River in Northwest Portland into a showplace for the nation. Cox, who had practiced law in Portland since 1886, died at age forty-five in 1901 and did not live to see his dream realized. Late in 1901, Portland attorney Frederick V. Holman launched a campaign in public speeches and newspaper articles to give the city a nickname. "We cannot hope to compete with the exposition at St. Louis, with the buildings and grounds of the exposition itself," he warned, "but every yard can be made attractive and all the residence parts of Portland be made park-like with trees and flowers."[1] A dedicated rose enthusiast, Holman realized that Portland had one of the best climates anywhere for growing his favorite flowers. Therefore, he suggested that Portland be known as the "Rose City." Holman's idea took root. By the start of the exposition, Portland had adopted the nickname that long outlasted the successful exposition. Holman, by the way, won the exposition's gold medal for roses.

Nationally, Theodore Roosevelt became the nation's youngest president when William McKinley was assassinated in 1901, and progressive new ideas in the political and social worlds dominated Congress as well as the corridors of power in Oregon. But at the dawn of this era of change, two pioneer lawyers still held leading roles in Portland. John H. Mitchell, who was the target of the infamous 1897 hold-up session of the legislature, in 1901 won his fourth election to the United States Senate in seven attempts.

Mitchell, then sixty-six years old, still maintained a law office in Portland with his partner, Albert H. Tanner. The other pioneer still in the public eye was George H. Williams, the former territorial judge and United States Attorney General under President Grant. Williams was recruited by the Mitchell faction in 1902 for a successful run for Portland mayor. At age seventy-nine, he became the oldest holder of Portland's highest municipal office. Williams took with him two primary goals as he entered city hall: beautification of the city and suppression of gambling and prostitution. Throughout its rapid growth, Portland had a history of gambling and prostitution, particularly at the northern edge of downtown between Burnside Street and Portland's impressive new railroad depot, finished in 1890. "The cribs on the streets between the railroad depot and the hotels and elsewhere on our main streets should be suppressed and their inmates compelled to quit their business or to move into more secluded quarters,"[2] Williams told the city council. He also urged enforcement of ordinances against public gambling.

Courtesy of *The Oregonian*

Frederick V. Holman.

Williams' election in 1902 coincided with Oregon's adoption of the initiative and referendum, designed by lawyer William S. U'Ren to kill off the kind of political machinery dominated by Oregon's two rival U.S. Senators, Mitchell and Simon. Since the early 1890s, the soft-spoken U'Ren had battled, cajoled, and negotiated to give more power directly to voters under the Oregon Constitution. "My sole purpose in this life is to secure for the people the direct control of the government and every officer in it," he declared.[3] Before the first decade of the new century was finished, U'Ren and his supporters had passed the initiative and referendum, and authority to recall elected officials from office. In addition, U'Ren spearheaded a major effort toward direct popular election of U.S. Senators. The package of reforms established Oregon as a national leader in citizens' political rights.

U'Ren's background made him an unlikely candidate for such sweeping influence. A native of Wisconsin, U'Ren was the son of an independent-minded itinerant farmer and blacksmith whose personal fortunes seemed to improve little despite numerous family moves westward. U'Ren studied law in Denver in the 1880s, but his wanderings took him to Iowa, California, and Hawaii before he landed in Oregon about 1890. He ventured into the nursery business in Milwaukie, but he was wiped out by the financial panic of 1893.

U'Ren then opened a law office in Oregon City and later practiced in Portland. He became engrossed in a Swiss concept of direct legis-

OHS OrHi 81789

William S. U'Ren.

lation, in which voters themselves could determine passage of proposed new laws. Under the direct legislation proposal, voters could pass new laws through the initiative and they could defeat or approve legislatively created acts through the referendum. Foiled in his first attempts to win the initiative and referendum through lobbying, U'Ren won election to the Oregon House of Representatives as a Populist in 1897. He controlled few votes as a leader of the minority party, but he bargained with the badly split Republican factions to advance his own goals. U'Ren played a major role in the hold-up session of 1897. He calculated that the political stalemate between the Mitchell and Simon factions would prove to the public the corruption of Oregon's party machinery. Under the state constitution at the time, the legislature had to approve the initiative and referendum proposal in consecutive sessions before voters could consider the amendment. Having won Joseph Simon's support in 1897, U'Ren quietly steered the initiative and referendum through the 1899 and 1901 sessions. Voters in 1902 approved it by a resounding 62,024 votes to 4,668.

When opponents challenged the initiative and referendum in the Oregon Supreme Court, U'Ren offered supporting briefs from every corner of Oregon's political landscape, including John Mitchell, George H. Williams, Joseph N. Teal, Governor George Chamberlain, and C.E.S. Wood. The court affirmed the measure in 1903.[4] Lincoln Steffens, an early investigative journalist, once asked U'Ren whether he should land in hell for bargaining with the political forces U'Ren struggled so hard to topple. U'Ren replied, "Well, I would go to hell for the people of Oregon."[5]

U'Ren's reforms included a primary election for Senate candidates and later a requirement asking state legislative candidates to declare if they would support the people's choice for the Senate. The first United States Senator elected under both reforms was Governor George Chamberlain, the former Multnomah County District Attorney and state attorney general, who narrowly defeated Portland lawyer Harry Cake in 1908. Legislators sent

Chamberlain to the Senate in 1909, where he supported the Seventeenth Amendment to the United States Constitution, which guaranteed popular election of Senators.

Oregon's political changes of the early 1900s unfolded amidst one of the biggest scandals in state history, the timber fraud cases that spanned 1904 to 1908. Congress in 1878 had passed the Timber and Stone Act, which allowed grants of federal timber lands to homesteaders who vowed to live on the land. Congress later adopted legislation allowing owners of land inside newly created federal forest preserves to trade for land outside those boundaries.

Transgressions of both those laws became the focus of investigations headed by Francis Heney, a special federal prosecutor who arrived in Portland in 1904. Heney, the son of a San Francisco furniture merchant, had already made a reputation for prosecuting fraudulent land-grant cases in Arizona. Heney's aggressive style was accompanied twice in his career by major violence. While in private practice in Arizona, Heney, acting in self defense, fatally shot a prominent physician whose wife had retained Heney to represent her in divorce proceedings. Later, while prosecuting municipal corruption in San Francisco in 1906, Heney was shot through the neck and cheek near the end of a sensational trial that convicted the city's political boss, Abe Reuf. Miraculously, Heney survived.

The investigation into possible timber fraud in Oregon was instigated by Secretary of the Interior Ethan Allen Hitchcock, who had heard rumors about misconduct in several western states. He first sent William J. Burns to Oregon to make preliminary inquiries. Burns was a federal investigator who, using unusual techniques and a penchant for publicity, gradually built a reputation as the nation's best private detective. He was joined later by Heney, who quickly decided that U.S. attorney John H. Hall wasn't acting aggressively with the evidence being found. Heney sought and obtained Hall's removal as the state's chief federal prosecutor. Hall eventually became one of the timber fraud defendants.

Heney learned that major timber companies had been paying people to sign up for the cheap land grants and then turn the land over immediately to the timber companies, which were amassing large tracts of timber. Heney also alleged that federal timber-preserve boundaries were being manipulated so that some owners could exchange their property for more valuable lands outside the federal preserves. Heney ultimately indicted thirty-four defendants on criminal charges, and convicted thirty-three. They included Senator John H. Mitchell, former U.S. attorney Hall, U.S. Representative John N. Williamson, who represented eastern Oregon in Congress, and prominent Portland lawyers Albert H. Tanner and Franklin Pierce Mays, then a state legislator.

Heney indicted Mitchell twice. The first indictment accused the senator on two occasions of receiving $1,000 in cash bribes from Stephen A. D. Puter, a land agent who later bragged about being "king" of the timber frauds. But Heney delayed that case to pursue one with stronger evidence, based on a written partnership agreement between Tanner and Mitchell. Federal law made it a criminal misdemeanor for members of Congress to receive fees for representing anyone with business involving a federal agency. The second indictment accused Mitchell of collecting payments for expediting several land-grant applications through the federal Land Office. Tanner testified before a federal grand jury that the legal fees in question had been routed to him, Tanner, and not to Mitchell. But Heney learned that the partnership agreement between Tanner and Mitchell called for Mitchell to retain all Land Office fees. Tanner then admitted perjuring himself before the grand jury and agreed to testify against his law partner.

Mitchell's trial in the summer of 1905 lasted two weeks, although the testimony took but a few days. Approximately half the time was taken by lengthy arguments by the lawyers to a jury composed of ten farmers and two merchants. Mitchell, who turned seventy as the trial began, was represented by two defense lawyers. Alfred S. Bennett, of The Dalles, had served as a Wasco County Circuit Court judge from 1882 to 1884. Bennett was considered one of Oregon's best trial lawyers of his era, and would serve on the Oregon Supreme Court late in his career from 1918 to 1920. Mitchell's other attorney was John M. Thurston, a former member of the United States Senate from Nebraska who also served as general counsel of the powerful Union Pacific Railroad. Mitchell, whose long white beard was trimmed to a sharp point, did not testify. The defense lawyers argued that Mitchell was confused about the payments and thought that Tanner was receiving them. Yet there was no confusion in Tanner's mind, and the amounts were not paltry. Heney contended that Mitchell had received $52,000 in illegal attorney fees over four years, a tidy sum considering that Mitchell's Senate salary at the time was only $5,000 per year. Mitchell tried to go for a walk while jurors deliberated on July 3, but he found no peace, as crowds assembling for a fireworks show forced him back to his hotel. When jurors returned the unanimous verdict of guilty late that night, Heney wasn't present. He was attending festivities at the centennial exposition.

Mitchell was sentenced to six months in jail and fined $1,000. The misdemeanor conviction, if it withstood appeals, carried even a more severe sanction: expulsion from the Senate. Mitchell's political supporters claimed that President Roosevelt had targeted Mitchell because Mitchell, as a senator, had opposed Roosevelt's strong-arm tactics in taking the Panama Canal Zone from Columbia. Mitchell, with Portland attorney Charles Carey working on the brief, filed an appeal but it was never argued or decided because Mitchell died later in 1905 from a diabetic coma after oral surgery. The U.S. Senate, breaking with tradition, neither adjourned nor declared a memorial resolution marking his death.

Tanner, a former municipal court judge, had been a close friend of Mitchell's since 1882 and Mitchell's law partner since 1890. When the Oregon Bar Association sought to disbar him for lying to the federal grand jury in the Mitchell case, Tanner explained that Mitchell "implored me, in the most pathetic manner, to stand between him and disgrace and ruin in his old age, after a lifetime of public service, and he represented that his fate was in my hands, and mine alone."[6] Tanner received a pardon from President Theodore Roosevelt after his federal conviction, and returned to practice after receiving a 90-day suspension from the Oregon Supreme Court.

John Hall, the former U.S. attorney, was convicted in 1908 on a conspiracy charge for failing to prosecute officials of the Butte Creek Company, who had built illegal fences on federal lands. Heney, who returned periodically to Portland to prosecute the land-fraud cases, contended that Hall decided to pursue a civil rather than a criminal penalty against the company because of Hall's friendship with company officials and their attorney, Franklin Pierce Mays. Williamson, the eastern Oregon congressman who was a large-scale Crook County rancher, and Mays were convicted in separate trials of conspiracy involving the creation of a 200,000-acre Blue Mountain Forest Preserve in eastern Oregon. Williamson, Mitchell, and Mays were accused of helping to create the forest preserve out of arid and generally worthless land, seeking transfers for land outside the preserve boundaries valued at an estimated $3 million. Williamson, according to the prosecution, was to receive 20,000 acres for his efforts. Mitchell had been accused of accepting bribes in connection with that case, but died before it came to trial. Mays, a prominent lawyer who had practiced in Hood River and Portland, had been U.S. Attorney for Oregon in 1891 to 1893. He retired from law practice when the timber scandals arose and spent much of the rest of his life in the Hood River area, where he became known as a local historian.

Heney, it turned out later, left little to chance in these high-profile prosecutions. Fearing that his efforts could be foiled by local Republican party officials, Heney had sought and gained removal of United States Marshal

Jack Matthews, a party boss who would have been in charge of subpoenaing federal jurors. But years later, evidence surfaced showing that detective Burns and Heney themselves seemingly stacked the jury deck for the 1906 trial that convicted Mays and Willard N. Jones, a state legislator, of conspiracy. President Taft in 1912, long after Heney had left Oregon, issued pardons after learning that Burns' associates had secretly interviewed all prospective jurors in those two trials. Publicly, Heney tried to brush the pardons aside as "all rot," contending they were merely the result of "political pull."[7] It turned out, however, that the prosecution's shenanigans violated the accepted rules of fair play. Burns, using a code, had sent a telegram to Interior Secretary Hitchcock stating, "Jury commissioners cleaned out old box from which trial jurors were selected and put in 600 names, every one of which was investigated before they were placed in the box. This is confidential."[8] The files of Heney and Burns revealed some of the jury investigation materials. One juror, for example, was described thus: "Conviction, by God, from the word go; would convict Christ."[9]

It also appeared that Heney had negotiated with the Roosevelt administration to keep W. W. Cotton, who had been nominated as U.S. District Court judge after Bellinger's death early in 1905, from presiding over Mitchell's trial. Cotton, a former partner of Joseph Teal, had overcome a serious stammering problem as a child to become one of the nation's leading railroad lawyers. His chief client was the powerful Oregon Railway & Navigation Co., and Heney feared that Cotton would be partial to the defense in the timber-fraud cases. District Court Judge John DeHaven of San Francisco presided over the Mitchell trial. Cotton, after meeting personally with President Roosevelt in July 1905, "resigned" from the judicial post he never held and resumed representing railroads.[10] Cotton gave no public explanation.

The United States Supreme Court in 1908 dealt another blow to the timber-fraud cases when it reversed the conviction of Williamson, the congressman. Jurors in 1905 had convicted Williamson of conspiring to commit subornation of perjury in proceedings for purchase of federal lands. The Ninth Circuit Court of Appeals affirmed the conviction, but the Supreme Court said the trial was tainted by irrelevant evidence. The high court said that the trial should have been limited to procurement of perjury in connection with the original land-grant applications and not in regard to the final proof for land patents after publication. In the meantime, however, Oregon voters in 1907 had replaced Williamson in Congress.

Regardless of the prosecutorial blemishes in the timber-fraud cases, Burns' burgeoning career continued without a misstep. In private business dealings, Burns set up an international network of private investigation offices bearing his name. As a public official, he served as director of the U.S. Department of Justice Bureau of Investigation, a forerunner of the FBI, from 1921 to 1924. Heney's prospects proved less grandiose than he wanted. He had hoped that his crime-fighting fame would propel him to state office in California or even at the national level, but those dreams never came true. Heney ended his career as a Los Angeles County Superior Court judge from 1931 until his death in 1937.

Mitchell had one year remaining on his Senate term at his death in 1905. Governor George Chamberlain appointed John M. Gearin, a former Multnomah County district attorney and a partner in the Dolph law firm, to fill the vacancy. Gearin became the fourth and last member of the Dolph office to hold the title of United States Senator, following Joseph Dolph, Joseph Simon, and Mitchell. Gearin's term lasted little more than a year, however. Voters in 1906 expressed a preference for Fred W. Mulkey, son of the former veteran county prosecutor Marion F. Mulkey, to finish the final few weeks of Mitchell's term. Like his pioneer father, Fred Mulkey had served on the Portland City Council. He also belonged to virtually every prominent social club in the city. Voters in the same election favored Jonathan Bourne, one of the old-school power brokers who nevertheless supported popular election of senators, to succeed Mulkey for the full six-year term. Mulkey's tenure as senator lasted but six weeks, ending in March 1907, when Bourne began his six-year term. Bourne, described much later by Governor Oswald West as being "unhampered by religion or morals,"[11] proved that it would take more than structural reform to eliminate the excesses of Oregon's nineteenth-century politics. Bourne's own party ended his political career after one term when Oregon Republicans failed to renominate him for a second term. Bourne, who died in 1940, spent much of the rest of his life living in the East.

Coincidentally, the end of Mitchell's career in 1905 also marked the end of the lengthy public career of George H. Williams, who had been elected to a three-year term as mayor in 1902. Critics claimed that fines imposed during his crackdown on gambling and prostitution amounted to little more than a systematic new source of municipal revenue, paid repeatedly by the same offenders. At age eighty-two, Williams was defeated by an aggressive young reform candidate, Harry Lane. Lane later won election to the U.S. Senate, but he died near the end of his term in 1917, opening the way for a second brief senatorial stint by Portland attorney Fred W. Mulkey. Governor James Withycombe appointed Charles L. McNary to fill Lane's vacancy immediately, but that 1918 election gave voters a chance to elect a candidate to fill the remaining few weeks of Lane's term. Mulkey announced himself as a candidate for the shortened term, and said he would resign immediately in favor of the candidate who won the full term. That method, Mulkey said, would assure that Oregon's senator would hold an advantage in seniority over any other newly elected senators in 1918. McNary won the full term and Mulkey the short term. Good to his word, Mulkey stepped down after holding the title of Senator only from November 5, to December 17, 1918. McNary, the brother of John McNary, who became a U.S. District Court judge in 1927, was one of Oregon's most popular senators. He held office until his death in February 1944. By comparison, Fred Mulkey's two senatorial victories put him in office for a combined total of twelve weeks.

George Williams died at age eighty-seven, five years after leaving the mayor's office. His death broke one of the final living links with Oregon's pioneer era. C.E.S. Wood wrote a memorial recalling Williams' contributions in national, state, and Portland affairs. "His life covers the most active part of the history of this country," Wood wrote. "When it began, there were neither railways nor telegraph lines. Travel was by river, canal and coach. Chicago did not exist. Pittsburgh and St. Louis were the western frontier and in all that has gone to the making of the country and of the State of Oregon he has had a conspicuous part."[12]

While the new era was bringing major changes to Oregon's political environment, progressives who worried about the effects of the Industrial Revolution began trying to invoke new workplace regulations. William Wallace Banks, a Portland lawyer and state legislator, successfully sponsored a bill in 1903 limiting the working hours of women employed in laundries to no more than ten hours per day. Banks, a native of Illinois, had come to Portland as a teenager and graduated from the University of Oregon law department in 1896. He served as an assistant U.S. attorney from 1904 to 1906, assisting Heney in the Mitchell trial, and began his long state legislative career as a Republican in 1903.

One of the first women to claim protection under Banks' legislation was Emma Gotcher, an employee in Portland's Grand Laundry. She complained that the laundry's owner, Curt Muller, ordered her to work more than ten hours on Labor Day, 1905. Circuit Court Judge Alfred F. Sears, Jr., expressed doubts about the new law when Muller came to court, but he convicted Muller and imposed a $10 fine. William D. Fenton, one of Portland's leading business lawyers who was at the peak of his career, viewed the new law as an unconstitutional intrusion into Muller's right to enter into contracts with his employees. After the Oregon Supreme Court affirmed Sears' ruling, Fenton appealed to the United States Supreme Court. The case set a national precedent when the nation's top court unanimously affirmed the laundry regulations in 1908.[13] But the case also became famous for another reason: Louis Brandeis.

Brandeis was the Boston lawyer, and later U.S. Supreme Court justice, who aimed his impressive legal skills toward social reform and consumer advocacy. He was a brother-in-law of Josephine Goldmark, a leader of the National Consumers' League, who had endorsed Oregon's new workplace laws. Goldmark recruited Brandeis to defend against Muller's attack in the U.S. Supreme Court. Goldmark and Brandeis crammed their Supreme Court brief with statutes, statistics, and medical and social science studies showing physical differences between men and women and the harmful effects of long working hours on women. Of the 113-page brief, Brandeis devoted only a few pages to legal analyses that are the routine grist of appellate briefs. Social data compiled by Goldmark comprised the rest. The document became known as the first "Brandeis brief," a tool of legal advocacy that went far beyond the customary legal research for an appellate brief.

The bulky brief was filled with material that would be criticized later in the century as sexist, but it had the desired effect for Brandeis. Justice David J. Brewer, writing for the unanimous Court, noted, "The legislation and opinions referred to… are significant of a widespread belief that woman's physical structure, and the functions she performs in consequence thereof, justify special legislation restricting or qualifying the conditions under which she should be permitted to toil…. "[14]

Fenton realized the significance of his defeat. "The decision may mark an epoch in this class of legislation," he noted soon after the decision. "It will have the effect of sustaining this trend in lawmaking and will probably go far toward establishing a general eight or ten-hour law."[15] Fenton soon was proved correct. In 1913, Brandeis argued another Oregon case before the U.S. Supreme Court, *Stettler v. O'Hara*,[16] that challenged new state wage-and-hour regulations for women. A primary drafter of those regulations was Dan J. Malarkey, a Portland lawyer and legislator who served as state senate president in 1913. Brandeis was appointed to the U.S. Supreme Court after the arguments and before the case was decided. So *Stettler* was reargued, this time by Felix Frankfurter, another prominent eastern social-reform lawyer who later also would sit on the nation's top court. Frankfurter also defended the state in *Bunting v. State of Oregon*,[17] which involved state legislation setting limits on work hours for all employees in mills, factories, and manufacturing. The new regulations in *Stettler* and *Bunting* were both affirmed by the U.S. Supreme Court in 1917. Years later, a friend asked Brandeis to suggest a name for the first Brandeis brief. He replied, "What Any Fool Knows."[18]

The *Muller* decision, social legislation affecting wages and hours, and the constitutional changes inspired by U'Ren were among matters mentioned by Charles H. Carey, president of the Oregon Bar Association, when he gave the president's speech to the bar in 1913. These changes amounted to nothing less than a "bloodless revolution," Carey said. He worried about what he saw as a move toward Socialism and the diminution of property rights. "For not being restrained by their Constitution, since it may be amended at will, the liberty of the person and the protection of property rights must necessarily rest, in the final analysis, upon the sobriety, the reasonableness and the substantial honesty of the voters themselves."[19] The changes to which he referred included the end of the machine-style party politics, in which Carey himself had been a vital player.

Using the relatively new muscle of the initiative, Oregon voters adopted a measure in 1914 outlawing the sale of liquor. However, citizens could still import spirits for their personal use at home. An expanded "bone dry" amendment was adopted in 1916, closing that loophole. One of the first prosecutions under the new bone-dry law in Multnomah County came before Circuit Court Judge Henry L. McGinn, a former district attorney. "If a man wants to make a short cut to hell across lots, I don't believe the state has any right to stop him," McGinn said from the bench in December 1916.[20]

Those views reflected the habits of one of Portland's most popular and colorful judges ever. McGinn was an early Portland native, born in 1859 to Irish pioneer parents. He became a successful trial lawyer, prone to quoting frequently from the Bible and Shakespeare. He was an early adherent of Joseph Simon's faction of the Republican party, and later admitted being familiar with corrupt voting practices of the late nineteenth century.

However, McGinn changed with the times. He turned his back on machine politics to become a prominent voice for reform in the Progressive era. He won a six-year term on the Multnomah County Circuit Court in 1910, and established himself as an unorthodox, often impatient judge. In trials without juries, McGinn ruled as soon as he had made up his mind, often after hearing testimony from a single witness. Faced one day with a long docket of pretrial motions, McGinn reportedly ascended to the bench, announced that all motions and demurrers were denied and quickly returned to his chambers.[21]

Courtesy of *The Oregonian*

Henry McGinn.

McGinn wasn't one to hide his feelings about the cases before him. In one case, a woman sued a railroad construction company, alleging that she had not been paid for meals she served to the company's laborers. In a heated exchange with the defense attorney, William Wallace Banks, during the jury trial, McGinn said he would make sure "that this infamous case will not be decided against this woman." The Oregon Supreme Court affirmed the outcome in 1913, notwithstanding McGinn's apparent prejudice.

Oregon Chief Justice Thomas A. McBride offered Judge McGinn some advice, however. "The writer knows from experience on the circuit bench that it is sometimes very difficult for a judge to refrain from making comments on a case," he wrote. "[B]ut after a reversal or two occasioned by this practice, he concluded to go, not to the ant, but to the meek and lowly oyster… and to keep the judicial mouth shut. He commends the example of the silent oyster to all trial judges."[22]

Oyster or not, McGinn wouldn't countenance injustice even if it came from the verdict of a jury. In a later case, he refused to accept a verdict on behalf of a man accused in a civil case of defaulting on two promissory notes to a Portland department store. "This man owes the money and every man on this jury knows it," Judge McGinn fumed. "Gentlemen, you will be dismissed from further consideration of this case. There will be a new trial granted. It takes 13 men to rob anybody in this court, and I want that understood."[23] The state high court in 1915 affirmed McGinn's decision to grant a new trial.

As McGinn's statement suggested in the prohibition case, his personal habits included drinking. At times he didn't show up for work at the courthouse, and lawyers knew why: McGinn was on a bender. But he remained wildly popular among his constituents. After he decided not to seek a new term on the circuit court, many of his supporters encouraged him to run for the U.S. Senate. McGinn chose instead to return to private practice. When he died at his favorite bawdy house in February 1928, *The Oregonian* charitably reported that McGinn collapsed on an early-morning walk. Chief Justice McBride, who had urged McGinn to follow the practices of a judicial oyster, served as a pallbearer.

McGinn's funeral was unlike any other lawyer's or judge's, McBride commented in a memorial. "There I saw not only the highest officers of the state, the judges of the courts, the leading citizens of the city where he was born, but . . . I saw the poor, the very poor of his community; I saw men and women of all colors looking for the last time upon the features of one who had been their champion and friend.... "[24]

Soon after McGinn's judicial career ended in 1916, Portland Mayor George Baker, a former vaudeville showman, launched a long-lasting judicial career by appointing George Rossman to a vacancy on the Portland Municipal Court. Rossman, who had been in private practice for seven years before his appointment in 1917, had planned to practice in Washington state, where he had grown up and worked his way through high school and college. But after he graduated from the University of Chicago Law School, Rossman found that he had missed the deadline for Washington's annual bar examination, so he took the Oregon examination instead. Rossman was promoted to Multnomah County Circuit Court in 1922, and to the Oregon Supreme Court in 1927. He remained on the state high court for more than thirty-seven years, setting a record for length of service, until retiring in 1964.

The spirit of reform that permeated the first years of the new century also affected Oregon's legal community. Lawyers grew concerned about qualifications and testing for bar membership and about policing the ethics of their profession. Early in the new century, Multnomah County was the last in Oregon not to have a county association of lawyers. One attempt to form a county association had died as a result of squabbling over political endorsements. But that changed in 1906 with the creation of the Multnomah Bar Association. William Fenton, who had just finished serving as a director for the Lewis and Clark Centennial Exposition, became the first president. He resigned from the association suddenly in 1907 without giving a reason, but lawyers speculated that he was unhappy about the bar's endorsement of proposed railroad regulations. William M. Cake, the brother of Harry Cake, succeeded Fenton as county bar president of 1907, and the new bar association claimed 169 members after its first year. The roster of new officials included as secretary Ralph B. Fisher, who soon thereafter became the tragic victim of a bar disciplinary matter.

Fisher in 1907 had prosecuted another Portland lawyer, James A. Finch, on ethics charges of appearing in court while drunk, writing bad checks, and illegally notarizing pension papers. As a result, the Oregon Supreme Court suspended Finch for one year. Finch wanted to apply for reinstatement sooner, but Fisher refused to sign his petition. On November 28, 1908, Finch, armed with a handgun, went to Fisher's office in the Mohawk Building. The brief confrontation ended with Finch fatally shooting Fisher in the back of his head.

Finch was charged with murder in December and went on trial only eight days after the indictment. Charles Carey volunteered a bright young member of his corporate law office, Omar C. Spencer, to assist the Multnomah County district attorney's office in prosecuting Finch. Spencer, who had become a member of the bar in 1905, eventually practiced for forty years in Portland and became one of the city's leading corporate lawyers. Besides community activities that included stints as president of the Oregon Historical Society and the Portland Community Chest, Spencer also served as an officer of Pacific Telephone and Telegraph.

Finch claimed he shot in self-defense after Fisher struck him on the head with a notary seal, but the prosecution showed that the seal was still locked in Fisher's desk after his death. At the end of a two-week trial, Finch's defense team, led by Charles Lord, a former Multnomah County district attorney who became a leading personal injury lawyer of his era, made closing arguments lasting fifteen hours spread over two days. Jurors deliberated for only thirty minutes, however, before convicting Finch of first-degree murder. "Word of the conviction spread rapidly about the city," *The*

Oregonian reported the next day. "General satisfaction was expressed at the outcome of the trial, for public sentiment has been strongly against Finch since the day he assassinated Ralph Fisher, and his clumsy story of self defense has found few believers."[25]

Circuit Court Judge Earl C. Bronaugh, who showed signs of impatience with Finch's defense during the trial, imposed a death sentence. Finch appealed to the Oregon Supreme Court, and included an attack on his lawyers as one ground for appeal. Justice Thomas McBride, writing for the court, found the criticism unjustified. "That they failed, after an intelligent and faithful effort, to secure his acquittal is not surprising in view of the testimony disclosed in the record," he wrote, affirming the conviction and penalty.[26]

Finch maintained his self-defense claim, but Governor Frank W. Benson found no justification for commuting the death sentence to a life term in prison. One year and a day after Fisher's death, Finch was hanged at the Oregon State Penitentiary. *The Oregonian*, which had criticized Finch editorially, noted that he "walked to his death with firm and steady steps."[27]

Another innovation of the era, although short-lived, was the creation of Portland's first public defender to represent indigent defendants charged with crimes. Municipal Court Judge John H. Stevenson first advocated representation for indigent defendants in January 1914. "Day after day men and women come before the court utterly unaware of their legal rights," he said. "It is the theory that the city and district attorneys act impartially, but the large volume of business and present conditions do not allow this impartial feeling."[28]

Stevenson himself was a former Multnomah County deputy district attorney, having started his legal career in that office in 1907 and 1908. The law was his second career. Stevenson had worked as a reporter and editorial writer for the Portland *Telegram* newspaper from 1901 to 1907, and attended night classes at the old University of Oregon law department. Stevenson later served on Multnomah County Circuit Court from 1925 until his death in 1930.

Stevenson helped establish a system of volunteer lawyers to appear in Municipal Court in 1914, but by the end of that year several Portland lawyers petitioned Mayor H. R. Albee to hire a permanent public defender. Although concerned about costs, the city council agreed. In March 1915, the city hired David Robinson, a young lawyer who was the son of a Portland painter.

Like his father, Robinson had been a union painter and served as president of a Portland local at age seventeen. As the new public defender, Robinson made daily rounds at the municipal jail, representing thieves, prostitutes, and drunks who could not afford to hire lawyers. He found few whom he believed to be completely innocent. But he viewed the importance of his job as arguing for sentences appropriate for the crimes: longer jail terms for the professional thieves and shorter ones for those who had been forced into crime as dupes of others or as a result of economic necessity. Although Robinson's contract called for him to provide assistance in criminal cases only, the young lawyer took it upon himself to help many defendants with civil matters, such as collecting back pay from employers and dealing with creditors.

Robinson's first lawyer job ended after a year and a half. The city council eliminated the public defender post in August 1917, as an economy measure. Mayor George Baker, the former vaudeville actor, saw no need for the position. "The purpose is to give these people justice," Baker said of the public defender. "That is work to be performed by the judge, it seems to me."[29]

Robinson's desire to practice public interest law didn't end so quickly, however. During a legal career that lasted nearly fifty years, Robinson remained an advocate for the downtrodden and for equal opportunity. For thirty years he worked as the western district manager of the Anti-Defamation League of B'Nai B'rith. Along the way, he campaigned to end prostitution and to help create a Legal Aid office. He served as president of the City Club, Congregation Beth Israel, and the Portland Rose Society. As a reflection of his interest in flowers and youngsters, Robinson over several years gave away thousands of rose bushes to children at his Northeast Portland home. "If nothing else," he said late in his life, "I have proven that a rose grows as beautifully for a Jew as it does for a gentile or a Negro, and to me that is a very important point."[30]

The first decade of the twentieth century brought rapid growth to Portland. Fueled in part by the success of the 1905 exposition, the city's population swelled to nearly 200,000 by 1910. One of the newcomers that year was Albert B. Ridgway, a native of Washington, D.C., who had just completed his undergraduate and legal studies at Georgetown University. Ridgway and a classmate, Everett A. Johnson, opened a civil law office. Johnson also worked in the U.S. attorney's office while their private practice was in its infancy. One of Ridgway's first clients was Carl Thielman, a Portland cigar manufacturer who needed speedy assistance early one morning when a customer departed with inventory without paying. Ridgway, who kept down expenses in his new practice by sleeping at his office, was the first lawyer Thielman could find. The office started by Ridgway and Johnson became the oldest of three Portland firms that merged in the late 1980s and then joined with a Seattle-based firm to create Davis Wright Tremaine LLP in 1989. Ridgway was active for many years in Oregon Bar Association affairs, and served as president in 1925. Ridgway and Johnson remained partners until Ridgway's death in 1940. Johnson died four years later.

Another legal newcomer of the era was McCants Stewart, the first black lawyer to be admitted to practice in Oregon. The son of T. McCants Stewart, a lawyer and ambassador to the Virgin Islands, Stewart arrived in Portland in 1902 after graduating from Tuskegee Institute in Alabama in 1896, and the University of Minnesota Law School in 1899. Stewart was admitted to practice in Minnesota in 1899. After his admission to the

Oregon bar in 1903, he practiced as a sole practitioner in Portland until 1917. Among other activities, Stewart in 1903 helped found *The Advocate*, which was Portland's second newspaper for the city's black community. Stewart also lobbied for state legislation that would end discrimination against minorities in public accommodations, such as hotels and restaurants. However, no such bill was passed until 1953, long after Stewart's departure from Portland. Building a successful practice in Portland—a city with relatively few minority residents—proved difficult for Stewart. He moved to San Francisco, hoping for better economic opportunities, but took his own life at age forty-two and still in debt.[31]

As Portland's population and legal community grew, so did the judiciary. By 1910, legislators had increased the number of Multnomah County Circuit Court judges to five. Congress added a second U.S. District Court seat in 1909, and the addition of two wings at the west end of the Federal

OHS OrHi 81964

McCants Stewart and daughter Mary Stewart

Building in 1904 had already nearly doubled the size of that building. U.S. District Court Judge Charles Bellinger, who died in 1905, was succeeded by Judge Charles E. Wolverton. Wolverton had practiced for twenty years in Albany before advancing to the Oregon Supreme Court in 1894. He was joined on the federal bench by a close friend, Judge Robert S. Bean, who was appointed to fill the new judgeship in 1909. The two had met as undergraduates at Christian College in Monmouth, a predecessor to Western Oregon University. Later, Bean practiced briefly in Lane County before becoming a circuit court judge for Lane, Douglas, Curry, and Coos counties in 1882. In 1890, Bean joined his friend Wolverton on the Oregon Supreme Court.

Another bond between the two federal judges was their dedication to higher education. Bean served as a regent for the University of Oregon from 1882 to 1920, and spent the final twenty-one years as president of the board of regents. He also was recognized as one of the university's most avid football fans. Wolverton also taught night law school classes in Portland from 1912 to 1915. The legal and personal friendship between Judges Wolverton and Bean spanned five decades, ending in 1926 when Wolverton died at age seventy-five while reading a book in front of the fireplace at the Gearhart Hotel.

By 1910, planning was underway for a bigger Multnomah County Courthouse. The courthouse was to occupy the same site as the first courthouse, built in 1866, which, despite a number of additions, had become woefully inadequate. A key supporter for a new courthouse was Lionel R. Webster, one of the state's leading trial lawyers, who served as a Multnomah County judge from 1902 to 1910. The position of county judge in those days was comparable to a modern county commissioner.

Webster was a Connecticut native who migrated to southern Oregon, where he served for four years as a circuit court judge for Klamath and Jackson counties in the late 1880s. He moved to Portland in 1895, where he was a law partner with Charles Carey and Franklin Pierce Mays for two years. In 1897, Webster returned to southern Oregon, where he defended Ed Oliver, who was accused of murdering a prosperous but unpopular pioneer cattleman, Peter French. Webster won an acquittal in one of the most heavily publicized murder cases of the era. After his return to Portland, Webster spent the rest of his career practicing law, engaging in local politics, and volunteering for social causes. He defended former U.S. attorney John Hall in the timber-fraud cases, but with a less successful outcome than the Peter French case.

As a public official, Webster stood for honesty and clean government. The county was $700,000 in debt when he took office in 1902, and high-ranking county officials were paid by percentages of public funds they collected rather than by established salaries. Opportunities for corruption were rife. Webster hired accountants to examine county books. As the *Oregon Journal* reported, "Revelations, frequently of startling nature, followed in rapid succession. In some instances suits were instituted to recover amounts due, and improperly taken or withheld from the county. The Webster administration ushered in a new day and set up a new standard for the administration of Multnomah County's business."[32] The county's books were balanced and plans for a new courthouse were complete when Webster resigned from county government in 1910.

Among his other interests, Webster was an early-day advocate for automobile safety. After leaving county office, Webster headed the Oregon Good Roads Association, an organization that lobbied for paved roads. He also was credited with drafting the state's first widow's pension law, which, in 1913, allowed single mothers to seek funds from county juvenile courts if they could prove need to support children under age sixteen. The law allowed $10 per month for the first child and $7.50 for each additional child.

Webster, still at the peak of his career at age sixty-four, met a peculiar death one evening in September 1918: he was crushed by an elevator at his fourth-floor office in the Columbia Building. An inexperienced elevator operator stopped the cage a few feet above the floor, and Webster somehow fell into the gap. He was crushed by the elevator cage and then fell to the bottom of the shaft. A coroner's inquest blamed both the operator and the building management for employing inexperienced help.

The new courthouse that Webster championed was designed by Ion Lewis and William Whidden, two of Portland's most prominent architects. The pair had designed the Portland City Hall two blocks to the south, and several other prominent downtown buildings. Construction of the new $1.6 million courthouse spanned nearly four years. Builders erected two separate L-shaped sections, each running flush to the lot lines on two sides of the block, which converged into a square building when it was finished in 1914. The old courthouse was demolished as the new construction unfolded. Brick foundations from the original 1866 building were incorporated into the basement of its successor.

Although clad in limestone with classical Ionic columns, the new courthouse was built with the relatively new technique of riveting a structural

OHS OrHi 97134

Workmen tore down remains of the original Multnomah County Courthouse while the new courthouse, which can be seen on the left, was constructed around the edge of the block.

cage of steel beams and wrapping them in concrete. The region's economy had been built on timber, but architects wanted to reduce the risk of fire. The only wood used throughout the new building was in the furnishings and doors.

When it was finished, the new eight-story courthouse, with its wide, dazzling hallways of black and white marble, was the largest courthouse on the West Coast and one of the largest buildings of any type in Portland. Besides the impressive lobby and hallways, citizens were fascinated by four public elevators, driven by hydraulic plungers designed to provide safe, smooth service. Thousands of Portlanders crowded into the new courthouse during the week before its official opening to test the mechanical marvels that transported them from the first floor to the upper floors and back down. The building originally contained eleven elegant circuit courtrooms, each two stories high, and three smaller courtrooms for justices of the peace. Given that Multnomah County had only six circuit court departments when the building was completed, county officials were looking ahead. News accounts said that the eleven courtrooms would be enough to serve the county's growth indefinitely. When it opened, the new building housed virtually all county offices in addition to the courts.

As years went by, all but four of the two-story courtrooms were remodeled into smaller spaces to make more room for courts and offices, and the original central courtyard was filled in with three floors of office space. After eighty years, nearly all county offices except the courts had moved out, and various remodelings had resulted in twenty-two circuit and fourteen district courtrooms. One fact remained immutable: like its predecessor, the courthouse stood on the former homesite of the pioneer Portland booster and lawyer, William W. Chapman.

The new courthouse soon had new occupants. The legislature in 1913 allowed cities of more than 100,000 population—Portland being the only city meeting that requirement—to abolish justices of the peace and establish district courts as new courts of limited jurisdiction. The new district court judges were entitled to hear civil cases involving less than $300, forcible entry and detainer matters, and misdemeanor criminal cases. Appeals from district court rulings were routed to circuit court. The first three district court judges, paid $2,400 per year, were the city's three former justices of the peace, J. W. Bell, Jos. H. Jones, and Arthur C. Dayton.

The new courthouse also became the home of the Northwestern College of Law, run by Calvin Gantenbein, who in 1908 became a Multnomah County Circuit Court judge. Gantenbein remained as dean until his death in 1919, when he was succeeded by Multnomah County District Court Judge J. Hunt Hendrickson. Hendrickson kept the night classes at the courthouse until 1924, when he rented quarters in the Sherlock Building, an office building near Southwest Third Avenue and Oak Street. The Sherlock Building was cater-cornered from police headquarters and Portland Municipal Court. For many years, the Sherlock Building also was the home of the Embassy Club, a nightclub that entertained a rich mixture of police, law students, and colorful local figures.

Despite Portland's rapid growth, the Oregon Supreme Court was still admitting lawyers by individual testing, the practice instituted in pioneer days. By 1913, members of the Oregon Bar Association concluded that the old method was outdated and that educational standards for admission should be enhanced. A bar committee proposed creation of a five-member Board of Bar Examiners to plan, conduct, and grade annual bar examinations. As a new educational requirement, the committee proposed that applicants have completed three years of law school or at least three years of law-office apprenticeship. These changes, the committee contended, "will at once place the standard of requirements for admission to the Oregon bar on a basis equal to the requirements already adopted in many older and larger states."[33] The Oregon Supreme Court, heavily burdened with its appellate caseload, agreed to the plan. In 1917, state legislators appropriated $1,200 for the Board of Bar Examiners to conduct tests in 1917 and 1918.

Growth during the era brought several new high-rise buildings to Portland's skyline, including the Yeon, Spalding, and Northwestern National Bank buildings, the latter now known as the American Bank Building. All were in walking distance of the federal and county courthouses, and these new structures became the homes of Portland's most prominent law firms. Charles Carey, the Oregon historian, law-library founder, and behind-the-scenes politician, moved into the fourteenth floor of the Yeon Building with his latest partner, James B. Kerr. Kerr had come to Portland in 1905 from St. Paul, Minnesota, to represent the Northern Pacific Railroad when it joined with the Great Northern to build the Spokane, Portland & Seattle Railroad line along the north bank of the Columbia River. Carey, who also represented Northern Pacific, had worked with several other partners dating back to 1883. Carey and Kerr became partners in 1907. During the next few years, they were joined by lawyers Charles A. Hart, Omar Spencer, and Charles E. McCulloch, each of whom had lengthy legal careers

OHS OrHi 83698

Trains still operated on Southwest Fourth Avenue in 1912, when the second Multnomah County Courthouse was under construction. The City of Portland and Southern Pacific Railroad were headed for a legal showdown over the downtown tracks.

in the same firm. In 1913, Kerr helped draft Oregon's first workers' compensation legislation, which provided compensation for injured workers without their having to sue their employers in court.

Portland's continuing growth spelled trouble for the Southern Pacific Railroad, an enterprise that had been vital to Portland's development. By 1910, the city had grown tired of the noise and dirt generated by steam trains using Fourth Avenue as their route through downtown Portland to Union Station. Starting in 1907, the city council passed an ordinance barring steam locomotives or freight trains from using Fourth Avenue, to become effective eighteen months later. When the city charged the railroad with violating that ordinance in November 1908, Southern Pacific, represented by William D. Fenton, sought an injunction against the city in U.S. District Court. The litigation lasted five years, ending with a United States Supreme Court decision in 1913.

U.S. District Court Judge Robert S. Bean, sitting with the Ninth Circuit Court of Appeals, ruled in the city's favor in 1910. When Portland officials had approved use of the street by the old Oregon & California Railroad in 1869, Bean noted that Fourth Avenue was an unimproved back street. "It is now practically in the heart of the business district," he noted. The rail line passed the front door of the Multnomah County Courthouse, and only a block away from the U.S. Building where Bean presided over U.S. District Court. Bean said that "noise, vibration, smoke, cinders and soot from the moving trains seriously interfere with the transaction of public and private business, and it is a constant source of danger and inconvenience to the public."[34]

Southern Pacific appealed to the United States Supreme Court. By this time, William Fenton, one of the elder statesmen of Portland's legal community, had finally taken on partners. In 1915 he formed Fenton, Dey, Hampson & Fenton. Ben C. Dey had been an associate since 1906, and Dey lured a college classmate from Stanford University, Alfred Hampson, an associate of utility lawyer Fred V. Holman, to join the firm. Their opponents in the Supreme Court were Frank S. Grant and Lyman E. Latourette, who between them spent a total of twenty-seven years as Portland's city attorney between 1911 and 1948. The U.S. Supreme Court in 1913 rejected the Fentons' constitutional arguments and held that the city had reserved the option of regulating use of the rail line.[35] With that precedent established, city officials granted permission for steam engines to run on downtown streets for several more years.

During their early years of development, the railroads also had acquired substantial portions of waterfront property along both sides of the Willamette River. Joseph N. Teal, whose law practice included representation of waterborne shippers before the Interstate Commerce Commission, believed that public ownership and development of docks and wharves were essential to Portland's future as a transportation center. He based his conclusions on personal visits to major ports throughout North America, Great Britain, and Europe. "No city with which I am acquainted, situated as Portland is, had better opportunities for the creation of an ideal port, and at comparatively small costs,"[35] Teal reported to the Portland Chamber of Commerce in 1910. He envisioned substantial increases in water trade with the completion of the Panama Canal and

OHS CN01562

Joseph N. Teal.

development of inland waterways serving the Pacific Northwest. But he noted that virtually all property on both sides of the Willamette from Portland to its mouth was held in private or corporate ownership, including much land owned by railroads, which wouldn't want shipping competition. "It is intolerable that the waterfront and entrance of and to a city should be in any hands but those of the city," Teal said. He believed that private interests alone should not be trusted with building and managing dock facilities. "We find that substantially everywhere this work is undertaken by the city or State," he wrote. "In other words, it is looked upon as a public function."[37]

Teal's concern about Portland's future as a port was more than merely professional. He was the son of Joseph N. Teal, a pioneer steamboat captain who operated vessels on the Willamette and Columbia rivers. The elder Teal, who came to Oregon in 1851 after prospecting for gold in California, was credited with planning the locks at Oregon City. And like his son, the elder Teal was active in Portland civic affairs before his death in 1905.

The younger Teal wasn't alone in seeking public involvement in docks. City voters in 1909 had approved a $500,000 bond measure to buy waterfront land, but Mayor Joseph Simon squelched the sale. Simon, the former law partner in the politically strong Dolph law firm, had returned to power as

Courtesy of *The Oregonian*

Joseph Simon.

Portland mayor in 1909 after losing his U.S. Senate seat in 1903. With Teal's backing, another initiative in 1910 created a separate Portland Commission of Public Docks, backed with $2.5 million in bonds. When Portland's first public dock was opened in 1914, Teal was recognized as its father. "Upon the

OHS CN021697

C.E.S. Wood with Sara Bard Field.

water, rests the foundation of Portland's future," Teal declared.[38] Many years after Teal's death in 1929, the municipal dock commission was merged with the Port of Portland Commission, which had been created by legislators in 1891 to dredge and maintain a shipping channel in the Willamette and Columbia rivers.

The teen years of the new century also marked the close of the law career of C.E.S. Wood, one of Portland's most talented and controversial lawyers. Wood, who had come to Portland to practice with George Williams in 1887, quickly established himself as one of the city's top legal minds in matters of corporate law and admiralty. He won three major cases before the United States Supreme Court between 1890 and 1903. One involved a maritime collision, the second was a massive land-grant dispute over the construction of a wagon road from Albany to the Oregon border at Ontario, and the third was a harbor-line dispute between a builder and the Port of Portland. The Willamette Valley and Cascade Road Land Grant case, as the second case was called, was the most significant for Wood personally. He netted a $50,000 legal fee from his client, the Lazard Freres international banking house, for handling the case. Later, Wood became independently wealthy when the banking firm gave him a commission on the $6 million sale of more than 800,000 acres involved in the matter. Meanwhile, Wood was also busy profitably representing major corporate clients and banks.

Yet for all his establishment connections, Wood described himself politically as an anarchist. He offered legal advice to the so-called Wobblies during the early days of the International Workers of the World, the labor movement that sparked civil unrest in some parts of the Pacific Northwest. His opponents accused him of being a Bolshevik. With his full beard and robust crown of unkempt hair, Wood was a dramatic figure on Portland's conservative streets. The fact that he was still married to his first wife while he carried on a close personal relationship with the wife of a Baptist minister, Sara Bard Field, antagonized the city's prim social circles. Wood was, quite simply, like no other lawyer Portland had known.

Wood's relationship with Mrs. Field began in 1910, when he was introduced to her by Clarence Darrow, the Chicago lawyer believed by some to be the greatest attorney in the nation. Darrow had come to the West Coast that year to defend two brothers accused of blowing up the *Los Angeles Times* building during intense labor strife. Darrow had known Wood for years, and believed Wood to be one of the best lawyers he knew. In addition to using their exemplary legal skills representing business interests to earn their respective fortunes, Wood and Darrow shared an interest in the labor movement and in literature and poetry. And as a result of Darrow's introduction of Wood to Sara Field, the two men also shared women companions from the same family. Darrow, who like Wood was married at the time, was maintaining an affair with Mary Field at the time he introduced Wood to Mary Field's younger sister, Sara.

Darrow invited Wood to help him defend the brothers in the *Times* bombing case, but Wood declined. Wood wrote privately to others that he feared Darrow would exceed the bounds of legal ethics by going to any length to win the case. Wood's opinion proved prescient. Darrow's clients pleaded guilty soon after police accused Darrow of bribing two prospective jurors. Darrow later was acquitted in one bribery trial, and the case against him was dropped after another jury couldn't reach a decision on the second bribery charge.[39]

As a writer and lawyer, Wood put great value on the First Amendment. His support for free speech, coupled with his political views, led him to the defense in two prominent cases shortly before he retired from law practice. Neither ended to his satisfaction.

The first, in 1916, involved the arrest of Margaret Sanger, a national birth-control advocate and founder of Planned Parenthood. She and others were accused of violating a municipal obscenity ordinance by possessing and selling pamphlets based on Sanger's book, *Family Limitation*, at the Heilig

Theatre. Wood declared that he would demand a trial before an all-woman jury, but the case was decided by Municipal Court Judge Arthur Langguth without a jury.

Langguth said that birth control was not on trial, only certain photographs and descriptions in the pamphlet. He noted that if the pamphlet were "used in a clinic and not put forth into general and promiscuous distribution, I am quite sure even the most sensitive and modest man or woman would not for one moment question its publication and use." But he said general distribution by those "not having the high and lofty motives of Margaret Sanger" would produce thoughts "of impure and libidinous character." Despite Wood's protestations that the obscenity ordinance was unconstitutional, Langguth found the pamphlet obscene.[40]

Among those who objected with Wood to the obscenity ordinance was attorney William S. U'Ren, who at the turn of the century had played a major role in amending the Oregon Constitution. In a letter to Portland Mayor H. R. Albee, U'Ren said the ordinance should be struck down under the free-speech clause of the state constitution, which preserves the right "to speak, write or print freely on any subject whatever." Decades later, the Oregon Supreme Court followed U'Ren's legal reasoning by interpreting the state provision as giving broader protection to free expression than the First Amendment.

The Sanger case faded quickly after Judge Langguth imposed $10 fines but suspended payment. However, consequences were far more dire for Dr. Marie Equi, a Portland physician and anarchist, who was charged in 1918 with violating the federal Espionage Act as a result of a speech presented at a meeting of the International Workers of the World. Equi, who also had been a defendant with Sanger in the obscenity case, was accused of trying to incite insubordination and of obstructing military recruiting. In the speech that led to her arrest, she contended that the ruling class had pulled the working class into World War I against its will. She said workers shouldn't kill or injure each other.[41]

Following her conviction in U.S. District Court, where she had been defended by James E. Fenton, the younger brother of William Fenton, Dr. Equi was sentenced to three years in prison. Wood took the case on appeal with the belief that the Espionage Act violated free speech protections. In a stinging, sometimes satirical brief, Wood said that the purpose of the Bill of Rights was to protect the few against the many. "Any court that permits it to fail of this high purpose has raped the Goddess of Liberty," he declared.

Legal precedents, however, weighed against Dr. Equi. The appeals court affirmed her conviction and the United States Supreme Court refused to consider it. President Woodrow Wilson later reduced her sentence to one year, and Dr. Equi served ten months in San Quentin.

Independently wealthy and tired of law, Wood retired from practice at age sixty-seven and moved in 1919, first to San Francisco and later to Los Gatos, California, where he lived with his lover who became his second wife, Sara Bard Field. During his California years, Wood wrote a collection of satires, *Heavenly Discourse*, which sold out two dozen printings. It featured historic and religious figures in Heaven discussing World War I and other political and social matters of the early twentieth century, with Wood immodestly expressing his personal views through the voice of God. But Wood's favorite form of expression was poetry, which proved much less marketable. He once wrote to his son, "I think poetry is the immortal branch of literature (not mine but poetry in general) but as I have said, this is not a poetic age."[42] Wood died in 1944 at the age of ninety-two.

Wood's departure, like Fenton's retirement from active practice a few years earlier, signaled a changing of the guard in Portland's legal community. A new generation of lawyers was on its way, many of them now boasting of being Portland natives. The village that Wood and William Fenton had discovered in the nineteenth century had grown to 200,000 in population by 1920, including about 550 lawyers. Teal, Minor & Winfree was the largest firm, with six attorneys.

Other firms that would grow into giants later in the century were smaller. Carey & Kerr, the predecessor to Stoel Rives LLP, had five lawyers at the beginning of the Roaring Twenties. Upon his retirement, William D. Fenton donated his extensive law library to the University of Oregon, which named a building in his honor. Fenton's successors, Dey and Hampson, added Roscoe C. Nelson to form Dey, Hampson & Nelson, a predecessor of Lane Powell Spears Lubersky LLP. Dey remained with the firm until 1930, when he moved to New York City to accept Southern Pacific's offer to become the railroad's general counsel. McCamant, Bronaugh & Thompson, a forerunner of Miller Nash Wiener Hager & Carlsen LLP, included Earl C. Bronaugh, who had served as Multnomah County Circuit Court judge from 1907 to 1910, and Wallace McCamant, who soon was headed for a controversial nomination to the Ninth U.S. Circuit Court of Appeals. Harry Beckett in 1915 became a partner with the insurance defense firm of Wilbur & Spencer, and began adding corporate clients to the firm that grew into Schwabe Williamson & Wyatt.

CHAPTER FOUR

Between the Wars

World War I—the Great War—marked the end of the Progressive Era. The mood of the 1920s was dramatically different in Portland and elsewhere, and the change was reflected by voters and by court cases. The new decade was only two months old when one of those symbolic landmarks occurred. A three-judge panel of the Ninth Circuit Court of Appeals, including one of its original members from Portland, Judge William B. Gilbert, affirmed the conviction of J. Henry Albers for violating the federal Espionage Act of 1917.

That was the same law under which Dr. Marie Equi had been prosecuted earlier. But unlike Equi, who had a long history of radical political involvement, Albers was a successful businessman not accustomed to publicity or to outspoken political activity. His big mistake, in retrospect, was drinking too much alcohol on a passenger train. Albers was president of the Albers Brothers Milling Company, a family business established in 1893 by one of his three German-born brothers. The firm grew from a family enterprise into a major mill and flour-shipping operation, with approximately 1,000 employees.

Albers had several drinks while returning on the Southern Pacific Railroad from a business trip to San Francisco on October 8, 1918. Seated in the smoking section of a Pullman car, somewhere between Grants Pass and Roseburg, Albers rankled some other travelers with comments about his

German origins and about his native country. Statements such as "A German can never be beaten by a Yank," "You can never lick the Kaiser—never in a thousand years," and "I could take a gun myself and fight right here"[1] were among several statements attributed to him by the passengers. Albers was arrested when he arrived in Portland, and was accused of seven counts of violating the law against inciting resistance to the United States or promoting the cause of its enemies.

Henry McGinn, the colorful Multnomah County judge who had returned to private practice after one judicial term, defended Albers in a jury trial in U.S. District Court. McGinn contended that Albers was so drunk that his statements were not intentional attempts to incite resistance. Evidence differed about Albers' state of intoxication. A porter testified that he hoisted Albers into his sleeping compartment while he was still fully clothed and wearing his shoes. But prosecutors bolstered their case by offering statements from acquaintances of Albers who said the businessman had made pro-German statements on occasions four and five years earlier. Jurors acquitted Albers on five of the seven charges, but Judge Charles Wolverton imposed a three-year prison term and a $10,000 fine on the two convictions. The Ninth Circuit Court of Appeals, citing Dr. Equi's trial where statements made two years before her arrest under the Espionage Act were admitted at trial, refused to overturn Albers' convictions.

Charles H. Carey and James B. Kerr appealed the Albers case to the United States Supreme Court. The government conceded error before arguments and the Court reversed the convictions in April 1921. The reversal was little consolation for Albers, however, who had been disgraced in the community. He suffered a stroke and died in July 1921, while prosecutors were considering whether to try him again.

If anti-German prejudice was a factor in the Albers case, those feelings were not limited to America's former war enemies. A burst of "100 percent Americanism" swept Oregon in the early 1920s, which brought the secretive

Ku Klux Klan to political power and led to voter approval of a measure that would have outlawed parochial and private elementary and secondary schools. The Klan, which claimed 9,000 secret members after its first year of organizing in Portland in 1921, launched a campaign for "native, white and Protestant supremacy." Catholics, owing their religious allegiance to the Pope in the Vatican City, were included as anti-American Klan targets. Using the initiative process championed at the turn of the century by William S. U'Ren, the Klan backed the Compulsory Education Act drafted by the Scottish Rite Masons. On its face, the bill simply mandated public education for all Oregon elementary students from ages eight to sixteen. However, its unstated purpose was to put church-run schools out of business.

Oregon's electorate, which was eighty percent Protestant, heard strenuous debate over the school bill. Governor Ben Olcott, a former accountant, was adamantly opposed to the school bill and its Klan supporters. He made his position clear early in his race for re-election: "Dangerous forces are insidiously gaining a foothold in Oregon. In the guise of a secret society parading under the name of the Ku Klux Klan, these forces are endeavoring to usurp the reign of government, are stirring up fanaticism, race hatred, religious prejudice, and all of those evil influences which tend towards factional strife and civil terror."[2]

Nevertheless, the school bill passed by 106,910 votes to 92,530, and Olcott was defeated as governor by Walter M. Pierce, a former public schools superintendent who endorsed the school measure. Another victim of the 1922 election was Multnomah County Circuit Court Judge William N. Gatens, a Catholic who had been on the bench since 1909.

As the new governor, Pierce became the chief defendant when attorneys in Portland representing the Society of the Sisters of the Holy Names of Jesus and Mary in Oregon filed suit in U.S. District Court to enjoin the school law, which was to take effect in 1926. The legal talent lined up against the Compulsory Education Act included some of Portland's finest attorneys. John P. Kavanaugh was a former Portland city attorney and Multnomah County Circuit Court judge for thirteen years who had returned to private practice. Kavanaugh's partner was Jay Bowerman, himself a former short-term Oregon governor. Bowerman, state senate president in 1909, held the governor's office for six months ending in 1911 after Governor George E. Chamberlain won a seat in the U.S. Senate. In the decade after his brief gubernatorial term, Bowerman became a leading business lawyer in Portland. Others who assisted in the lawsuit included Dan J. Malarkey, a highly respected trial lawyer, Hall S. Lusk, a young lawyer with a long, distinguished judicial career ahead of him, and Frank J. Lonergan, a former star football halfback at Notre Dame, who later would spend sixteen years as a judge in the Multnomah County Circuit Court.

U.S. District Judges Robert S. Bean and Charles Wolverton, the two close friends who were nearing the ends of their judicial careers, and Judge Gilbert of the Ninth Circuit Court of Appeals, heard arguments on the school bill in the United States Building. The decision issued by Wolverton in March 1924 suggests that the case gave the court little trouble. The judges enjoined enforcement of the law, stating that "its purpose being to take utterly away from complainants their constitutional right and privilege to teach in the grammar grades has and will deprive them of their property without due process of law."[3]

OHS CN 008840

U.S. District Judges Charles Wolverton left, and Robert S. Bean right, flanked William B. Gilbert of the Ninth U.S. Circuit Court of Appeals to hear the Pierce v. Society of Sisters *case.*

That decision was affirmed by the United States Supreme Court a year later in *Pierce v. Society of Sisters*.[4] Justice James C. McReynolds wrote that the law violated the Fourteenth Amendment because it "unreasonably interferes with the liberty of parents and guardians to direct the upbringing and education of children under their control."

Even faster than the courts disposed of the school bill, the Ku Klux Klan disposed of itself as a political force in Oregon. Although boasting enough muscle to elect a speaker of the house during the 1923 legislative session, a man named K. K. Kubli of Portland, Klan adherents fell to bickering among themselves. The Klan was unable to pass several proposals at the 1923 session. By the 1924 elections, the secret organization had lost its political appeal.

The early 1920s brought another legislative dispute, this one fought outside the limelight of the press, over the Multnomah County Law Library. The quarrel arose after the library barred William Wallace Banks from checking out a book because he had not paid his annual library dues. Banks was the Portland lawyer and legislator who had introduced the law limiting hours for working women that had gone to the U.S. Supreme Court. As a state senator in the 1921 session, Banks retaliated against the law library by proposing legislation that would require the library to be open to all lawyers without dues or fees. Unless the library was opened to all lawyers, it would not be able to collect the $1 fee from civil complaints approved by legislators in 1907, according to the Banks plan.

The librarian was Fred M. Salway, a 1908 graduate of the University of Oregon law department, who had been librarian since 1910. By 1920, the library membership had grown to 391 lawyers. With expanded space available in the new courthouse, Salway had increased the library's materials to 18,000 volumes. Without the membership dues, however, Salway feared that the library would be ruined. But a compromise evolved. Legislators required the library association to permit use of its library by all lawyers in the state without fees or dues. At the same time, legislators doubled to $2 the fee collected from each civil complaint filed in the county to be paid to the library.

Although the Progressive Era was long over by the mid-1920s, memories of those who lived through it remained vivid. A political slight not forgotten by a powerful U.S. senator from California cost Wallace McCamant, a prominent Portland lawyer, a seat on the Ninth Circuit Court of Appeals. McCamant was a Pennsylvania native who came to Portland in 1890, where he began working as a clerk for the firm of Gilbert & Snow. Two years later he became a partner. Except for two brief interludes, the association was long-lasting. McCamant spent more than fifty years with the firm that evolved into the modern-day law office of Miller Nash Wiener Hager & Carlsen LLP. Besides an interest in the law, McCamant had a knack for public speaking. He spoke on historical subjects at many civic occasions, sometimes speaking for as long as an hour from texts he had written and memorized. He also was active for many years in the Republican party, which eventually led to his showdown on Capitol Hill with Senator Hiram Johnson of California.

McCamant was nominated for a seat on the federal appeals court in 1925 by President Calvin Coolidge, whom McCamant had nominated for vice president at the 1920 Republican National Convention to run on the ticket with Warren Harding. Coolidge became president upon Harding's death in 1923. The appointment was McCamant's second to an appellate court. He was appointed to fill a vacancy on the Oregon Supreme Court in January 1918, and stepped down in June 1919 to return to his Portland law firm. Senator Johnson also had been a Republican presidential hopeful in 1920. Johnson was perturbed that McCamant had not supported him for president, even though Johnson had won a plurality of Republican votes in the 1920 Oregon primary. McCamant said he could never support Johnson because Johnson, as a vice-presidential candidate with Theodore Roosevelt in 1912, had supported a plank to allow voters the power to recall unpopular appellate judicial decisions. The concept had been advocated by Populists in the initiative and referendum movement who wanted a method to erase appellate rulings that reversed jury decisions. Oregon never adopted the judicial-decision recall, but proponents, including C. E. S. Wood and Henry McGinn in 1910, successfully passed a state constitutional amendment that bolstered the power of jurors. The measure restricted appellate judges from overturning facts found by juries "unless the court can affirmatively say there is no evidence to support the verdict."[5]

While running as a delegate for the 1920 convention, McCamant had written to a supporter that he could never support Johnson, even if he won the Oregon primary. "He is an advocate of the recall of judicial decisions," McCamant wrote. "This means that he does not believe in the form of constitutional government which has come down to us from the fathers. In other words, he is not an American. Under no circumstances will I vote to send to the White House a man who is not an American."

OHS CN011944

Wallace McCamant.

Johnson had the letter at hand during the Senate confirmation hearing in January 1926. "In that letter you said I was not an American?" Johnson asked.

With his federal appointment at stake, McCamant did not back down. "Yes, I did," he answered. "Theodore Roosevelt was not an

American then?" Johnson asked.

"He was not a good American," McCamant replied.

"He was not a good American," the senator said, repeating the phrase to himself. "I stand on this man's statement. If any man can be confirmed in the Senate who says Theodore Roosevelt was not a good American, I will want to know why."[6] At Johnson's urging, the Senate refused to confirm McCamant, even though he had proved his ability with eleven months of service on Court of Appeals. McCamant returned to his Portland firm of McCamant & Thompson, where he practiced until his death in 1944.

The controversy over McCamant coincided with another unusual judicial development in Portland. Early in 1926, Governor Walter M. Pierce appointed Mary Jane Spurlin to a vacancy on the Multnomah County District Court. Spurlin was a native of Sparta, North Carolina, who had taught school in Virginia beginning at age eighteen. She moved to Oregon in 1916, where she worked in law offices before going to Northwestern College of Law, from which she graduated in 1925. Her pursuit of a legal career, she said years later, was opposed by her family. With Governor Pierce's appointment, Spurlin became the first woman to hold a county-wide judicial office in the state.

OHS CN013057

Mary Jane Spurlin.

Spurlin's appointment was unusual for another reason. An Oregon statute required a lawyer to have three years of practice before becoming a judge. Although Spurlin had worked in law offices for many years, she had been a member of the bar for only one year. Spurlin purportedly wasn't concerned about that statute. She contended that the law applied only to elected judges, and she was an appointee. Neither was Governor Pierce concerned about it. "The appointment stands," he said when the law was brought to his attention.[7]

Spurlin's swearing-in ceremony on April 1, 1926, was followed by a celebration in the Crystal Room at the Benson Hotel. Her appointment was heralded as a breakthrough by the small community of women lawyers in the Portland area. "We don't have to say Judge Spurlin was appointed because she was a woman; she was appointed in spite of the fact she was a woman because she was competent," declared Manche I. Langley.[8] Langley was one of the most outspoken women in a profession still overwhelmingly dominated by men. She was practicing in Forest Grove at the time of Judge Spurlin's appointment, but she later joined the Multnomah County district attorney's office, where she worked until her death at age eighty in 1963.

As a district court judge, Spurlin presided over small claims, misdemeanor criminal cases, traffic offenses, and civil disputes when the amount at issue was not more than $300. Her tenure as a judge, however, was brief. Fred L. Olson, a former justice of the peace and unsuccessful candidate for the Portland Municipal Court bench in 1913, defeated Spurlin in the November 1926 general election by 37,000 votes to 30,000. Olson remained on the bench until 1950. By then, however, a large segment of the bar had become dissatisfied with his judicial performance, as indicated by a large number of affidavits of prejudice filed by lawyers declining to take cases into his court. When Olson sought a sixth term at age eighty-two, four candidates lined up to challenge him. Olson's court, *The Oregonian* commented in a campaign editorial, "has degenerated into a state of virtual uselessness. Lawyers shun it whenever possible, fearing the unpredictable and crotchety whims of this 82-year old judicial anachronism."[9] Olson was beaten handily by John F. Gantenbein, who had been operating the Northwestern College of Law.

Spurlin was mentioned as a possibility for another appointment to a judicial vacancy in 1928, but by then Governor Pierce was no longer in office and she was not chosen. Spurlin never again served as a judge. She spent the rest of her lengthy legal career in Portland, working both in public law and in private practice. For a few years during the Depression, Spurlin worked as Multnomah County deputy district attorney along with Manche Langley, handling "morals" cases involving girls under the age of eighteen and child-support matters. Spurlin enjoyed recalling an incident in which she was prosecuting a juvenile rape case and an opposing lawyer tried to use her gender against her.

"What would Miss Spurlin know about rape?" challenged a male defense attorney.

"Assuming that opposing counsel is a gentleman," Spurlin shot back, "what would he know about rape?"[10]

Spurlin later returned to private practice and continued coming to her office in the Public Service Building well into her seventies. Ironically, she was sharing office space with Jean Lagerquist Lewis when Lewis was appointed by Governor Mark Hatfield to become the state's first woman judge on the circuit court bench in 1961. Spurlin lived for many years on a three-acre plot in Washington County where she raised a few sheep. She was active in many Portland community activities and served as a president of the City Federation of Women's Clubs. However, she told an interviewer many years later, "They didn't like me much—I was too tough."[11] By the time Spurlin died at age eighty-seven in 1970, her brief judicial tenure was largely forgotten.

Meanwhile, the 1920s brought a judicial controversy unlike any other to Portland. It began with a contest in Multnomah County Circuit Court over the will of Harry E. Wemme, a successful tent and awning maker who left an estate valued at approximately $1 million when he died in 1914. Wemme's will, written by Portland lawyer George W. Joseph, left half of the estate to heirs in Germany and half to the Christian Science Church for the construction of a maternity home for "unfortunate or wayward girls."

The church built the White Shield Home for unwed mothers and briefly operated it. But the church closed it after deciding not to provide medical services contrary to its religious tenets. The church sold the home to the Salvation Army, which reopened it for its original purpose. Wemme's heirs, represented by Portland attorney Thomas Mannix, alleged that the church had breached its trust and that the assets should revert to the surviving relatives. The Oregon Supreme Court, in a decision written by Justice John L. Rand of Baker, interpreted the will in 1924 as establishing a charitable trust. The court ordered that trustees be appointed to take the property and carry out the charitable purposes expressed in Wemme's will. The court also awarded $15,000 in attorney fees to Mannix and a second lawyer, Dan Powers.

Joseph, convinced that he had drafted Wemme's will so that it would leave the church in control of the assets to do as it wished, was outraged by the decision and by the size of the attorney fees charged against the estate. His anger grew as Mannix tried repeatedly, both in federal and state courts, to overturn the charitable trust and to win the second half of the estate for the German heirs. As it turned out, the heirs had sold their interests to E. W. Wickey, an Indiana lawyer who agreed to pay Mannix a contingent fee for any recovery. But what turned the case into a statewide political controversy was a land-sale option between Justice Rand and Mannix executed in 1926.

Henry M. Hanzen, a political reporter for the Portland *Telegram* newspaper and a close friend of Joseph's, found an option allowing Mannix an opportunity to buy an undeveloped mine in eastern Oregon from Rand and a partner for $300,000. Joseph suspected that Mannix and Wickey planned to use money won from the Wemme estate to buy the mine from Rand and keep the substantial amount left over. Joseph wondered aloud why Mannix was considering paying so much for what Joseph called "an undeveloped hole in the ground."[12]

The revelation about the mine option surfaced shortly before Rand began seeking a new term on the supreme court in 1928. Joseph, who had been an outspoken politician since his first election as a state senator from Portland in 1910, decided not to seek reelection in 1928 so that he could attack Rand without being accused of political aggrandizement. He made speeches on a major Portland radio station attacking Rand's decision in the Wemme case as "so outrageous it is without parallel in the judicial history of Oregon."[13] Joseph collected other supreme court decisions of which he was critical and issued a pamphlet entitled, "The Truth about Rand. A few reasons why John H. Rand is unfit to be a justice on the Oregon Supreme Court."

Joseph's frustration with the top Oregon court also extended to Justice Thomas A. McBride, the senior member of the court who had been appointed in 1909. McBride earlier had been a Clackamas County Circuit Court judge for eighteen years, and had practiced before that in Lafayette and Oregon City. Joseph submitted an affidavit in

OHS CN012033

George W. Joseph.

an unrelated civil case suggesting that McBride, then in his late seventies, had been seen drinking whiskey in Mannix's office. With Prohibition in effect, the allegation was more than a mere suggestion of social impropriety.

Joseph's attack on the court failed. A secret inquiry commissioned by the court cleared Rand of wrongdoing. Joseph brushed aside those proceedings as political chicanery. Voters renominated Rand in a contested primary election and reelected him to a six-year term over opposition in the November general election.

However, passage of the elections did not quell Joseph's attacks on the court. Both Mannix and Joseph filed ethics complaints against each other, and Joseph's allegations against Rand and McBride stayed alive in the press while three circuit court judges from other counties presided over disciplinary hearings late in 1929. Joseph, hearing informally that the disciplinary panel intended to recommend his disbarment, decided to run for governor in the Republican primary. His campaign pamphlets recalled his birth in a log cabin in Modoc County, California, and his early years in Lake County, Oregon, where he worked his way through high school herding sheep. The disciplinary panel's formal disbarment recommendation, issued shortly before the 1930 primary election, fueled Joseph's successful gubernatorial nomination as a Populist reformer who battled Oregon's entrenched political machinery.

The primary election was only a few weeks behind Joseph when the Oregon Supreme Court, in May 1930, disbarred both Mannix[14] and Joseph.[15] Mannix, the court concluded, had engaged in "a long continued course of misrepresentations" in both state and federal courts involving the Wemme litigation. Joseph, however, had done nothing wrong but attack the court. The decision was written by Justice Harry Belt, a former circuit court judge for Marion and Polk counties. Ironically, it was Judge Belt who had upheld Wemme's original will nearly a decade earlier while sitting as a temporary Multnomah County Circuit Court judge. "Joseph, as a lawyer and an

American citizen, undoubtedly had the right freely to criticize Justice Rand, who was a candidate for re-election," Belt wrote. "Joseph, however, is not permitted under the guise of a qualified privilege to so transcend the limits of decent and legitimate criticism as to falsely and maliciously impute to a candidate the commission of a crime." The court also disapproved of the whiskey-drinking allegation against Chief Justice McBride, "who will be long remembered as one of [the court's] greatest and most beloved jurists."

But while both Mannix and Joseph were disbarred, the court left Joseph an unusual opportunity. It said he could apply for reinstatement as a lawyer "whenever he files a fair and honorable retraction, not of his criticism, but of his charge of corruption which reflects on the honor and integrity of this court. It is sincerely hoped that such retraction will be made, in which event he will be reinstated."[16]

Whether Joseph would accept the court's offer would remain a mystery. Three weeks after the court issued its disbarment order, he died at age fifty-eight of a stroke while campaigning for governor in Clatsop County. Two days later, the Oregon Supreme Court withdrew its disbarment opinion involving Joseph, and it was never published in the official Oregon Reports. Justice McBride died a few months after Joseph at age eighty-one. Justice Rand remained on the state supreme court until his death in 1942.

Julius Meier, a former law partner of Joseph's and head of the Meier & Frank department store, decided to run for governor in Joseph's stead as an Independent. He shared many of Joseph's political views, including a preference for publicly owned electric power. Meier won the 1930 general election and went on to become one of the state's most popular governors. Among the achievements during his tenure was legislation that made Oregon judicial races nonpartisan, a change that had been advocated unsuccessfully since the Progressive Era by the Oregon Bar Association.

By the end of the 1920s, Portland's community of lawyers had grown to nearly 800. The decade's newcomers included several who would lay groundwork for major firms of the future. The earliest of them to enter practice was Victor V. Pendergrass, an Arkansas native whose family moved to Portland while he was an infant. Pendergrass passed the Oregon bar examination even before finishing course work at the Northwestern College of Law. Nevertheless, he went ahead and finished his final year at the Portland night law school. "There is still more to learn," he explained.[17] Within a year of opening a law office in 1921, Pendergrass relocated to the First National Bank and began a relationship with the bank that lasted for decades, including more than twenty years as a member of the bank's board of directors. Pendergrass became one of the leading banking lawyers in the Pacific Northwest. In 1938, he formed a partnership with Charles R. Spackman and Rupert R. Bullivant, then the president of the Oregon State Bar, to create a firm that concentrated on banking, corporate, and commercial law. Pendergrass' son, Walter H. Pendergrass, joined the firm in 1950. As years passed, the firm expanded into many other areas of law and grew into Bullivant Houser Bailey Pendergrass & Hoffman PC., one of the city's largest firms. Although he retired from practice in 1969, Victor Pendergrass lived until 1991, when he died at age ninety-five.

The year that Pendergrass opened his first office, 1921, also marked the start of the legal career of Lamar Tooze. Tooze, who had been student-body president as an undergraduate at the University of Oregon, had his legal studies interrupted by World War I, where he fought for the U.S. Army in the Argonne Forest. His identical twin , Leslie Tooze, who had attended Harvard Law School with Lamar, was killed in the same battle shortly before the war ended. Lamar Tooze returned to combat in World War II and fought in the Battle of the Bulge, approximately twenty miles from the site of his brother's death. He worked for several years in the Cake & Cake law firm, and later founded the firm known today as Tooze, Shenker, Duden, Creamer, Frank & Hutchison. His son, Lamar Tooze, Jr., joined him in the practice in 1928. The elder Tooze also taught night classes at the Northwestern College of Law between 1925 and 1942.

Another brother of Lamar Tooze, Walter L. Tooze, Jr., also achieved legal distinction. Eight years older than Lamar, Walter Tooze practiced in Dallas and McMinnville before World War I and moved to Portland after his military service. He won a seat on the Multnomah County Circuit Court in 1948, and two years later advanced to the Oregon Supreme Court. He died in 1956 while serving as an associate justice.

Gunther Krause, a Portland native who graduated from Reed College and then the Columbia University Law School, returned home in 1922 to start a forty-five-year legal career. Krause concentrated on maritime law, labor relations, and litigation. He limited his interests outside the office to Reed College, where he served as a trustee, and to Oregon State Bar activities, including a term as president in 1942-1943. At his death in 1967, the firm of Krause Lindsay & Nahstoll included eight lawyers. The firm later grew to nearly 100 lawyers when, in 1990, it split into separate firms of Lindsay, Hart, Neil & Weigler and Ater Wynne Hewitt Dodson & Skerritt LLP.

In 1926, the early signs of the Great Depression prompted a Montana lawyer, Verne Dusenbery, to pack up his family at age forty-one and seek better opportunities on the West Coast. Dusenbery settled in Portland, where he first entered a law partnership with Virgil Crum. Crum later left the office and Dusenbery took on other partners to establish the firm that evolved in the 1990s into Martin, Bischoff, Templeton, Langslet & Hoffman. Dusenbery's partners over the years included Herbert M. Schwab, and John C. Beatty, Jr., both of whom served as judges in Multnomah County Circuit Court. Schwab later became the first Chief Judge of the Oregon Court of Appeals. Another of Dusenbery's partners was Sidney Teiser, who came to Portland in 1911 after practicing in Norfolk, Virginia. Teiser practiced business law in Portland at various times until 1972, when he retired at age ninety. Teiser was active with the American Bar Association in many capacities for more than fifty years, including a term on the ABA Board of Governors. Among his other interests, Teiser wrote history articles about Oregon's early territorial judges, and invented an early form of microfilm camera and reading equipment for storing and retrieving miniaturized legal publications.

Another newcomer of the 1920s was Moe M. Tonkon, who opened his one-man office in 1928 after attending Reed College and Northwestern College of Law. Tonkon, the son of a hat and cap maker, was born in Bender, Russia. His family came to Portland when he was an infant. Tonkon practiced business and commercial law and, later in his career, joined with others to create the firm of Tonkon, Torp, Galen, Marmaduke & Booth, a firm of thirty lawyers at the time of his death in 1984. Tonkon's clients included Pro Basketball, Inc., otherwise known as the Portland Trailblazers, Portland's first major-league professional sports franchise. Among numerous civic affairs, Tonkon maintained a close association with Reed College and served as a college trustee from 1951 to 1966, the final three years as board chairman. Tonkon also quietly became the first Jewish member of three of Portland's most prominent private clubs, the Arlington Club, the University Club, and the Waverley Club. "I guess it boils down to this," he once told an interviewer. "I haven't stood aloof, I suppose, as a lot of our people have."[18]

Tonkon's first year in practice also marked the start of the legal career of Robert T. Mautz, who perhaps was Portland's most famous young lawyer starting practice in the 1920s. Mautz established himself as a star football player at the University of Oregon, and finished his undergraduate career as captain of the team in 1925. But much of his fame arose from a single play in Oregon's 1924 game against the Oregon Agricultural College, now Oregon State University. As Oregon drove toward OAC's end of the field, Mautz fell down near the right sideline and remained on the ground while the rest of the players veered with a runner carrying the ball to the left side. On the next play, Mautz leaped to his feet and slanted toward the goal line.

Before the OAC defense could react to his sudden appearance, Mautz caught a game-winning touchdown pass. The "deadman" play won wide notoriety. Mautz was recognized as one of the best ends on the West Coast, and after the 1925 season he was invited to play in the first East-West Shrine Game at Palo Alto, California.

Mautz drifted into insurance defense work and in 1934 joined the Wilbur, Beckett, Howell & Oppenheimer firm, a predecessor to the modern firm of Schwabe Williamson & Wyatt. Mautz became a leading tort defense trial lawyer. He also became well known for his role in a series of humorous radio programs, the "Circus Court on the Air," which raised funds for the Shriner's Crippled Children's Hospital. Prominent Portlanders accused of preposterous crimes had their fictitious trials on the radio, with Mautz acting as the defense lawyer. He always lost, and each citizen was then "fined" for the benefit of the charity.

The new lawyers of the 1920s had an edge on the newcomers of the 1930s: they could find jobs. Although lumber and agricultural prices had been slumping in Portland since 1927, the market collapse on Wall Street in October 1929 brought on the full force of the Depression. At the outset, many lawyers believed that the crash would be short-lived. However, the focus of practice for Portland's business lawyers turned quickly from business creation and expansion to one of struggling to keep existing enterprises alive. One example was Ralph Cake, the son of William Cake, a founder of the pioneer Cake & Cake firm, who had been a member of the Equitable Savings & Loan Association board of directors since 1922. Cake ascended to the association's vice presidency in 1933 and to the presidency in 1938, as the Portland-based savings and residential lender successfully struggled to keep its doors open. Ralph Cake, who had joined his father's practice in 1921, was one of the industry leaders who helped draft plans for the Federal Home Loan Bank and the Federal Savings and Loan Insurance Corporation. Cake also played an active role in Republican party politics through much of his career. He was a national committeeman from 1940 to 1952 and later served as a political advisor to President Dwight D. Eisenhower.

Another lawyer enlisted to grapple with the era's economic hardships was Charles H. Carey, the noted historian, founder of the Multnomah County Law Library, and senior partner in the state's largest firm. In 1933, at age seventy-five, he retired from practice with Carey, Hart, Spencer & McCulloch to serve as state corporation commissioner at the request of Governor Julius Meier. Carey held the post until his resignation in 1937. Meier's successor, Governor Charles Martin, offered this praise: "He has rendered outstanding service to the people of Oregon in adjusting the difficult and troubled affairs of the corporation department, taking office in the midst of the depression. No corporation commissioner in recent years faced a more difficult task than did Judge Carey. He has fulfilled this high trust with honor to himself and with great benefit to the people of Oregon."[19] Carey died four years later at age eighty-three.

One of Portland's most complicated financial messes to surface during the Depression was the bankruptcy of Portland Electric Power Company, known as PEPCO, a forerunner of Portland General Electric. PEPCO sought voluntary bankruptcy in 1934 and again in 1939. The long-standing troubles had arisen with sale of PEPCO in 1929 to the Public Utility Holding Corporation of New York, which in turn sold PEPCO to the Central Public Service Corporation of Chicago, in 1930. The absentee owners profited by millions of dollars from stock manipulations and bond sales, while leaving the Portland power provider with inadequate capital for its operations. The second bankruptcy proceeding occurred under the supervision of U.S. District Court Judge James Alger Fee and a recently appointed bankruptcy referee selected by Fee, Estes Snedecor. Fee was a native of Pendleton and had served as judge on the Umatilla County Circuit Court from 1927 until his appointment to U.S. District Court in 1931 after the death of Judge Robert S. Bean. After twenty-three years on the federal trial bench, Fee was elevated to the Ninth Circuit Court of Appeals, where he served until his death in 1959. He died while attending an American Bar Association meeting in Miami.

In 1936, Fee appointed Snedecor as bankruptcy referee, a position Snedecor held for thirty-three years until retiring in 1969 at age eighty-one. By the time of his bankruptcy appointment, Snedecor had already served as president of Rotary International in 1921, had been elected to a term in the Oregon House of Representatives in 1933, had served as legal counsel to Governor Charles Martin in 1935, and had practiced law for twenty-six years. But he was best known for his athletic pursuits despite the loss of a leg at age twelve due to polio. It was assumed that the young Snedecor would spend the rest of his life in a wheelchair. But Snedecor preferred crutches. In 1910 he became the first person to climb Mt. Hood on crutches, and he received national attention for his prowess on the golf course, where he often shot in the mid-eighties for eighteen holes. "My philosophy has always been, 'One-legged, but not crippled,'" Snedecor said.[20] Based on his experience in bankruptcy proceedings, Snedecor successfully lobbied state legislators to temper the state's harsh garnishment laws with legislation that protected greater percentages of wages from garnishment.

OHS CN015056

Estes Snedecor.

PEPCO's second round of bankruptcy proceedings lasted more than a decade. Although Snedecor supervised most of the hearings, Fee closely watched the complicated case and wrote the final orders. Attorney Ralph King, a partner in the firm that became Miller Nash Wiener Hager & Carlsen LLP, was appointed as counsel for PEPCO's independent trustees in the second case. Fee had a reputation as a stickler for legal procedure and courtroom etiquette. King's careful efforts in sorting out the financial machinations of the PEPCO case impressed Judge Fee, who delivered a rare public compliment as the lengthy matters ended. "Great praise must be given to Mr. King for his untiring effort . . . in discovering uncontroverted evidence of dealings herein outlined by legal process from adverse and hostile sources."[21]

While lawyers struggled for economic survival during the Depression, students at the Northwestern School of Law made unusual sacrifices to finish their schooling. Ralph Holman, who later spent fifteen years as a Clackamas County Circuit Court judge and another fifteen years on the Oregon Supreme Court, remembered that some students in the Depression years shared books rather than buying their own.[22] Nels Peterson, who became one of Portland's leading personal injury and workers' compensation lawyers, worked his way through Northwestern by selling shoes during the day and working as a security guard at the Multnomah Kennel Club dog races during summer evenings.[23] But there were virtually no law jobs in Portland for the new graduates. Peterson, for example, moved to Toledo, a mill town that provided him a foothold with injury cases. Thomas J. White, a 1937 graduate,[24] went to work for a full year with a Portland firm for no pay, until deciding to open his own small office in the Jackson Tower. White's office furniture was nearly repossessed by a creditor, but then he began representing clients in the trucking and shipping industries. White gradually took on partners and associates as the workload expanded, and his tiny office eventually evolved into the firm of Brownstein Rask Arenz Sweeney Kerr & Grim LLP.

Perhaps relief from difficult economic times was one reason Portlanders expressed so much interest when, in October 1931, a large marine creature spouting water appeared in the Columbia Slough near the Interstate Bridge. Hundreds of people lined the banks to take a look at the creature, believed to be thirty or forty feet long. Experts suspected that it was a whale, but they couldn't be sure without a closer look. Quickly the creature became known as Jim McCool's whale, after a newspaper reporter who first wrote about it. Someone tried to shoot the whale soon after its appearance, prompting Governor Julius Meier to order a halt on the use of firearms against it. But the young whale, which turned

Courtesy of *The Oregonian*

McCool's whale on display at the Multnomah County Courthouse courtyard.

out to be about twelve and a half feet long, was killed days later by a Portland man, Edward O. Lessard, and his son, Joe, using home-made harpoons. The whale's appearance in Portland and its demise rated international news coverage. The Lessards were promptly charged with criminal violations of Oregon fish and game laws.

Portland lawyer Delmore Lessard, a brother and uncle of the defendants, quickly deflected criminal charges against the whale killers because state fish and game laws did not outlaw the killing of a whale. But the case refused to die when the state filed a civil case claiming that the embalmed carcass belonged to the state, not to its killers. The whale was lodged in the courtyard of the Multnomah County Courthouse, open to public view, while the legal dispute unfolded in circuit court.

Judge James W. Crawford had been on the bench less than a year when the whale case arose. He would serve a total of thirty-one years before his retirement in 1962, making him the longest-sitting judge ever on the Multnomah County circuit bench. He held another prominent role in Portland legal circles as well. After two years of teaching at the Northwestern College of Law, Crawford became the school's dean in 1924. He held that position until 1965 when the night law school merged with Lewis and Clark College.

Crawford dismissed the state's suit to take possession of the carcass. He concluded that the state had no restriction against killing whales and that none could be implied from the state's relationship to wildlife. But he made sure that no one thought he approved of the whale's demise. "The legal considerations rendering these conclusions inescapable are not to be taken as any expression of personal approval of, or sympathy with, the act of the defendants in the unnecessary killing of Jim McCool's whale in the waters of the Oregon Slough," Crawford wrote.[25] However, the Lessards' victory before Judge Crawford was short-lived. The Oregon Supreme Court in 1934 accepted the state attorney general's contention that, under the common law, the whale was a "royal fish"[26] while in coastal or inland waters. On remand, a different judge awarded the whale to the state.

Delmore Lessard went on to serve two terms in the Oregon Legislature, but his life and career ended tragically two decades later at age fifty-seven. Lessard traveled to Heppner in June 1955 to regain custody of a thirteen-year-old boy whose father, represented by Lessard, had won custody in a divorce case. The mother, a barmaid at O'Donnell's restaurant and bar, fired three shots at Lessard in the establishment. The third shot killed him.

Economic pressures of the mid-1930s helped stimulate creation of two new legal institutions, the integrated Oregon State Bar and the Multnomah County Legal Aid office. Discussion of an integrated bar—to which all Oregon lawyers would be required to belong, unlike a voluntary association—had surfaced as early as 1924 when the subject arose in California and other western states. But the idea met a chilly reception from members of the voluntary Oregon Bar Association and the suggestion lay dormant until 1929. A formal proposal for an integrated bar advanced to the legislature in 1933 but was narrowly defeated. Defeat turned into victory in the 1935 session, when legislators created the Oregon State Bar and its Board of Bar Governors to supervise attorney admissions and to enforce professional discipline. Legislators envisioned the integrated bar as a consumer service to protect the public from unethical conduct. The voluntary bar association, which attempted to police professional ethics, had difficulty raising money to pay for disciplinary proceedings. The association's powers were also weaker in rural areas of the state where even voluntary bar membership was less popular. Lawyers who backed creation of the integrated bar also saw the new agency as a tool for cracking down on the unauthorized practice of law.

Mandatory dues the first year were $3 for each of the bar's 1,800 members. Portland lawyer Robert F. Maguire, who was the founding partner of the firm known later as Cosgrave Vergeer & Kester LLP, was the integrated bar's first president. Maguire had come to Portland as a young lawyer in

1910. He spent his first three years as an assistant U.S. Attorney, then worked as a deputy Multnomah County district attorney. He spent many years as a bankruptcy chancellor before forming a partnership in 1934 with Roy F. Shields, then assistant general solicitor for the Union Pacific Railroad. Within a few years, Maguire and Shields built a firm that rivaled the Carey firm as Portland's largest.

Outlining the function of the nine-member Board of Bar Governors at the first general meeting in Salem in September 1935, Maguire said, "The organization presents an opportunity to the bar to render a service real and substantial to the profession, to the courts and to the people of the state."[27] Portland attorney Fred M. Sercombe became the bar's first secretary and sole staff member of the organization. The bar's first office was in the Yeon Building. Sercombe's salary at the outset was $1,166.67 per year. It was better, Sercombe recalled many years later, than his first month of legal practice, when he took in $25.

OHS CN012986

Robert F. Maguire.

Soon after its inception, the Board of Bar Governors created a Legal Aid Commitee composed of Portland lawyers David Robinson, the one-time public defender in Portland Municipal Court, Gus J. Solomon, and George N. Woodley. Convinced of the need to provide legal assistance for citizens who couldn't afford it, the Multnomah Bar Association already had taken steps to open a legal aid office on

February 15, 1936. The original office was funded with a grant from the federal Works Progress Administration and by an $800 contribution from the Oregon State Bar. In its first four months, the two-lawyer staff received more than 1,000 inquiries. Volunteers from the Junior League of Portland helped answer the telephones.

Legal Aid's first supervising attorney was Janet W. Starkey, a graduate of the University of Denver Law School, who had been working as a municipal bond lawyer. Ironically, Starkey had skipped out of classes on domestic relations while in law school because she felt her presence as the only woman in the class inhibited the other students from discussing some of the factual unpleasantries in that field. But she saw the full scope of domestic turmoil at Legal Aid, where Starkey remained until resigning twenty-six year later in 1961.[28]

Child custody and divorces dominated the Legal Aid cases of the era. The office expanded to five lawyers in 1938, when the Community Chest, a forerunner of United Way, became a continuing contributor to the program. Many Portland lawyers had feared that Legal Aid would deprive them of some fee-paying clients, but the new office screened prospective clients to assure that other attorneys would not be losing paying business.

Starkey was succeeded as Legal Aid director by Ronald I. Gevurtz, who held the position for eight years. Gevurtz resigned in 1969 and went on to form Portland's largest law firm devoted to domestic relations, Gevurtz, Menashe, Larson, Yates & Howe PC. By the late 1990s, the Gevurtz firm grew to twenty lawyers and claimed to be the largest in the nation devoted solely to domestic relations matters.

The Depression nearly halted construction in downtown Portland but the federal government pressed ahead with construction of a new U.S. Courthouse at Broadway and Salmon Street. Besides U.S. District Court, which had outgrown the cramped courthouse built in the Matthew Deady era, the new building was designed to house several other agencies in the

OHS OrHi 97133, *Oregon Journal* photo

Construction of the U.S. Courthouse in July 1932 on SW Broadway.

growing federal bureaucracy. Portland architects Morris H. Whitehouse and Walter Church were commissioned in 1930 to design the courthouse. Whitehouse had designed Jefferson and Lincoln high schools, as well as buildings for important local institutions such as the Multnomah Athletic Club and the University Club. Completed in 1933, the new courthouse featured a sedate, substantially flat exterior with classical detailing, but the interior offered elaborately paneled courtrooms with high ceilings, and a post office in the lobby filled with intricate bronze art deco decoration.

After the U.S. District Court moved into its new headquarters, the original United States Building fell into disuse. City officials talked of tearing it down to make way for a downtown park or parking lot. Another generation would pass before its fate was decided.

The first judicial tenants in the new federal courthouse were Judge Fee and Judge John H. McNary, who took the federal bench after the death of Judge Charles E. Wolverton in 1926. A native of the Salem area, McNary

OHS OrHi 43057

Portland's new U.S. Courthouse, completed in 1933, moved Oregon's federal judiciary out of the old United States Building.

studied law after being elected Marion County recorder. He served as a prosecutor for seventeen years before entering private practice with his brother, Charles L. McNary, in Salem. Charles McNary was appointed to the U.S. Senate in 1918, and became one of the state's most popular senators, holding office until his death in 1944. John McNary remained on the U.S. District Court bench until his death in 1936 at age sixty-nine.

The Depression years also rekindled interest in organized labor, which had waned during the prosperity of the 1920s. Passage of the Wagner Act granted unions the right to organize. Dock workers in Portland, like their counterparts at other major West Coast ports, quickly expressed support for the International Longshoreman's Association. The association signed up more than 1,100 Portland workers within a few months. But Portland shipping companies declined to negotiate, prompting a tense, eighty-two-day dock strike beginning in May 1934. Dock strikes in other cities led to fatal violence. Shots were fired on occasion in Portland, but no fatalities occurred. Portland attorney Burl A. Green, who represented the union, tried to act as a moderating force by keeping lines of communication open with employers. Green met with New York Senator Robert Wagner, chairman of the new National Labor Relations Board, for a tour of the docks on July 18, 1934, when strike tensions had reached their peak. Someone fired bullets near and above the car carrying Green and Wagner, but no one was injured. Several days after Wagner's visit, dock employers finally agreed to settle the strike by mediation.

Labor supporters and local Communist party members had felt harassed during the strike by Portland police, under the direction of Portland mayor Joseph K. Carson, Jr., and by a volunteer group, the Citizens Emergency League, which offered its assistance to police "in cases of extreme emergency to maintain law and order."[29] Carson, a cherubic-looking lawyer who had practiced in Portland since returning from World War I in 1919, was elected mayor in 1932. Portland's population surpassed the 300,000 mark during Carson's two terms. Given the state of the economy, Carson's tenure as mayor was not a time for new programs. He concentrated on balancing municipal budgets and improving efficiency. The dock turmoil of 1934 was Carson's biggest mayoral headache. Although a Democrat with traditional labor support, Carson believed that maintaining order was his highest priority during the labor unrest. Ultimately, Carson's relations with labor survived the stress of the Depression. Labor groups backed him in 1947 when President Harry Truman nominated Carson to the U.S. Maritime Commission, a position Carson held for three years.

A public meeting sponsored by the Communist party to protest conduct by police and the Citizens Emergency League during the dock strike eventually led to another major case to be decided by the United States Supreme Court. The meeting was held on July 27, 1934, at the party's offices at 68 Southwest Alder Street. Although the meeting was entirely peaceful, police raided it and accused several people, including one of the speakers, Dirk DeJonge, of violating Oregon's criminal syndicalism laws. Those laws, adopted in many states after the red scare following World War I, made it a felony to espouse or to belong to any organization that advocated "crime, physical violence, sabotage or any unlawful acts or methods as a means of accomplishing or effecting industrial or political change or revolution."

Because DeJonge, a Communist party candidate for mayor, had not advocated or engaged in violence during the speech leading to his arrest, his three-week trial in Multnomah County Circuit Court was composed mostly of Communist party documents that referred to violent overthrow of the United States government. Jurors, after twenty-four hours of deliberations, returned a ten-to-two verdict convicting DeJonge, but they asked that he be treated leniently. Circuit Court Judge Jacob Kanzler, an infantry veteran of World War I and an active member of the American Legion and Veterans of Foreign Wars, imposed a seven-year penitentiary term on DeJonge out of a possible ten-year maximum. Some members of the Oregon Supreme Court questioned the severity of Kanzler's sentence, but the court affirmed DeJonge's conviction.[30]

The American Civil Liberties Union did not have a chapter in Oregon at the time; however, a handful of Portland lawyers sympathetic with the association's views on civil liberties occasionally volunteered to take on cases. One of those lawyers was Gus J. Solomon, the son of two eastern Europe immigrants, who had felt the sting of discrimination as a Jew growing up and later working in Portland. Solomon entered legal practice in 1929 and built his practice representing businesses, unions, farm organizations, and rural cooperatives. He agreed to write the brief for DeJonge's appeal to the United States Supreme Court.

In January 1937, a unanimous Supreme Court in *DeJonge v. Oregon* adopted Solomon's view that rights of free speech and assembly were violated by the syndicalism law when a defendant arrested under them had not engaged in otherwise illegal conduct. "The holding of meetings for peaceable political action cannot be proscribed," wrote Chief Justice Charles Evans Hughes. "Those who assist in the conduct of such meetings cannot be branded as criminals on that score."[31] DeJonge was released after nine months in prison and later found employment as a laborer for Portland Traction Company. Syndicalism laws in Oregon and elsewhere were repealed, to be replaced instead with criminal laws on conspiracy. Gus Solomon, however, would learn a dozen years later that the *DeJonge* case was not yet through with him.

Turmoil on Portland's docks coincided with the 1934 elections. Governor Julius Meier decided not to seek a second term, but another Portland lawyer, Multnomah County Circuit Court Judge William A. Ekwall, wanted to run for Congress for the seat encompassing Portland. Ekwall, a 1912 graduate of the old University of Oregon night law school, had followed Judge George Rossman on the Portland Municipal Court bench in 1922, and had taken Rossman's seat in circuit court five years later when Rossman was appointed to the state supreme court. By 1934, Ekwall was the presiding circuit court judge.

When Ekwall tried to file as a congressional candidate, Secretary of State P. J. Stadelman refused to let him. Stadelman contended that Ekwall's oath as a judge barred him from accepting "any other office, except judicial offices" during his elected term. Ekwall filed a mandamus action with the Oregon Supreme Court. The court agreed that Oregon lacked the power to add qualifications for federal candidates, and ordered Ekwall's name to be placed on the ballot.[32] Ekwall, a Republican, narrowly won the Congressional seat, but some members of his party accused him of giving too much support to President Franklin D. Roosevelt. In 1936, Ekwall was defeated by Nan Wood Honeyman, daughter of former prominent Portland lawyer C. E. S. Wood, who became the first woman from Oregon to serve in Congress. President Roosevelt did not forget Ekwall. The president appointed him in

1942 to the United States Customs Court in New York, a position Ekwall held until his death at age sixty-nine in 1956.

President Roosevelt also turned to the ranks of Portland's legal profession to select Bert E. Haney as the state's second judge, after William B. Gilbert, to sit on the Ninth Circuit Court of Appeals. Haney, a native of tiny Lafayette, began his legal career in 1904 as a Multnomah County deputy district attorney. Haney left that office in 1908 and spent ten years in private practice with the firm headed by George W. Joseph before being appointed United States attorney in 1918 by President Woodrow Wilson. Haney returned to private practice in 1920, and in 1923 was appointed to the United States Shipping Board by President Calvin Coolidge. He left that national post in 1926 to make an unsuccessful run for the U.S. Senate from Oregon on the Democratic ticket. Haney then returned to private practice in Portland and served on the Port of Portland Commission before he was appointed to the federal appeals court in 1935. Haney held the post until his death at age sixty-four in 1943.

By 1930, the Multnomah County Circuit Court bench had grown to eight positions. The decade brought two new judges who would leave lasting marks on the state and local judicial systems, Hall Lusk and Donald E. Long. A native of Washington, D.C., Lusk arrived in Oregon in 1909 and went to work as an associate with Portland's oldest law firm at the time, Dolph, Mallory, Simon & Gearin. He served as an assistant United States attorney from 1918 to 1920, and then returned to private practice with political aspirations. Lusk's first attempt at elective office, however, was a dismal failure. He ran for state representative from Multnomah County in 1922, the year the Ku Klux Klan exerted its greatest influence. Lusk, a Democrat and a Catholic, challenged the Klan and lost decisively. He won a measure of revenge by working on the U.S. Supreme Court brief in *Pierce v. Society of Sisters*, the case that struck down the ban on parochial education supported by the Klan.

Lusk was appointed to the Multnomah County Circuit Court bench in 1930, and served until his appointment to the Oregon Supreme Court in 1937. He remained on the state high court until 1960, when Governor Mark Hatfield appointed Lusk to finish the U.S. Senate term of Richard L. Neuberger, who died with nine months remaining before the 1960 general election. Lusk returned to the Oregon Supreme Court in 1961, where he served until retiring in 1968 at age eighty-five. With thirty-one years on the appellate bench, Lusk's lengthy service ranked just behind Justice George Rossman's thirty-seven years on the supreme court. The two Portland lawyers served twenty-eight of those years at the same time, between 1937 and Rossman's retirement in 1965.

Donald E. Long's judicial career began in 1934 when Mayor Joseph Carson, Jr., appointed him to the Portland Municipal Court. Long, the son of a Hillsboro newspaper editor, spent two years as an FBI agent before completing Georgetown University Law School in 1924. Long had interrupted his schooling in 1916 to join the Army protecting the U.S.-Mexico border during World War I. After two years as a municipal court judge, Long in

OHS CN012203

Multnomah County Circuit Judge Donald E. Long at the juvenile detention facility named in his honor. The building shown here was replaced a larger successor in 1995.

1936 won election to the domestic relations seat on Multnomah County Circuit Court.

With time out for a return to active military duty during World War II, Long remained on the bench until retiring in 1963. He earned wide respect as a domestic relations and juvenile court judge, including a term as president of the National Council of Juvenile Court Judges. He lobbied for many improvements in the Multnomah County juvenile system, including construction of new detention and juvenile court facilities approved by county commissioners in 1952. After his retirement, county officials named the juvenile facility the Donald E. Long Juvenile Home in his honor.

During World War II, Long returned to active duty as an artillery officer, serving in Africa, Italy, France, Germany, and Austria. He was wounded in France and was awarded the Bronze Star for meritorious service during the Allied landing on the Anzio beachhead. At the end of his career in 1963, Long offered a simple explanation for his colorful life: "All I have tried to do over the years," he said, "is to do my duty as a citizen, as a soldier and as a judge."[33]

CHAPTER FIVE

Post-War Growth

Economic pressures of the Depression reduced the ranks of Portland lawyers from roughly 800 in 1930 to 650 at America's entrance to World War II in 1941. Within three years, some 125 Portland attorneys, or roughly twenty percent of the city's roster of lawyers, had joined military service. McCamant & Thompson, which ranked as one of Portland's largest firms in 1940 with nine lawyers, saw its legal staff reduced to four lawyers during the war.[1] Other large firms felt similar cutbacks, as did the Northwestern College of Law.

Portland's night law school had been graduating twenty to thirty lawyers per year during the 1920s and 1930s. But total enrollment fell to as few as sixteen during World War II, when Dean John Gantenbein worked for three years without pay to help keep the doors open. The son of Calvin Gantenbein, who had bought the few physical assets of the old University of Oregon law department in 1915, John Gantenbein had graduated from the law school in 1934. Four years later he became dean. In 1947, Gantenbein bought out the rest of his family to become sole owner of the law school, which held its classes in the Sherlock Building. Gantenbein turned over the deanship to Circuit Court Judge James Crawford in 1946. John Gantenbein finished his legal career as Multnomah County District Court judge from 1950 to 1975.

Lawyers who remained in Portland during the war assisted in blood drives, in war bond sales, and in a program offering free legal help to members of the armed services. News of these events circulated through the Oregon State Bar in a new monthly periodical, the *Bar Bulletin*, begun in July 1941 under the editorship of Alexander G. Brown, a Portland deputy city attorney. Brown, who held an undergraduate degree in journalism, had worked for several newspapers, including the Portland *Telegram*, the *Oregon Journal*, and *The Oregonian*, before graduating from the Northwestern College of Law in 1931. He began his legal career as a deputy city attorney in 1935, and by 1938 was chief deputy.

Brown entered active military duty in 1942. Upon his return to civilian life in 1947, he resumed editing the monthly *Bar Bulletin* from his office in City Hall, a practice he continued until his retirement in 1968. Brown was appointed city attorney in 1947 and served at that post for twenty-one years, longer than any other Portland city attorney. His office became a training ground for many deputies who continued with successful careers. They included Marian C. Rushing, the first woman ever to hold the position of Portland city attorney, who succeeded Brown; Virgil Langtry, who served for eighteen years as a Multnomah County Circuit Court judge and then became one of the first judges of the Oregon Court of Appeals when it was created in 1969; Richard L. Unis, who served as a Portland Municipal Court judge and later as Multnomah County District Court and Circuit Court judge before joining the Oregon Supreme Court in 1990; Philip T. Abraham, who served on the Portland Municipal Court and Multnomah County District Court before joining the Multnomah County Circuit Court bench in 1981; Phillip J. Roth, who won election to the circuit court bench in 1964, a seat he held for thirty years; and William C. Beers, who served as a district court judge for twenty years, ending in 1982.

America's involvement in the war was three months old when Minoru Yasui, a graduate of the University of Oregon Law School and recent admittee to the Oregon State Bar, walked into Portland's central police precinct at 11:20 p.m. on March 28, 1942. That peaceful act of Yasui, the American-born son of Japanese parents, challenged a new federal law that gave military officials the power to set curfews for "enemy aliens and persons of Japanese ancestry." Yasui believed the law was void against him because he was an American citizen. He was promptly charged in U.S. District Court with a federal misdemeanor.

Portland attorney Earle F. Bernard, a former county prosecutor, led Yasui's defense. A graduate of the University of Oregon law department in 1913, Bernard had established himself as a prominent lawyer in both civil and criminal litigation. He was joined in practice in 1947 by his son, William F. Bernard, and the firm evolved into the modern office of Duffy Kekel Jones & Bernard LLP. In addition to Earle Bernard, some of Portland's most notable lawyers of the era— including Burl A. Green, Omar Spencer, and Manley Strayer—filed a friend-of-the-court brief on Yasui's behalf. U.S. District Court Judge Alger Fee tried the matter without a jury. Fee, in a carefully worded opinion in November 1942, found Yasui guilty. He outlined his reasoning and his findings of fact in detail because, he explained, "Grave danger exists that otherwise the findings might be used as a basis for unwarrantable action in other times."[2] Fee concluded that the curfew was void against American citizens without a declaration of martial law. But he went on to find that Yasui had renounced his U.S. citizenship by working for the office of Consul General of Japan in Chicago until shortly after the attack on Pearl Harbor.

Yasui told the judge that he would "prefer a thousand times over to die as an American in defense of American principles rather than live in comparative comfort of an internment camp as an alien Japanese."[3] Nevertheless, Fee imposed a sentence of one year in prison and a $5,000 fine. "The court can only view this as a proceeding to embarrass the military authority of the United States," he declared.[4]

Bernard appealed Fee's decision to the United States Supreme Court. In

June 1943, the Court issued its ruling with a companion case involving Gordon Hirabayashi, a University of Washington student who had failed to register for evacuation in Seattle. In decisions widely criticized after the war, the Supreme Court affirmed the curfew and internment of Japanese aliens and American citizens of Japanese descent in *Hirabayashi v. United States*[5] and *Yasui v. United States*.[6] Chief Justice Harlan F. Stone justified the decision in part on the speedy progress of Japanese military forces in their South Pacific attacks. Unlike Judge Fee, the U.S. Supreme Court failed to recognize a distinction between aliens and American citizens of Japanese descent. By war's end, more than 110,000 Japanese were removed from the West Coast, including 4,500 from Oregon and Washington state.

One of the FBI officers assigned to protect the West from espionage and sabotage by the Japanese was Alan F. Davis, a 1939 University of Oregon law graduate who chose federal service over private practice as the Depression wore on. Davis was ordered to help round up Japanese citizens for placement in internment camps. He quit the FBI in 1943, partly in protest over that policy. Davis entered private practice after the war. He was elected Oregon State Bar president in 1956, and served as Multnomah County Circuit Court judge for twenty-three years starting in 1959.

Yasui, meanwhile, settled in Denver, Colorado, where he practiced law and served as executive director of the Denver Commission on Community Relations. He continued his fight to have his federal conviction reversed. In January 1984, two years before his death, the federal government agreed to vacate his conviction. But U.S. District Court Judge Robert C. Belloni, a former Coos and Curry County Circuit Court judge appointed by President Lyndon Johnson to the federal bench in 1967, declined to find that there was no necessity for the curfew and that the curfew and internment laws were based on racism, as Yasui had urged. With the conviction vacated, Belloni said, there was nothing further on which to rule.

Another round of Japanese race-related litigation surfaced in 1947 when

Portland lawyers Verne Dusenbery and Allan Hart challenged Oregon's alien land laws. Influenced by fears of a "Yellow Peril," Oregon legislators in 1923 had followed California's lead in adopting laws that barred Japanese aliens from owning agricultural land. Oregon extended its laws in 1945 to prohibit leasing of agricultural land to Japanese aliens, who at the time were ineligible for citizenship under federal law. Dusenbery and Hart represented Kenji Namba, an American citizen who had fought in combat in Italy during World War II, and his father, Etsuo Namba, who was a native of Japan and who had lived in the United States since 1908. The father and son had negotiated to lease sixty-two acres in east Multnomah County. When they checked with Multnomah County district attorney John B. McCourt before signing the lease, McCourt said he would enforce the alien land law. Prospective penalties against the Nambas and the lessor included forfeiture of the land to the state, $5,000 in fines, and two years in prison.

Dusenbery and Hart appealed to the Oregon Supreme Court after losing a declaratory judgement in Multnomah County Circuit Court. The lawyers contended that the law violated state and federal constitutional rights, including equal protection and due process of law. In their brief to the Oregon Supreme Court, Hart and Dusenbery said that the purpose of the discriminatory law was to harass Japanese aliens and to discourage them from residing in Oregon. The Oregon high court, in March 1949, unanimously reversed Judge James Crawford, who had ruled against the Nambas. Chief Justice George Rossman, writing for the unanimous court, said, "The American people have an increasing consciousness that since we are a heterogeneous people, we must not discriminate against anyone on account of his race, color or creed."[7] Dusenbery and Hart were honored by the Emperor of Japan in 1968 for their work on the case.

While many lawyers were returning to their homes and careers in Portland after the war, former Oregon State Bar president Robert F. Maguire left Oregon to serve as one of three judges of an International Military

Tribunal in Nuremberg, Germany. Maguire spent eighteen months with justices from the supreme courts of Minnesota and Iowa, working their way through 79,000 pages of testimony involving alleged war crimes of several German officials. Maguire's tribunal reviewed evidence and issued its findings in a written decision of 838 pages. The three-judge panel on which he served imposed twenty-five-year prison sentences on two high-ranking Nazi figures and lesser terms on several other Nazi planning officials. Maguire returned to Portland in 1949.

Maguire's service in the Nuremburg trials came to be overshadowed in the public's mind by that of another Oregon lawyer, James T. Brand. A native of Oberlin, Ohio, Brand finished undergraduate studies at Oberlin College and had completed his first year of law school at Harvard University when he came to Oregon during portions of 1910 and 1911 to improve his health by working as a forest ranger. After graduating from Harvard in 1914, Brand opened a law office in Coos Bay. He then served as a circuit court judge in Coos and Curry counties from 1927 until his appointment to the Oregon Supreme Court in 1941. Brand left Oregon for fifteen months to serve as a judge at Nuremburg, where he tried judges who had served under Hitler's regime. Brand's role in the trials was memorialized in a Hollywood movie, *Judgment at Nuremburg*, in which Spencer Tracy played Brand. Brand worked with Tracy in preparing him for the role. Brand remained on the Oregon Supreme Court until resigning in 1958. He then opened a law office in Salem, where he practiced until his death in 1964.

Many changes were at hand as lawyers came home from the war. The Oregon State Bar, believing many returning veterans would need to refresh their legal skills after lengthy military service, instituted brush-up courses under the name of Continuing Legal Education. The courses were planned as a temporary measure, but lawyers quickly appreciated their value. Continuing Legal Education became a permanent function of the bar.

Fred M. Sercombe, who had served as secretary of the bar since its integration in 1935, retired in 1949. Lee Karr, the new secretary, moved the bar headquarters from the Yeon Building to a larger office in the Pittock Block. Dues were raised to $12 per year, in part to help pay for the move. However, Karr's tenure as bar executive ended tragically in October 1953. Karr was thrown from a truck being used for a hay ride during a bar function in Klamath Falls. Karr, age thirty-six, suffered fatal head injuries after the truck lost its brakes and crashed into a tree. The only other passenger on the truck at the time was Wendell Wyatt, who suffered superficial injuries. Wyatt, an Astoria lawyer, later served five terms in the U.S. House of Representatives before becoming a senior partner in the Portland firm of Schwabe Williamson & Wyatt in 1975. Karr was succeeded as bar executive by lawyer John H. Holloway, who held the post for twenty-four years until retiring in 1978.

Another postwar development with a lasting significance occurred in August 1946 in a room at the old Portland Hotel. A small group of Portland lawyers met there with Sam Horovitz, a Boston attorney concerned about legal representation for injured workers. Horovitz came to Portland to attend the 1946 meeting of the International Association of Industrial Accident Boards and Commissions, a group that had been dominated by manufacturers and insurance companies. Horovitz believed injured workers needed lawyers to stand up against insurers. Accounts vary as to how many attorneys were in the room with Horvitz, but the total was fewer than a dozen. The lawyers assessed themselves $1 dues and formed the National Association of Claimants' Compensation Attorneys (NACCA). Ben Marcus, a friend of Horovitz's and a labor lawyer from Detroit, was selected as an informal president.[8] As years went by, NACCA grew quickly and later changed its name to the Association of Trial Lawyers of America.

Others in the Portland Hotel room that day in 1946 included James T. Landye, then a partner of prominent Portland labor lawyer Burl A. Green, and Portland lawyers Nels Peterson and Ben Anderson. Gus Solomon attended briefly but left for another appointment. Other informal meetings were held around the nation, and the new organization held its first formal convention in 1947 in Toronto. Landye became NACCA's first formally elected president. A native of Wales, Landye had come to Portland in his early teens, and joined the bar in 1935. He practiced in Portland and San Francisco at different times and became one of the West Coast's leading labor lawyers. Landye served as president of the Multnomah Bar Association in 1947-1948. He died at age forty-five of a heart attack suffered while attending a Multnomah Bar Association meeting in 1956. Twenty-five years after its founding in Portland, the Association of Trial Lawyers of America returned to Portland to hold its annual convention. Membership in the national organization by 1971 had climbed to 28,000.

Another postwar change was the creation by Congress of a third U.S. District Court seat for Oregon in 1948. President Harry S. Truman nominated Gus J. Solomon, son of a Russian-born merchant, to the position. Solomon's confirmation wasn't perfunctory. A growing fear of Communists in the United States had already taken firm root when Daniel C. Mahoney, a former federal law clerk, and W. B. O'Dale, a retired Portland policemen, suggested to U.S. Senate investigators that Solomon in the 1930s had been a member of at least two Communist-front organizations. Those suspect bodies included the National Lawyers Guild and the American Civil Liberties Union. Furthermore, Solomon's assistance on behalf of Dirk DeJonge, the Communist party mayoral candidate whose criminal syndicalism case set a U.S. Supreme Court precedent, bolstered the possibility that Solomon was a Communist sympathizer.

Several of Portland's leading lawyers rallied to Solomon's defense at a Senate judiciary subcommittee meeting held in Salt Lake City, Utah, in May 1950. Lamar Tooze, who then worked in the law firm of Republican National Committeeman Ralph Cake, told the committee, "I wouldn't be here if I had the slightest doubt as to his loyalty or ability."[9] Chester

McCarty, another lawyer with outstanding military credentials, also backed Solomon, as did Burl A. Green and Gunther Krause. In a later hearing, Solomon submitted a statement reflecting his devotion to the law as protector of personal liberty and property rights. "I am uncompromisingly opposed to any government which, like the Communist state, is predicated upon the suspension of liberty or upon a reign of lawlessness," he said.[10] Solomon ultimately was confirmed without dissent. He served in U.S. District Court longer than any other judge in Portland history, ending with his death in 1987.

Solomon joined Judges James Alger Fee and Claude McColloch on the federal bench. McColloch, nominated and confirmed in 1937 following the death of John McNary, came to Oregon as a small boy from Red Bluff, California. His family had lived in both Baker and Portland by the time McColloch went off to Stanford University in 1904. McColloch later practiced in both cities before joining the federal bench. His younger brother, Frank McColloch, after serving as state public utility commissioner, also became a prominent Portland lawyer in the firm now known as Lane Powell Spears Lubersky LLP.

OHS CN014751

Gus J. Solomon

Judge McColloch earned a reputation for humor and a relaxed style in running his courtroom. A notable example of McColloch's wit surfaced in 1949 when the federal government accused a food-packing company of violating federal standards in its canned asparagus. The issue was whether the canned stalks were too fibrous. Predictably, evidence from the government and the packer was contradictory.

With the consent of the parties, Judge McColloch assigned himself to a personal test. "I took three days to eat the can," he reported. "That, I can now state, is as much as an old protein user should attempt on his first venture into herbalism. I suspect the Government witnesses tried to eat their cans all at one time, and that may explain the severity of their judgment about the defendant's asparagus."[11] Judge McColloch ruled for the canning company.

The postwar years saw the reemergence of an old public problem in Portland and the rise of a prominent lawyer to fight it. The problem was vice; the lawyer was Dorothy McCullough Lee. The battle was long and controversial, and in the end, perhaps, a stalemate.

Perhaps because of its status as a river and shipping town, gambling and prostitution had a long history in Portland, dating back well into the nineteenth century. Mayor George H. Williams was not the first to rail against vice, nor the first to be unable to eradicate it during his tenure at city hall after the turn of the century. World War II, which drew thousands of new residents to work in Portland's shipyards, brought more people and more money to the city's after-hours clubs, prostitution cribs, and drinking establishments.

Upon her arrival in Portland in 1924, Lee, the recent bride of a Standard Oil chemical engineer, would have seemed an unlikely candidate to tackle Portland's long tradition with social crime. But she was an unusual woman. The daughter of a U.S. Navy surgeon, the young Dorothy McCullough had traveled around much of the world by the time she began undergraduate studies at the University of California at Berkeley. She then advanced to law school in Berkeley and practiced in San Francisco for a year before coming to Portland with her husband.

Unlike San Francisco, Portland offered little opportunity for women in the law. "There were stenographer jobs, but there was no place in law firms as a lawyer for me," Lee once recalled. "The law firms told me it couldn't be done, but I had come from San Francisco where it had been done, so I knew better."[12] Lee opened her own office, joined numerous civic clubs, and ran for the legislature. She lost her first race in 1926, but in 1928 won a seat in the Oregon House of Representatives.

In 1931, Lee formed a law partnership with Gladys M. Everett, establishing Oregon's first all-woman firm, and one of the first on the West Coast. Like Lee, Everett was a tradition-breaker. After graduating from the University of Oregon Law School in 1923, she opened a practice in Portland the next year. In 1935, the Portland City Council selected Everett to preside over the Portland Municipal Court for three days while Judge Donald E. Long was away from the city, making her the first woman to sit on the municipal bench. Lee served briefly, too, as a temporary municipal judge in 1940.

Lee advanced to the Oregon Senate in 1932, where she became the state's first woman to preside over a branch of the legislature. She was defeated in 1936 and returned again in 1938 to fill a vacancy, but her biggest impact would prove to be in municipal government. When a vacancy arose on the Portland City Council in 1943, Fred Peterson, a pharmacist and city commissioner, proposed Lee's name. Mayor Earl Riley agreed and appointed Lee to the city council. Lee closed her law practice and became Portland's first woman to serve as a city commissioner.

Riley had announced plans to seek a third mayoral term in 1948, when the Portland City Club released a report on crime suggesting that underworld figures were paying thousands of dollars per month to Portland police for protection. A Multnomah County grand jury undertook an investigation and issued no indictments, but crime became the major issue in the mayor's race. Lee and several other candidates entered the race against Riley in the

May primary. As a candidate, Lee repeated little more than one sentence about crime throughout the May primary election campaign: "I will enforce the law."[13] Portlanders liked what they saw in candidate Lee: she won a resounding seventy percent of the vote in the May primary, eliminating the need for a November runoff. Dorothy Lee became mayor in January 1949. She was the first woman to hold that job.

Lee quickly lived up to her campaign promise about enforcing the law. She hired a new police chief and ordered police to go after punchboards, slot machines, pinball games, betting pools, and gambling games wherever they were found. Gambling proved not to be restricted to after-hours joints and taverns. Many of the city's prominent private clubs used gambling revenue to bolster their operating budgets, and they, too, had to halt those games. The mayor also prevailed on John B. McCourt, the county district attorney, to use abatement laws to close down cheap hotels north of Burnside where prostitution had been rampant. "Dottie-Do-Good," as she was called by many, shook Portland like no mayor before her. "She was a real lady," said Tom McCall, a television news reporter of the era who went on to become a two-term Oregon governor. "But she had an iron will."[14]

Lee's tireless drive carried political costs, however. Compromise was difficult for her. Before Lee's first year as mayor was finished, opponents circulated a petition seeking her recall. Maxwell Donnelly, a Portland lawyer, led the initiative drive. Ultimately, Donnelly failed to raise enough signatures to force a recall election. He sent the mayor a dozen roses as a means of making up, but Lee took no solace in Donnelly's gesture. She refused the flowers.

Lee was not a single-issue mayor. During the rest of her term, she hastened the removal of trolley tracks from downtown streets and instituted the one-way traffic pattern as the automobile became the prevalent mode of urban transportation. Lee bolstered the Housing Authority of Portland and took a stand for equal-housing opportunity for minorities. She lobbied strenuously but unsuccessfully for modernizing the structure of municipal government. But above all, Lee was noted for enforcing vice laws and for attempting to toughen them. The toll of her diligence was reflected in November 1952, when pharmacist Fred Peterson, who had first recommended Lee as a city council appointee in 1943, defeated her in a mayoral runoff election.

The loss was only a brief setback in Lee's career. After a trip to Europe, President Dwight D. Eisenhower, who had met Lee during his 1952 campaign, appointed her to the federal Parole Board in Washington, D.C., a position she held until 1956. Oregon's young and upwardly mobile secretary of state, Mark O. Hatfield, suggested to Eisenhower that year that he should appoint Lee to the United States Supreme Court. Eisenhower had other plans, however. He called on Lee instead to serve on the Subversive Activities Control Board, a presidential commission investigating the Communist party. Lee became the board's chairwoman in 1957 and retained that title until resigning in 1962. She then returned to Portland and resumed private law practice in estate and probate work. She died in 1981.

Courtesy of *The Oregonian*

Dorothy McCullough Lee in the Rose Festival Parade in 1952, her last year as mayor.

The prosperous 1950s sparked fast growth for Portland's business-oriented law firms. Companies engaged in fields such as logging and forest products, food processing, aluminum, and transportation grew quickly, and so did their need for legal help. The successors to William D. Fenton's old firm grew from a twelve-lawyer staff in 1945, then the largest in Portland, to twenty by 1955, when the firm was known as Koerner, Young, McColloch & Dezendorf. During the same decade, the firm founded by Charles H. Carey leapfrogged from ten lawyers to the twenty-six-lawyer office of Hart, Spencer, McColloch, Rockwood & Davies, taking the lead as Portland's largest. The firm of King, Miller, Anderson, Nash & Yerke grew to fifteen lawyers by 1955, and Mautz, Souther, Spaulding, Denecke & Kinsey was close behind with fourteen lawyers.

Although most business negotiations took place in office buildings cloaked with attorney-client secrecy, the takeover of a major Oregon timber company by the fast-growing Georgia-Pacific Corporation involved unusual circumstances. Robert S. Miller of the King firm represented the C.D. Johnson Lumber Company in 1951 when Georgia-Pacific cast its corporate eye on large-scale Johnson Lumber holdings in western Oregon. Two sons of C.D. Johnson traveled to Chicago in August 1951 to meet with Owen Cheatham, Georgia-Pacific's founder, to discuss the transaction. However, the commercial airliner bringing Dean and Ernest Johnson back from Chicago crashed in hills near Oakland, California, killing all passengers. Miller, knowing that Dean Johnson customarily took accurate notes of his business dealings, rushed to Oakland immediately after the crash. He found Johnson's damaged briefcase and notes that coincided with Cheatham's recollection of the negotiations. The $16.8 million transaction was completed later the same year, and Miller became Georgia-Pacific's counsel for Oregon.

Outside the privacy of board rooms and law offices, public interest in the law in the mid-1950s focused on a series of highly publicized trials. The first was instigated late on the night of April 21, 1955, when Portland lawyer Kermit Smith turned the ignition key in his car in the parking lot of the Columbia Edgewater Country Club. Unbeknownst to the handsome thirty-four year old lawyer and state amateur golf champion, the ignition was wired to ten sticks of dynamite. The ensuing blast killed him immediately.

Within two days police obtained and released to the press a detailed confession from Victor L. Wolf, a handyman with some knowledge of electrical work who had done repair work for Smith's wife, Marjorie E. Smith. Wolf claimed that he and Mrs. Smith conspired to kill her husband so that she and Wolf could flee to Alaska and share the proceeds of Kermit Smith's estate and life insurance. Portland newspapers liberally splashed the case across front pages, and declared Wolf to be a "love slave" of Marjorie Smith. Police aggressively interrogated Marjorie Smith for two days after the bombing. She made no admissions, but nevertheless she was indicted for murder.

Smith's defense was headed by Bruce Spaulding, a former three-term Polk County district attorney who had joined Robert Mautz in 1951, creating the law firm of Mautz, Souther, Spaulding, Denecke & Kinsey. After twenty-five years in practice, Spaulding had established himself as a leading trial lawyer in both civil and criminal cases. The Smith case was one of his toughest. Victor Wolf, the codefendant, quickly pleaded guilty to murder and agreed to testify against Marjorie Smith. The defense also was burdened with Marjorie Smith's complex marital history. Kermit Smith was her third husband, and she had left him for a time to rejoin her second husband, who had remarried in the meantime.

Spaulding's first imperative was to have the case transferred out of Multnomah County. He pointed to the intensive press coverage of the murder, and cited articles "in part untrue and largely twisting and warping other facts partially true, in order to create a sensational, perfect sounding detective story."[15] The thrust of the news coverage, he contended, was that Mrs. Smith was guilty but wouldn't admit it. Circuit Court Judge James R. Bain, himself a former district attorney, stopped short of criticizing the press, but noted that some of the information widely distributed about the case would not be admissible in evidence. Bain granted Spaulding's motion.

Marjorie Smith went on trial in October 1955, in Yamhill County. The trial lasted thirteen days. Mrs. Smith testified over three days, including intense cross-examination by Willis West, chief criminal deputy to Multnomah County district attorney William Langley. Her account never changed. "I very definitely did not have anything to do with killing my husband," she insisted.[16] Virgil Crum, who had been Kermit Smith's partner in a practice of general law and domestic relations, testified that he saw Mrs. Smith within hours after the bombing. He said her behavior was consistent with that of a grieving widow.[17]

Courtesy of *The Oregonian*

Marjorie Smith with Bruce Spaulding moments after her acquittal.

Jurors deliberated for fifteen hours over three days. As tension mounted during deliberations after dinner one evening, Spaulding gave the impression of calm as he napped on a courtroom bench. But the tension broke on November 4, when jurors returned with a verdict of not guilty. Tears flowed down the faces of both Marjorie Smith and Spaulding, who said they had prayed together before entering the courtroom to receive the verdict. It turned out that the jurors, from their opening vote of seven to five, had favored Spaulding's view that the state had not proved beyond a reasonable doubt its case against Mrs. Smith.

Mrs. Smith walked out of the Yamhill county Courthouse a free woman for the first time in six months. Spaulding had yet another quarter-century of trials ahead of him, many of them defending doctors against medical negligence claims. He made a statement at the end of the Smith case summarizing an attitude he held during his long career. "I have great confidence in the courts and in what I believed to be the truth," he said. "In spite of all the prejudice about this case, I've had faith in this court. My faith has been justified."[18]

Intense though it was, the level of publicity surrounding the Smith case soon was surpassed by yet another vice scandal in Portland. This one was fueled by a series of articles by two reporters from *The Oregonian*, Wallace Turner and William Lambert. Their articles alleged that a Portland gambling figure, James "Big Jim" Elkins, had plotted with certain union leaders and local public officials to keep Portland "wide open" as a gambling town. The articles led to a Pulitzer Prize for *The Oregonian* in 1957, and to a total of 114 special grand jury indictments against forty-one defendants. In the end, however, there was but one conviction—and it came nowhere close to matching the far-reaching allegations spread by the newspaper investigations. Indictments eventually were issued against Multnomah County district attorney William Langley, Portland Police Chief James W. Purcell, and Portland's new mayor and former Multnomah County sheriff, Terry D. Schrunk.

Charges against Purcell were dismissed because he had resigned as police chief in the new Schrunk administration. The first big trial was that of district attorney Langley, who had taken office in 1955. Langley was the son of a former county district attorney, Lotus L. Langley, who held the office from 1931 to 1934. The younger Langley was arraigned in August 1956, and it wasn't a pleasant experience. "If you take one more shot I'll smash that thing," he warned a newspaper photographer in the courthouse hallway.[19] The photographer snapped the shutter again and Langley, true to his word, jerked the camera from the photographer and broke it.

Courtesy of *The Oregonian*

Multnomah County District Attorney William Langley.

Langley was accused of willfully neglecting to prosecute William B. Nettleton for gambling. The misdemeanor charge arose from a brief visit by Langley to Jack & Jill's restaurant in March 1955, to attend a party sponsored by the Portland Paint, Varnish and Lacquer Association. Gambling to raise funds for charity, which wasn't illegal, was one event of the evening. Langley had been invited to attend the event by his secretary, Dorothea Anderson, whose husband was a member of the paint association. Anderson had come to the district attorney's office at Langley's request in 1955. She eventually spent twenty-seven years in the office as a valued clerical worker and advisor to deputy district attorneys on matters of criminal forms and procedure.

What Langley didn't know during his twenty-minute visit to the restaurant was that Nettleton, who provided the gambling equipment, was an employee of Big Jim Elkins, and that the gamblers were receiving half the profits of the charity gambling. Trial evidence indicated that Elkins had been a large contributor to Langley's successful campaign for district attorney, and that Langley had performed some legal work for Elkins in the mid-1940s. Elkins claimed that he had profit-sharing agreements from some gambling operations with Langley. Langley heatedly denied any such deals. As for Nettleton, Langley testified he had never seen the man until he came to court. Nevertheless, a Multnomah County Circuit Court jury convicted Langley of the neglect-of-duty charge. Judge Frank J. Lonergan imposed a $100 fine and declared the office of district attorney vacant.

Langley lost his appeal to the Oregon Supreme Court, which rejected Langley's contention, among others, that his case was prejudiced by Judge Lonergan's decision to allow news cameras in front of the bar in the courtroom.[20] The U.S. Supreme Court refused to hear the case, thus ending Langley's attempts to set aside the conviction. However, Langley later achieved a measure of vindication. The Oregon Supreme Court, after two professional disciplinary hearings conducted by the Oregon State Bar, failed to find any "corrupt motive" from Langley's behavior that would have justified disbarment or any lesser professional sanction.[21] Langley returned to private practice.

Langley's trial was followed quickly by that of Terry D. Schrunk, Portland's newly elected mayor, who had been Multnomah County sheriff from 1949 until he defeated Mayor Fred Peterson in 1956. The special grand jury on vice, relying in part on testimony from Elkins, accused Schrunk of picking up a $500 bribe in an envelope during a late-night raid on an after-hours club in September 1955. Schrunk also was accused of perjury for denying the incident before the grand jury.

The two charges were separated for trial. In June 1956, Schrunk faced the perjury charge before a jury in the courtroom of Multnomah County Circuit Court Judge James Crawford. Elkins testified that he saw the bribe placed in an envelope by another gambling figure, Clifford O. Bennett. A policeman testified that he saw Schrunk stoop down near a utility pole near the intersection of North Denver Avenue and Kilpatrick Street. The new mayor's position was clear: "So help me God, there was no package picked up," he testified. "There was no bribe offered or accepted."[22] Chief defense attorney Edwin D. Hicks and his partner, Thomas H. Tongue, who later served on the Oregon Supreme Court from 1969 to 1982, contended that Elkins framed Schrunk in an attempt to remove him from office.

The two-week trial, played out under intense scrutiny from the news media, was notable for the nonappearance of one potential witness, and by the surprise appearance of another. Bennett, the man who allegedly placed the bribe in the envelope, sat in the hallway throughout the trial but never was called to testify. Bennett's shady background, it appeared, made him too much of a liability for either side to put on the stand. The surprise witness was Robert F. Kennedy, the younger brother of the dashing young United States Senator from Massachusetts, John F. Kennedy.

Robert Kennedy, then age thirty-one, was chief counsel for a U.S. Senate committee investigating racketeering. Kennedy had been investigating Teamsters activity in California and other states on behalf of the committee when he learned about the allegations of corruption in Portland. Mayor Schrunk had appeared before Kennedy's committee in Washington, D.C., where Schrunk accused the committee of intimidating Clifford Bennett from telling the truth.

Called as a rebuttal witness at Schrunk's trial, Kennedy testified that he had heard of Portland's vice allegations from police in Los Angeles and he had visited Portland to discuss matters with *The Oregonian*'s investigative reporters. Kennedy's testimony added little to the case. Yet the tanned, handsome, and sharply-dressed young lawyer impressed courthouse observers—Judge Crawford included. As Kennedy rose to leave the witness stand at the end of his testimony, he extended his right hand toward Judge Crawford. The veteran judge of twenty-six years extended his arm across the bench and shook Kennedy's hand as the jury sat watching.

In Judge Crawford's chambers, Hicks and Tongue protested the unusual judicial gesture and demanded a mistrial. The next day Judge Crawford issued a special instruction to jurors regarding the surprise handshake: "As far as the court is concerned, it was purely instinctive reaction and is not to be regarded as any personal or judicial expression of approval or disapproval of the witness."[23]

OHS CN001332

Multnomah County Circuit Judge James Crawford

During closing arguments, defense lawyer Hicks draped the courtroom with large sheets of butcher paper. In large black letters, he posed twenty-three questions for jurors to consider, all of them suggesting that it wasn't plausible for Schrunk to pick up a bribe on a public street, in plain view of police and at the expense of his public career. Jurors deliberated only one hour and fifty minutes before returning their verdict acquitting the new mayor.

Terry Schrunk shook hands and thanked each juror as the panel left the courtroom. In the gallery behind him, the mayor's fifteen-year old son, Michael, had absorbed the drama and tension of the trial. Given the speedy acquittal on the perjury charge, the state dismissed the remaining count against Terry Schrunk, who went on to serve a record-setting sixteen years—four full terms—as Portland mayor. His son Michael became a lawyer and set a record for length of service as Multnomah County district attorney.

When the so-called vice scandal finished its course, the only significant conviction was Langley's. And although it cost Langley his job, the conviction itself was a misdemeanor. *The Oregonian*, which had provided the impetus for the investigation, found itself the target of several civil lawsuits, including two filed by Langley. The civil damages sought against the newspaper totaled $3.6 million. The company was defended by George Black, Jr., and the firm of Black, Kendall & Tremaine. All claims ultimately were dis-

Courtesy of *The Oregonian*

Mayor Terry D. Schrunk, center, with defense lawyer Edwin Hicks, left, shook hands with jurors after his acquittal in Multnomah County Circuit Court.

missed without any payment from the newspaper.

Although the Portland vice trials commanded the headlines, other changes of a less tumultuous nature were taking place. Several lawyers concerned about protecting civil liberties convened in Portland to form the Oregon chapter of the American Civil Liberties Union (ACLU). One of their concerns was the growing fear of Communism that led to the so-called witch-hunts of suspected Communists led by Wisconsin Senator Joseph McCarthy. A local committee dating back to 1935, including Gus Solomon and a well-respected lawyer who shared office space with him, Leo Levenson, had worked on several ACLU cases. Judah Bierman, a professor of literature at Portland State College, was the first chairman of the new affiliate, elected in November 1955. The first secretary was Jonathan U. Newman, who later served on the Portland School Board from 1968 to 1979, and on the Oregon Court of Appeals from 1983 to 1991. Other founding members included Richard W. Nahstoll, vice chairman, and Paul R. Meyer, who was elected to serve on the executive committee of the ACLU's national board of directors in 1976, and who later was elected a national vice president.

One near-victim of the red-scare days was Bernard Jolles, a Northwestern College of Law student who finished at the top of his class in 1961. Jolles passed the bar exam but the Board of Bar Examiners, noting that he had been a Communist party member from 1949 to 1957, recommended by a six-to-three vote against admitting him to the Oregon State Bar. Jolles appealed to the Oregon Supreme Court, which, by a four-to two vote, found him morally fit to practice law.[24] Jolles eventually became the senior partner in the firm of Jolles, Bernstein & Garone, and served as president of the Oregon State Bar in 1987.

By the early 1950s, many lawyers were becoming dissatisfied with the inability of the Multnomah County Law Library to provide up-to-date materials in fast-moving fields such as labor law, tax, and business law. A

Multnomah Bar Association committee in 1954 gently reported on "a personnel problem which must be resolved"—a not-so-veiled reference to the advancing age of Fred M. Salway, the law librarian.[25]

Salway, who graduated from the old University of Oregon law department in 1908, had been the librarian since 1910. After four decades, Salway was often absent from the library and had delegated many duties to an assistant who lacked training in law or librarianship. Yet Salway showed no inclination to retire, and he had outlived many of the library directors such as Charles H. Carey, one of the founders, who died in 1941. Pleas to Wilbur Henderson, the library chairman, for updated materials also were unsuccessful.

Henderson had been a colorful Portland lawyer since 1911. His career had almost ended early when he took off from Northwest Portland in a hot air balloon race as part of the 1914 Rose Festival. Henderson's balloon crashed near Bull Run Lake, and nothing was heard from him for six days. He spent four of those days fighting starvation as he hiked out of the remote wilderness. Still practicing law into his seventies, Henderson saw little need for practicing law other than he had always done it. "What the lawyers ought to do is get back to Blackstone and Kent," Henderson told the younger generation.[26]

By 1960, there had been no formal shareholder meetings of the library corporation for many years. Portland lawyers Herbert Anderson, a former Multnomah Bar Association president, and Francis Harrington devised a plan to replace the moribund library board, including Wilbur Henderson. Anderson formed the Multnomah Bar Foundation to hold stock that the pair planned to acquire. Harrington in 1961 obtained a share of library stock from the son of an original shareholder, but Salway refused to record it in the corporate records.[27] Salway also refused Harrington's request to see the membership list and other records. Harrington eventually filed a lawsuit against Salway, but in the meantime the bar foundation was marshaling supporters one shareholder at a time. In 1964, the reformers finally won control of the library board and Salway, then eighty-seven years of age, was forced into retirement after fifty-three years as librarian.

Salway was replaced by Jacquelyn Jurkins, a lawyer and professional librarian who had been working for the Colorado Supreme Court. When she was hired in 1964, Jurkins made no personal commitment to the library board beyond two years. But changes occurred quickly under her supervision. The new board liked Jurkins and Jurkins liked the library and Portland. She gradually built the library into a leading facility for practicing lawyers. Her stature in the law library field was reflected in 1984 when she served as president of the American Association of Law Libraries. That same year, Jurkins doubled the library's space by adding an 8,000-square-foot research facility in the Standard Insurance Center, on the block immediately north of the Multnomah County Courthouse. Jurkins continued as the library administrator as the library celebrated its centennial in 1992 and headed toward the new century.

Courtesy of *The Oregonian*

Multnomah County Law Librarian Jacquelyn Jurkins.

Opportunities for women in the legal profession were still limited in the 1960s. Governor Mark O. Hatfield opened one door in 1961 by appointing Jean Lagerquist Lewis to a vacancy on the circuit court bench. She became the first woman in Oregon to hold office as a circuit court judge, and the first woman to serve full-time on the bench since Judge Mary Jane Spurlin's brief tenure in district court in 1926. It was another of many "firsts" in Lewis's impressive career.

Lewis had earned her expenses for Northwestern College of Law by working in a department store. She graduated first in her class in 1939 and opened a law office with $50 in capital. She worked as a lawyer for the federal government from 1942 to 1945, then returned to private practice and politics after World War II. She was selected as a temporary circuit court judge in 1954, but she withdrew after she was elected to the Oregon House of Representatives later that year. Lewis advanced to the state senate in 1956. As a legislator, she was the first woman to serve on the Ways and Means Committee and on the State Emergency Board, the committee of legislators that handles state business between legislative sessions. As a legislator, Lewis supported the expansion of Portland State College into Portland State University and helped create the community college system.

OHS CN012171

Multnomah County Circuit Judge Jean Lewis.

As a judge in the domestic relations department, Lewis reportedly was the first judge in the nation to grant an adoption to an unmarried man. She also supported the expansion of conciliation services aimed at reuniting couples or smoothing the difficulties of child custody. At the start of her career, lawyers weren't used to addressing a woman as judge. Lewis once recalled a young lawyer who, in bumbling confusion, touched all the bases by referring to her as "Judge, Your honor, Ma'am, Sir."[28] Lewis retired from the bench in 1978.

Major Portland law firms hired few women, and partnership for women in the big firms remained out of the question. Despite those limitations, Lewis and several other women lawyers in Portland established excellent legal reputations. The most senior of them was Manche I. Langley, who continued working in the district attorney's office until her death in 1963 at age eighty. She became chief deputy for domestic relations in 1961 following the retirement of Olive Zimmerman, who had held that title for twenty-five years. Langley, who had begun in the office during the administration of her brother, Lotus Langley, in the mid 1930s, also served as area director for the Works Progress Administration for six years until its closure in 1943. She was the aunt of William Langley, who was removed from office by the misdemeanor conviction during the so-called vice scandal.

At city hall, Marian Rushing signed on as a deputy city attorney in 1944 and advanced to chief deputy in 1950. With the retirement of Alex Brown in 1968, she became Portland's first woman city attorney. Another deputy city attorney, Helen F. Althaus, former law clerk to U.S. District Court Judge James A. Fee and the first woman to work as a federal law clerk in Oregon, went to work for the King, Wood, Miller, Anderson & Nash firm in 1953 after four years as a deputy city attorney. For her first five years, Althaus was listed on firm stationery and on her door by her first two initials because senior partners feared clients might be upset by the presence of a woman lawyer.[29] Althaus remained at the Miller firm for more than fifteen years, always as an associate, in an era in which no large firms had yet accepted a woman as a partner.

The 1960s marked the start of several other important judicial careers, as several judges who had served since the pre-World War II era died or retired. Dean F. Bryson, a former Oregon State Bar president with twenty-five years of private practice, was appointed to Multnomah County Circuit Court in October 1961, after the death of Judge Frank Lonergan. After nine years as circuit court judge, Bryson challenged and defeated Justice Gordon Sloan for an Oregon Supreme Court seat, which Bryson held until retiring in 1979.

Charles S. Crookham, who had worked for ten years in the firm of Vergeer, Samuels & Crookham, was appointed by Governor Hatfield in December 1962 to replace Judge Arno Denecke on the circuit court bench. Denecke was a former member of the Mautz, Souther & Spaulding firm who, after three years on the circuit court bench, was elected in 1962 to the Oregon Supreme Court. Denecke served on the high court for nineteen years, including six years as chief justice.

Crookham remained on the circuit court bench for twenty-six years, and spent eight years, from 1978 to 1986, as presiding judge. After his retirement from the bench, Crookham was appointed by Governor Barbara Roberts to fill a vacancy as state attorney general in 1991 and 1992.

Crookham's tenure as presiding judge ranked in duration only behind that of Judge Charles W. Redding, a thirty-year circuit court veteran, who served as presiding judge from 1957 to 1966. Redding, who was appointed to the bench in 1941, also served two stints as a temporary Oregon Supreme Court justice in 1959 and again in 1966-1967. Redding was active in many civic affairs and held a special interest in children's activities. Among his volunteer efforts, Redding was a board member of the Portland Area Council of Boy Scouts, the Boys and Girls Aid Society, and Camp Fire Girls. He died in his court chambers in April 1971, at age sixty-six. His son, Robert

W. Redding, was appointed to the Multnomah County District Court bench in 1973, and advanced to the circuit court bench by election in 1982.

The retirement of Judge Donald E. Long in 1963 led to the appointment of Robert E. Jones, a former state legislator, who arrived on the bench at age thirty-six. Jones served nineteen years on the circuit court bench before being appointed to the Oregon Supreme Court in 1983. Jones, who for many years taught evidence at the Northwestern School of Law with Circuit Judge Richard L. Unis, spent seven years on the top state court until he was nominated by President George Bush to fill a vacancy on the U.S. District Court.

William M. Dale, a member of the law firm that defended Mayor Terry Schrunk in the vice trials, was appointed to the circuit court bench in 1967, where he remained until 1984 when he was selected for an eight-year term as a U.S. magistrate. Like several other lawyers and judges, Dale was a devoted teacher at Northwestern School of Law, where he taught torts and trial practice for many years.

At the U.S. Courthouse, Robert C. Belloni was appointed by President Lyndon Johnson to succeed U.S. District Court Judge William G. East. East had been elevated to the federal bench in 1955 by President Eisenhower after Judge James A. Fee advanced to the Ninth Circuit Court of Appeals. East had served for six years on the Lane County Circuit Court. In 1964, Judge East presided in Los Angeles over the trial stemming from the kidnapping of Frank Sinatra, Jr., the son of the famous singer. Ill health forced East to announce his resignation at the end of 1965 at age fifty-seven.

Belloni had worked in hospital administration and in his father's trucking company in Myrtle Point before going to law school. He started his law practice in 1951 in Myrtle Point and served as city council member and mayor of that city before being appointed to the circuit court bench of Coos and Curry Counties in 1957. Belloni in 1969 ruled that Indian tribes that had signed a federal treaty in 1855 were entitled to a "fair share" of fish caught in the Columbia River. The case, *Sohappy v. Smith*,[30] was a harbinger of many environmental battles to come in federal court involving Oregon's forests and wildlife. One of the lawyers representing the Warm Springs tribe in the 1969 case before Belloni was Owen M. Panner, who joined the U.S. District Court bench in 1980.

Another prominent face at the Multnomah County Courthouse, starting in 1962, was that of district attorney George A. Van Hoomissen, who had been a deputy prosecutor from 1957 to 1959. After entering private practice and winning a seat in the Oregon House of Representatives, Van Hoomissen saw a need to modernize management of the district attorney's office. He won the job in November 1962, at age thirty-two, by challenging incumbent Charles L. Raymond, who died before the general election.

Van Hoomissen launched new recruitment practices to attract bright young deputies and improved training programs for both newcomers and veteran prosecutors. He also established a formal rotation system to channel deputies through the various prosecutorial departments. Van Hoomissen resigned from the office late in 1970 to become dean of the new National College of District Attorneys in Houston, Texas. One of the last new deputies Van Hoomissen hired was Michael D. Schrunk, son of Portland mayor Terry D. Schrunk, who had graduated from the University of Oregon Law School and served in the Marine Corps. At his departure, Van Hoomissen said he was leaving behind "one of the finest professional staffs in any prosecutor's office in the country."[31]

Van Hoomissen wasn't gone for long, however. He returned in 1973 to accept an appointment as a Multnomah County Circuit Court judge. Using the political clout he had gathered from his earlier days, Van Hoomissen successfully ran for a seat on the Oregon Court of Appeals in 1980, and eight years later advanced by election to the Oregon Supreme Court.

Meanwhile, another new prosecutor, Sidney I. Lezak, took control of the U.S. Attorney's office in June 1961, by appointment of President John F. Kennedy. Lezak came to Portland in 1949 after graduation from the

University of Chicago. He went into partnership with labor lawyer Paul T. Bailey. Lezak's service as U.S. Attorney lasted longer than any of his predecessors, and he held the singular distinction of working under five different presidential administrations.

Lezak's original appointment, however, was stalled for more than three years by a squabble between U.S. Congresswoman Edith Green, who had headed the Kennedy campaign in Oregon, and new U.S. Senator Maurine Neuberger. Neuberger had no objections to Lezak's qualifications, but Green had recommended Lezak to President Kennedy without consulting with Neuberger. Neuberger wanted to make sure she had a role in all future political appointments, particularly a prospective Ninth Circuit Court of Appeals position rumored to be going to an Oregon nominee. Robert F. Kennedy, the new U.S. Attorney General, used his authority to appoint Lezak as an assistant U.S. Attorney and gave him control of the office. The squabble between Neuberger and Green was finally resolved in 1964, allowing Lezak to earn his full salary as U.S. Attorney.

Courtesy of *The Oregonian*

Sidney Lezak.

Lezak remained through the administrations of Presidents Lyndon B. Johnson, Richard M. Nixon, Gerald R. Ford, and Jimmy Carter. He is the only U.S. Attorney for Oregon to serve both Republican and Democrat administrations. Lezak resigned in March 1982, following the election of President Ronald Reagan, and returned to private practice.

The 1960s brought dynamic change to another major legal institution in Portland, the Northwestern College of Law. The school had moved in 1950 from its home in the Sherlock Building to the Geisy Building, adjoining the rear of the Benson Hotel. By the early 1960s, enrollment had climbed to 200 students, and the school continued to graduate a substantial percentage of new Oregon lawyers. But national trends were shifting toward more stringent requirements for law school admittance and training. Without a full-time faculty and a permanent library, Northwestern wouldn't be recognized for accreditation by the American Bar Association. Without accreditation, Northwestern's students couldn't be eligible to take bar exams outside of Oregon.

Rumors about a sale of the law school surfaced in 1962, and the Oregon State Bar established a Committee on Standards and Admissions to study the matter. Late in 1964, Dr. Arthur Flemming, president of the University of Oregon, proposed a merger that would have reunited Northwestern as a Portland branch of the University of Oregon Law School. Talks between Northwestern and state officials occurred over several months without agreement. Northwestern trustees, including Portland lawyers Thomas H. Tongue and Jack Kennedy, feared that the University of Oregon Law School would not continue Northwestern's tradition of holding night classes for students working their way through school. State officials rejected Northwestern's suggestion of merging the law school with Portland State College.

A few months after discussions with the state collapsed, trustees of Northwestern and Lewis and Clark College reached unanimous agreement on a merger. John Howard, Lewis and Clark president, promised that night classes would continue and that day classes would be added. The college also vowed to build a new law school campus within four years on a woodsy site near the undergraduate campus on Palatine Hill in Southwest Portland. Sale of the Geisy Building in 1966 forced Northwestern students to temporary quarters at Lewis and Clark College, marking the first time Northwestern classes were not headquartered in downtown Portland. In 1970, modernistic concrete classrooms and a glass-walled library greeted students as the law school's permanent home. Northwestern School of Law at Lewis and Clark College, as it was renamed, won temporary accreditation in 1970 and was granted membership in the American Association of Law Schools in 1973.

Meanwhile, the physical environment began to change on the downtown blocks near the Multnomah County Courthouse and the U.S. Courthouse. There had been little major downtown construction since the 1920s. Standard Plaza, which opened in 1963, became the first downtown office building to be built on an entire city block. At seventeen stories, it served as a harbinger of larger towers, such as the Georgia-Pacific and First Interstate Bank towers, that would be completed within a decade and become home to several major law firms. Officials of the Standard Insurance Company, owners of the new building, planned to call it the Standard Insurance Center. But one of their first tenants, Robert Mautz, senior partner of Mautz, Souther, Spaulding & Kinsey, suggested they call it Standard Plaza, instead. Mautz was concerned that legal letterheads and envelopes not show up at courthouses where jurors by happenstance might see them and be influenced by the forbidden word "insurance." Until moving into the new Standard Plaza, the Mautz firm had been housed in the Board of Trade Building since 1909. Ironically, when Standard Insurance bought the Georgia-Pacific Building many years later, they renamed it the Standard Insurance Center.

Other tenants moving into the sleek new Standard Plaza included the law firms of Cake, Jaureguy, Hardy, Buttler & McEwen; Bernard, Bernard & Hurley; and Pozzi, Levin & Wilson. The latter firm was founded by Frank Pozzi, who was admitted to the bar in 1948 after graduating from Willamette

Law School. Pozzi had worked as a longshoreman before becoming a lawyer, and his practice from the start involved workers' compensation claims and personal injury. Before opening his own office, Pozzi worked with Nels Peterson and, like Peterson, he was an early member of the National Association of Claimants' Compensation Attorneys. Over time, Pozzi built the largest Portland firm devoted to representing injured workers and personal injury clients. The firm also served as a training ground for several leading personal injury lawyers who later opened their own offices, including Garry L. Kahn, who became a circuit court judge in 1992, Richard P. Noble, and Jan Thomas Baisch. Kahn resigned from the bench after only two years, after deciding that he preferred representing personal injury clients.

The early 1960s also saw the formation of another lasting partnership in Portland's legal community when Gilbert Sussman opened an office with Jerome B. Shank in 1962. Sussman received his law degree from Columbia University in 1929, and worked on the staff of Yale Law School until 1934, when he became a northwest regional attorney for the U.S. Department of Agriculture and then assistant general counsel for the Bonneville Power Administration. After leaving government service in 1945, Sussman practiced with his younger brother, Maurice D. Sussman, in Portland. The younger Sussman was active in many Jewish community activities, and served as president of the Congregation Nevah Shalom and the Robison Jewish Home. Shank was a graduate of the University of Oregon and Northwestern College of Law who had an interest in bankruptcy. Their first associate was Norman Wapnick, who, after starting his legal career with the Federal Trade Commission in New York City, became a partner in 1965, creating Sussman, Shank & Wapnick. The firm concentrated on bankruptcy and business law, and grew over the years into Sussman Shank Wapnick Caplan & Stiles LLP.

Social forces pulling at the entire nation in the late 1960s, including the

Vietnam War and the assassinations of presidential candidate Robert F. Kennedy and civil rights leader Martin Luther King, Jr., made the 1968 election year one of the most tumultuous in Oregon history. Two Portland lawyers, Robert W. Packwood and Lee Johnson, ran victorious statewide races that made political and legal history.

Packwood was a grandson of a pioneer miner and businessman, William H. Packwood, who was a delegate to the Oregon Constitutional Convention of 1857. After finishing New York University Law School in 1957, Packwood joined the Portland firm of Koerner, Young, Swett & McColloch as an associate, but his real interest was politics. In 1962 he ran an unorthodox campaign as a Republican for a state representative seat from East Portland. Although he had little money, Packwood, then thirty years old, cultivated a group of volunteers selected for their dedication and tenacity.

Packwood's strategy consisted mainly of neighborhood coffee meetings with no more than two dozen voters attending any one session. The campaign volunteers adopted a slogan of "EPS"—Elect Packwood Somehow.[32] To the surprise of the political establishment, Packwood won. He was reelected to the Oregon House of Representatives in 1964 and 1966. But his eye all along was set on the U.S. Senate seat held by Wayne Morse, a Democrat.

The steely, combative Morse, a former dean of the University of Oregon Law School, was the only Oregonian ever to be elected to the U.S. Senate at different times as a Republican, an Independent, and a Democrat. Morse in 1968 was seeking a fifth term in Washington, where he had won the nickname "Tiger of the Senate" for his blunt outspokenness on many issues, including his opposition to the Vietnam War. Morse started the race as the heavy favorite.

By 1968, Packwood had left the large Koerner firm and formed a partnership with Garry P. McMurry, a prominent business litigator. Besides his corps of dedicated volunteers, Packwood was now able to raise substantial campaign funds as well. The race was tight as Packwood and Morse squared off for a debate before a packed Portland City Club and a television and radio audience in October 1968. Morse, who was expected to be the superior debater, met at least his equal in Packwood. In one key exchange, Packwood shot back a quote Morse had used in another campaign fourteen years earlier: "Never confuse seniority with ability because when you go to the mat ability will win every time."[33]

Assessing the debate's outcome, *The Oregonian*'s chief political reporter noted "the general reaction was that the youthful Republican had twisted the tail of the Tiger of the Senate."[34] Packwood won the race by a slim 3,500 votes out of some 750,000 votes cast. Packwood went on to surpass Morse's longevity in the Senate, but the start of his fifth Senate term in 1993 was stained by allegations of sexual harassment against women spanning many years, ultimately leading to his resignation from the Senate.

The other Portland lawyer involved in a successful statewide race in 1968 was Lee Johnson, who defeated Attorney General Robert Y. Thornton and then had the victory taken away from him and later restored in court. Johnson, an heir of the C.D. Johnson lumber-holding family, spent much of his youth in Toledo, Oregon, before graduating from Princeton University

Courtesy of *The Oregonian*

Bob Packwood during his first campaign for the U.S. Senate.

and Stanford Law School. After two years with the U.S. Department of Justice in Washington, D.C., Johnson returned to Portland and joined the law firm of Mautz, Souther, Spaulding, Kinsey & Williamson. He won election to the Oregon House of Representatives from Southwest Portland in 1962 and 1964.

Johnson was not well-known statewide when he challenged the well-entrenched Thornton, a Democratic incumbent seeking a fifth term as attorney general. Johnson attacked Thornton for not doing enough to fight crime and raised a campaign fund of $140,000—a hefty amount at the time for a statewide race. Thornton also tried to appear as a law-and-order candidate, although he complained later that the attorney general had little crime-fighting authority. Johnson won the race handily.

Johnson's victory appeared to be short-lived, however. A three-judge panel in Marion County Circuit Court declared Thornton the winner based on Thornton's accusations that Johnson had filed inaccurate campaign finance reports. Thornton also contended that Johnson had violated election laws by making false statements on the crime issue, but the Marion County judges rejected that claim. Johnson appealed to the Oregon Supreme Court, seeking to take the office he had won at the polls; Thornton also appealed over his allegations of false statements.

Johnson was represented by John R. Faust, then a young partner in the Cake, Jaureguy, Hardy, Buttler & McEwen firm, who became a major figure in Republican party politics. Faust also became one of the most visible lawyers in the community as host of a lively, weekly public-issues television program for thirteen years, ending in 1993. In April 1969, nearly four months after Johnson was supposed to have taken office, the Oregon Supreme Court reinstated Johnson as the winner. The court, in an unsigned opinion, said Johnson had not deliberately filed false campaign finance reports because he had signed blank papers to be filled in by others. The court also rejected Thornton's claims of alleged false statements. "Courts are, and should be, most reluctant to interfere in the political process and will not do so unless compelled by a clear legislative directive," the court said.[35]

Johnson served two terms as attorney general. He modernized office management and, among other achievements, supervised the first massive rewriting of the state's criminal laws since those drafted by Matthew Deady in the pioneer era. At the end of his second term, Johnson won a seat on the Oregon Court of Appeals, where he joined Judge Robert Y.Thornton, who had won election to the same court in 1970. Johnson left the appeals court after two years to become executive assistant to Governor Victor Atiyeh. He quit Atiyeh's staff in mid-1981, and at the end of 1983 was appointed by Governor Atiyeh to the Multnomah County Circuit Court.

In the narrow world of lawyers who appeared before him, Judge Johnson remained a controversial figure during his tenure on the trial court bench. He made decisions quickly, but some lawyers believed that Johnson's decision were based on his own views rather than on law. Johnson retired from the bench in 1995.

CHAPTER SIX

A Decade of Tumult

Judges, lawyers, and municipal officials gathered in November 1969 at the run-down United States Building with its quaint cupola in the heart of downtown Portland. The one-time home of U.S. District Court and Judge Matthew Deady, abandoned by the federal courts in 1933, had been declared surplus property by the federal government in the middle 1960s. City officials had talked since the 1950s about tearing down the architectural antique to make way for a park, an office building, or a hotel. Meier & Frank Company, the big department store located on the adjoining block to the north, at one time had cast its corporate eyes on the old building as a site for a parking garage.

None of those possibilities was acceptable to John F. Kilkenny, a Pendleton lawyer who had tried his first federal case in the old building in the late 1920s. Kilkenny wanted to save the building. And he had the clout and persistence to see it done. Kilkenny knew about persistence, from his upbringing in an eastern Oregon sheep-raising family and from his football days at Notre Dame, where he played for the famous coach, Knute Rockne. Kilkenny had served as U.S. District Court judge from 1959, when he replaced Judge Claude McColloch, to 1969, when he was appointed by President Richard M. Nixon to the Ninth Circuit Court of Appeals.

Kilkenny began lobbying to save the old building in the middle 1960s. In 1967, he convinced the Ninth Circuit Court of Appeals to recommend its preservation. After a search, the federal General Services Administration found the blueprints to the old building in an archive in Washington, D.C. Kilkenny's persistence paid off in 1969, when federal officials agreed to restore the oldest public building still standing in the Pacific Northwest.

"This magnificent structure of the past will become an even more magnificent structure of the future," Kilkenny predicted in November 1969, at the beginning of the restoration project when the building was rechristened as the Pioneer Courthouse.[1] Many thanked Kilkenny for his efforts, including Hall Lusk, a former Portland lawyer and Multnomah County Circuit Court judge then sitting on the Oregon Supreme Court. "It took a man from Umatilla County to preserve the building and keep it from being turned into a parking lot," Lusk noted.[2]

The restoration project was finished early in 1973 at a cost of $1,265,000. Unfortunately, none of the original furnishings remained, but donors contributed items appropriate for the era to complete the nineteenth-century charm of the building. Pioneer Courthouse became the home of Oregon's representatives on the Ninth

Courtesy of *The Oregonian*

Ninth U.S. Circuit Court of Appeals Judge John F. Kilkenny in the cupola of the building he fought to preserve, Pioneer Courthouse.

Circuit Court of Appeals. Fittingly, Judge Kilkenny was one of the first new tenants.

Symbolically, the restored little courthouse reflected the start of a new era of development in downtown Portland, guided by a hard-driving lawyer in city hall, Neil Goldschmidt. It also coincided with the start of a period of fast growth and cataclysmic change for Portland's lawyers, judges, and law firms. Indeed, the 1970s changed the face of legal practice more than any other single decade before it.

While many of those changes were beginning to surface, however, an unfinished piece of legal business from the turbulent 1960s was wending its way through the courts. The case had begun in November 1968, when several protesters opposing the Vietnam War entered the privately owned Lloyd Center shopping mall to promote an event called "National Draft Card Turn-In Day." The protesters left peacefully after private security guards told them that Lloyd Corporation, which owned the mall, prohibited distribution of noncommercial literature on mall grounds.

Three of the protesters quickly filed suit in U.S. District Court in Portland, seeking an injunction to prevent the Lloyd Corporation from interfering with what they claimed was their constitutional right to engage in free speech. They were represented by Carl R. Neil, a partner in the fast-growing firm of Lindsay, Nahstoll, Hart, Duncan, Dafoe & Krause, the firm that dated its origins back to the 1920s and Gunther Krause. U.S. District Court Judge Gus J. Solomon, then in his twenty-first year on the bench, issued a ruling in January 1970 in favor of the young protesters. "I do not believe the Corporation may decide what groups may distribute literature in the Mall," Solomon wrote. He said owners who opened private land to the general public for business purposes gave up their right to prohibit the distribution of literature if the land became the "functional equivalent of a public business district."[3]

George Black, Jr., senior partner in the firm of Black, Kendall,

Tremaine, Boothe & Higgins, appealed Solomon's ruling to the Ninth Circuit Court of Appeals. A three-judge panel, including Judge John Kilkenny of Oregon, affirmed Judge Solomon in a brief, unsigned opinion.[4] Black then appealed to the United States Supreme Court. At age seventy-three, Black argued the case before the nation's highest court. He contended that owners of private shopping centers should be able to prevent distribution of handbills unrelated to the business of the center. He said that loss of business might follow, and customer goodwill was at risk, and that nonbusiness political activity competed for the time and attention of shoppers attracted to the mall at the corporation's expense. The Supreme Court in 1972 sided with Black in a five-to-four decision. Justice Lewis F. Powell, Jr., writing for the majority, said it would be an infringement on property owners' rights to require them to yield to the First Amendment rights of others when "adequate alternative avenues of communication exist."[5]

Although that decision ended the matter for the war protesters, a variation of that issue—whether gatherers of signatures for initiatives and referendum petitions could use private shopping-mall property (again the Lloyd Center)—was revived by Portland lawyer Gregory Kafoury, a sole practitioner who represented injured plaintiffs and many political activists. After many years of litigation, the Oregon Supreme Court in 1993 ruled that the Oregon Constitution allowed political petitioners to use major malls under reasonable restrictions.[6]

While the first Lloyd Center case percolated through the federal courts, major structural changes were at hand in all state, federal, and municipal court systems affecting Portland. Legislators in 1969 created a new intermediate appeals court, the Oregon Court of Appeals, to ease the voluminous caseload of the Oregon Supreme Court. It was the single biggest change in the state court system since creation of the circuit courts in 1878. The five new judges appointed by Governor Tom McCall became the initial appellate arbiters of most criminal, probate, juvenile, and domestic relations cases from the trial courts. Two of McCall's appointees to the new court were Portland lawyers, Virgil Langtry and Herbert Schwab. Langtry, an avid outdoorsman and former deputy city attorney, had been a Multnomah County Circuit Court judge for eighteen years. Schwab had served on the circuit court from 1959 to 1966, when he returned to private practice. He also had served as a temporary Oregon Supreme Court justice in 1965 and 1966. Schwab's commitment to public service had been established much earlier, however, during his tenure from 1950 to 1959 as a member of the Portland School Board. While on the circuit court bench, Schwab agreed in 1965 to chair the school board's Committee on Race in Education. The "Schwab Committee," as it was generally known, established the backbone of the Portland district's racial integration plan.

Schwab's colleagues chose him to serve as chief judge of the new court of appeals. As the load of appeals poured into the court, Schwab established a reputation as a diligent administrator as well as for impatience with any ill-prepared appellate lawyers. "I like the role of resolving disputes and keeping the railroad running," he once told a news reporter.[7] Schwab held the post as chief judge until his retirement in December 1980.

Portland lawyers continued to lead the court of appeals long after Schwab's retirement. George M. Joseph, a former Multnomah County deputy district attorney and county counsel, succeeded Schwab and held the position of chief judge until his retirement in 1992. Joseph, a second cousin once removed of the George W. Joseph who died while running for governor in 1930, had been appointed to the court of appeals in 1977 when it was expanded from six judges to ten. In 1993, Joseph was succeeded as chief judge by William L. Richardson, a former Multnomah County District Court judge, who first joined the appeals court in 1976 after defeating at the polls one of Governor McCall's original appointees, Judge William S. Fort.

At U.S. District Court, three new judges were sworn in between December 1969 and June 1972. The first was Alfred T. Goodwin, who had spent nearly a decade on the Oregon Supreme Court and five years as a Lane County Circuit Court judge before being appointed by President Richard Nixon to succeed Judge Kilkenny on the federal trial bench. Goodwin's investiture on December 22, 1969, coincided with the issuance of his most famous Oregon Supreme Court decision, *State of Oregon ex rel Thornton v. Hay*,[8] in which Goodwin and the court used the ancient English doctrine of custom to declare Oregon's dry sand ocean beaches open to the public along the state's entire coast.

Goodwin's tenure as a federal trial judge was brief. President Nixon elevated him to the Ninth Circuit Court of Appeals in 1972. Nixon replaced Goodwin in U.S. District Court with Otto Skopil, Jr., a Salem trial lawyer of twenty-six years' experience and trustee of Willamette University. At the same time, Nixon selected James M. Burns, a Multnomah County Circuit Court judge since 1966, to succeed Judge Gus Solomon. Despite his status as a senior judge, Solomon retained a full workload, giving Oregon the benefit of four U.S. District Court judges although the state formally was allotted only three.

Meanwhile, state legislators in 1971 opened the door for another major judicial change by allowing voters in Portland and Multnomah County to consider merging Multnomah County District Court with Portland Municipal Court. Backers believed merger of the separate criminal prosecutorial entities would allow greater efficiency in managing local courts, jails, probation and parole supervision, and prosecutors. It was a risky proposition for the seven judges of the Portland Municipal Court, who stood to lose their jobs if the consolidation were approved. Governor Tom McCall gave his word, however, that he would appoint the municipal court judges to the seven new vacancies on the district court.[9] Voters approved the measure by a decisive three-to-one ratio. Portland Municipal Court officially ended business on December 31, 1971. Governor McCall kept his promise to the municipal court judges. Multnomah County District Court began operating the following month with twelve judges. Former Municipal Court Judge Richard L. Unis was elected first presiding judge of the expanded district court.

The new district court brought together, for a brief time, the state's first two African-American judges, Aaron Brown, Jr., and Mercedes F. Deiz. The Portland City Council had added Brown to the municipal court in November 1969, after he had completed one year as a temporary judge. The son of a heavy-equipment operator, Brown spent his childhood years in Louisiana and Texas. He worked his way through Fisk University of Nashville, Tennessee, as a railroad porter and doing odd jobs. He later taught school before coming to Portland in 1955 as a social worker. Soon after his arrival, Brown decided he wanted to be a lawyer. He worked his way through the Northwestern College of Law, graduating in 1959. On the bench, Brown quickly established himself as a judge who spoke plain English in explaining the legal rights and responsibilities to defendants and litigants who appeared before him. For many years Brown presided over small claims court, where his explanations often entertained as well as educated the parties.

Courtesy of *The Oregonian*

Multnomah County District Judge Aaron Brown, Jr.

Like Brown, Deiz brought a variety of life experiences with her when she began law school. A native of Harlem in New York City, Deiz came to Portland in 1947. She had three children and was working as a legal secretary when she realized she had the ability to be a lawyer. Like Brown, she attended Northwestern School of Law, finishing in 1960. Although Deiz became the state's first African-American female lawyer, she was not Oregon's first African-American woman to finish law school. That precedent had been set by Beatrice Cannady, who graduated from Northwestern in 1922. Cannady, like Deiz after her, was married and a mother before she started law school. But Cannady was never admitted to practice by the Oregon Supreme Court. She continued working as an editor of *The Advocate*, a black newspaper whose founders included Portland's first black lawyer, McCants Stewart. She moved to California a dozen years later.

Deiz began a general private practice in 1960, and in 1967 became a part-time hearings officer for the state Workers' Compensation Board. Governor McCall appointed her to a vacancy on the Multnomah County District Court in December 1969. "I knew of course that as a young black woman I would have to be a bit better than if I were white . . . type faster, work harder, react more quickly," she said in an interview after her appointment. "So I did. It was good for me."[10]

Deiz in 1972 ran for a newly created circuit court seat in a race that attracted a field of eight in the May primary. Deiz placed first in that field, and defeated Portland lawyer Ronald Gevurtz in the November general election. She held

Courtesy of *The Oregonian*

Multnomah County Circuit Judge Mercedes F. Deiz.

that position until 1992, when she was forced into retirement by an unusual provision in the state constitution that prevents judges from continuing to work full-time after age seventy-five.

While serving on the circuit court in 1979, Deiz had the misfortune of witnessing a murder-suicide only a few feet in front of her bench. Elmer McClain, a fifty-nine year-old Astoria carpenter, had been accused of contempt for failing to make support payments to his estranged wife. After Deiz ordered an increase in support payments and began leaving the bench, McClain pulled a revolver from his clothing and fired one bullet at short range at Candise DuBoff Jones, a lawyer who had been representing McClain's estranged wife, Billie Lee McClain. Elmer McClain then fired one shot at his wife before pointing the gun at his own head and killing himself. The second bullet only grazed Billie Lee McClain, but the first shot was fatal for Jones, age twenty-six.[11] The young lawyer, whose older brother, Leonard DuBoff, was a professor at the Northwestern School of Law, had been practicing only one year. She was an associate of Robert McKee, a veteran North Portland attorney. McKee had planned to appear at the domestic relations hearing himself, but he sent Jones in his place after a schedule conflict arose.[12]

The same round of elections that elevated Mercedes Deiz to circuit court also installed a new Multnomah County district attorney, Harl H. Haas. Like other local public figures before him, Haas had built a political base as a state legislator, beginning in 1969, while he practiced personal injury law in Portland. In 1972, he narrowly defeated Desmond Connall, who had been appointed district attorney after George A. Van Hoomissen departed in 1970 to become dean of the National College of District Attorneys at the University of Houston. Haas held the district attorney's office for eight years and proved to be outspoken and innovative. Taking advantage of federal law-enforcement grants, Haas established a special unit to prosecute repeat offenders and reduce plea-bargain options for serious criminals. He also established Oregon's first victims' assistance program, in which social workers assisted crime victims as their cases advanced through the justice system.

Haas seemed likely to use his record as district attorney as a stepping stone for higher political office. But he suffered an unusual setback during his second term when he was arrested for drunken driving in Sacramento, California. Haas took his case to trial and testified that he refused to take a breath test because he didn't trust the arresting officers.[13] News of his testimony eroded his political support in Oregon's law enforcement community. Haas ran for state attorney general at the end of his second term as district attorney in 1980, but he was defeated by David Frohnmayer, a University of Oregon law professor. Haas returned to private practice and then won a seat on Multnomah County Circuit Court by an election in 1984. He continued to be an innovative public official and in 1990 helped establish a drug-diversion program in which hundreds of felons accused of drug possession could have their charges dismissed after one year of drug treatment and counseling.

Despite its demise at the end of 1971, Portland municipal court left a legacy that helped lead to a major change in the practice of criminal law. The case began in August 1967, when Ralph Stevenson, age eighteen, was arrested in Irving Park and accused of disorderly conduct. When Stevenson appeared before Municipal Judge Philip T. Abraham, the young defendant said he could not afford a lawyer. Stevenson, appearing without representation, was convicted and sentenced to 180 days in jail. Charles Merten, a lawyer in the Portland Legal Aid office, filed a writ of habeas corpus in Multnomah County Circuit Court, alleging that Stevenson was wrongly jailed because he should have been entitled to legal counsel. Circuit Court Judge Alfred T. Sulmonetti agreed. He signed the writ, freeing Stevenson.

The United States Supreme Court had not yet addressed whether the federal Constitution required a court-appointed lawyer for a "petty offense" such as Stevenson's. The state's appeal of Sulmonetti's decision caused a showdown before the Oregon Supreme Court. Merten, who later worked as a deputy district attorney before establishing his own office in private practice, wrote an exhaustive brief, including all similar rulings in every state. The district attorney's office and a friend-of-the-court brief from city attorney Marian Rushing raised, among other issues, the expense of providing counsel for indigents accused of misdemeanors. In September 1969, the top state court sided with Merten. "The denial of the assistance of counsel will preclude the imposition of a jail sentence," the court said in a six-to-one decision.[14]

The ruling forced local governments to consider new ways to provide legal defense for indigents. A committee of the Columbia Region Association of Governments proposed the creation of a nonprofit public defender agency and won a one-year federal grant. Officials wanted to see whether the new Metropolitan Public Defender, Inc., could handle a volume of criminal defense cases competently at less cost than appointing lawyers from private practice. James D. Hennings, a Multnomah County deputy district attorney and a former deputy public defender in Chicago, was hired in June 1971 to head the new office. He became the first full-time public defender in Portland since the brief tenure of David Robinson in municipal court in 1915. Hennings and a second lawyer, Douglas S. Green, began representing indigent misdemeanor defendants in municipal court and district court. By early 1972, the new office began representing felony defendants.

By the end of that first year, judges were complimenting the Metropolitan Public Defender staff for its competence and for the convenience of having lawyers readily available in court for appointments.[15] The office grew as criminal caseloads increased, and by 1992, still under Hennings' supervision, the staff had grown to forty lawyers. The office proved to be a training ground for many lawyers who rose to other positions of prominence, including Linda L. Bergman and Ancer L. Haggerty, who became judges in Multnomah County District Court and later circuit court; Jeffrey Rogers, who became a federal prosecutor and later Portland city attorney; Julie Frantz, who went into civil practice and in 1992 became the first woman to serve as president of the Oregon State Bar before becoming a Multnomah County judge two years later; Stephen Kanter, who became dean of the Northwestern School of Law at Lewis and Clark College; and Janet Hoffman and Stephen Houze, who became leading private practitioners in the criminal defense bar. The creation and fast growth of the public defender's office was a harbinger of specialization that would affect many sectors of the bar during the decade. General practitioners or lawyers engaged in other trial work began to appear more rarely in criminal cases.

One of the most outspoken proponents of the municipal court merger in 1971 was Neil Goldschmidt, the youngest and brashest member of the Portland City Council. Goldschmidt, a Eugene native, joined the Portland Legal Aid office after finishing law school at the University of California at Berkeley, in 1966. He engineered an easy victory to a seat on the city coun-

Courtesy of *The Oregonian*

Mayor Neil Goldschmidt.

cil in 1970 using the strategy of neighborhood coffees and dedicated volunteers pioneered earlier by Bob Packwood. Goldschmidt advanced to the mayor's office in the 1972 election after Mayor Terry Schrunk retired at the end of four terms. Goldschmidt's appointed replacement on the council was another outspoken Portland lawyer, Mildred A. Schwab.

Schwab, the sister of Herbert Schwab, had been a Depression-era student at Northwestern College of Law. Women graduating in that era were not yet accepted in major firms or as trial lawyers. Schwab opened her own office and developed a practice in real property, contracts, and the performing arts. For many years she represented the booking agent who brought national and international talent to the Civic Auditorium. Schwab, herself an accomplished pianist, included among her closest friends some of the leading musical artists of the era. At the time of her appointment to the city council, Schwab was president of the Portland Planning Commission.

Goldschmidt's achievements during six years as mayor included a major revitalization of downtown Portland. With frequent support from Schwab, Goldschmidt supervised adoption of a new downtown plan, which focused growth during the next two decades. Many of the ideas had been raised by the Citizens Advisory Committee to the Downtown Plan, chaired by Dean Gisvold, a lawyer in the firm of McEwen, Gisvold, Rankin & Stewart. The plan was approved by the City Planning Commission, whose president was Hardy Myers, a partner in the firm later known as Stoel Rives LLP. The downtown plans carried out by Goldschmidt included creation of Tom McCall Waterfront Park on land where the city was first created in the pioneer era, demolition of a parking garage to make way for Pioneer Courthouse Square on the block directly west of the Pioneer Courthouse, construction of bus transit malls traversing downtown on Southwest Fifth and Sixth avenues, and approval for the return of electric rail transit between Gresham and Portland.

The light-rail transit project was the most controversial of

Goldschmidt's tenure as mayor. At one time, Portland had one of the most enviable electric trolley systems in the United States. However, the takeover of the automobile had been completed in the early 1950s, when Mayor Dorothy McCullough Lee encouraged removal of the last of the downtown trolley tracks. The automobile, alas, had not proved to be the best means of transportation for the congested downtown area. City planners and Goldschmidt realized that the sheer physical space needed for parking and the air pollution from thousands of vehicles were antithetical to a lively commercial and retail core. By the early 1970s, a new option had emerged. It was light rail—a bigger, faster, and quieter version of the old trolley cars.

By a controversial four-to-one vote in 1974, the city council decided to use federal money that had been earmarked for a proposed Mt. Hood Freeway through Southeast Portland to instead improve the existing Banfield Freeway and build a parallel fifteen-mile rail transit line. Supporters of the Mt. Hood freeway, harking back to the political reforms instituted early in the century by William S. U'Ren, led a successful initiative petition drive asking voters to affirm the city's preference for the new freeway. But supporters of the transit plan filed suit in Multnomah County Circuit Court, alleging that the city's "administrative" decision to reroute the federal funds didn't qualify as a "legislative" enactment as required by the constitutional amendment creating the initiative. Multnomah County Circuit Court Judge Clifford B. Olsen ruled for the transit supporters and removed the initiative from the ballot. His decision was affirmed in January 1975 by a two-to-one decision of Oregon Court of Appeals written by Judge Virgil Langtry.[16]

Goldschmidt left office in the middle of his second term in 1978 to become secretary of transportation under President Carter. He later served one term as Oregon governor, from 1986 to 1990, but chose not to seek reelection because of the breakup of his first marriage.[17] Goldschmidt then entered private practice in Portland. Mildred Schwab, whose tight-fisted approach to municipal fiscal matters made her one of Portland's most popular city commissioners ever, remained on the city council until she retired in 1986.

Among other distinctions, Schwab in 1973 became the first woman admitted as a member to the Portland City Club after a lengthy, divisive dispute about the civic club's all-male membership policy. Club members on three occasions in 1971 and 1972 had rejected proposals suggesting that women members be allowed. The third failure, in 1972, led to the resignation in protest of the club's president Sidney Lezak, the U.S. Attorney for Oregon. Portland lawyers William McLennan, who became a Multnomah County Circuit Court judge in 1972, and Jonathan U. Newman, who later served on the Oregon Court of Appeals, were among proponents who helped plot the change. Club voters narrowly scrapped the men-only policy in October 1973.

While the Goldschmidt administration was changing the face of downtown Portland, forces were at work that changed long-standing traditions of legal practice. In four dramatic years beginning in 1974, Oregon lawyers witnessed the demise of attorney fee schedules set by the Oregon State Bar, saw traditional prohibitions against advertising disappear, watched lawyer disciplinary files become open to public inspection, and began paying mandatory fees to a unique legal malpractice insurance program.

The U.S. Justice Department sued the Oregon State Bar in May 1974, alleging that fee schedules recommended by the bar for routine office work and court appearances violated federal antitrust laws.[18] Fee schedules had been adopted annually by the bar since its integration in 1935. Although lawyers were not prevented from charging less than the recommended fees, excessive fees could be grounds for professional discipline. Most Oregon lawyers followed the approved schedules. The Justice Department, estimating that the bar's 3,700 lawyers annually collected some $150 million in fees, contended that the schedules assured that legal fees were "maintained at artificial and noncompetitive levels." Manley B. Strayer, a partner in

Portland's largest firm, then known as Davies, Biggs, Strayer, Stoel & Boley, represented the bar during the Justice Department's investigation. Strayer had come to Portland in 1935 as an assistant U.S. Attorney where he succeeded Hugh L. Biggs, who later became his law partner. From 1932 to 1935, Strayer served as district attorney of Baker County. During his long career, Strayer was noted for his litigation skills and for a rollicking sense of humor, which he displayed in poems he wrote for the entertaining tent shows at Oregon State Bar conventions during the 1950s and early 1960s. Strayer told antitrust officials he knew of no case in which a lawyer had been disciplined for charging less than the bar recommended fees, but Strayer's contention didn't stop the Justice Department's attack.

The U.S. District Court complaint marked the first time that the government challenged a state bar on the fee issue. However, a similar issue involving the Virginia Bar Association already was far along in its route through the federal court system. It was prompted by a Virginia couple who complained they were being charged an excessive fee for a title search when they wanted to buy a house. In December 1975, the U.S. Supreme Court, ruling in *Goldfarb v. Virginia Bar Association*,[19] held that "anticompetitive" conduct by lawyers fell within the federal antitrust Sherman Act. As a result, Manley Strayer never had to litigate the Oregon case that had been pending. Two years later, Strayer celebrated a personal landmark by writing a poem he called, "Fifty Years in the Wrong Profession." In typical Strayer fashion, he teased his firm and the profession, but mostly himself and his rural roots. One chorus went:

Fifty years in the wrong profession
Filled with the worst kind of luck,
Fifty long years and I'm guessin'
I'd be better off driving a truck.
I'd like to go back to the prairie
Where the deer and the antelope play,

Where the birds and the bees charge no minimum fees
For the things they are doing all day.[20]

Surprisingly, the *Goldfarb* decision caused little consternation among Portland lawyers— unlike the next professional upheaval. In 1976, a new member of the Oregon State Bar practicing in Portland, Magar E. Magar, placed a small advertisement in newspaper classified ads listing his fees for uncontested divorces and wills. The Oregon State Bar notified Magar that his advertisement violated the bar's code of professional ethics. Magar contended that he had a right under the free-speech clause of the First Amendment to run his advertisements.

Ironically, a similar small newspaper advertisement had caught the attention of the grievance committee of the old Oregon Bar Association in 1892, the first year of that voluntary organization's history. "Divorces a specialty; reliable advice, prompt attention and moderate fee; no fee until after divorce," the old ad said. It listed an address, but not the name of the attorney. After brief debate, the bar association sent the matter to the Oregon Supreme Court. C.E.S. Wood, despite being one of the outstanding civil libertarians of his time, summarized the general feeling of the bar in that era: "[I]t seems to me that for a man to advertise himself in that manner, as aiding and assisting in, and encouraging, the procuring of divorces, is prima facie unprofessional and immoral."[21] Decades later, many lawyers still held similar views against professional advertising.

Like the antitrust case the year before, the advertising controversy involving Magar was not limited to Oregon; a similar case from Arizona was already pending before the United States Supreme Court. After negotiations, Magar agreed to stop running his advertisement and the bar agreed to halt disciplinary proceedings against him until the Arizona case was decided. A divided Supreme Court in June 1977, ruling in *Bates v. State Bar of Arizona*,[22] struck down as unconstitutional total bans against lawyer advertising. Justice Harry Blackmun, writing for the majority, left the door open for state bar associations to "weed out those few who abuse their trust" with deceptive or misleading advertising. Blackmun added, "We suspect that, with advertising, most lawyers will behave as they always have: They will abide by their solemn oaths to uphold the integrity and honor of their profession and of the legal system."

Magar's tiny classified ad paled in comparison to advertising strategies tried by many lawyers after the *Bates* ruling. Lawyers experimented with newspaper display ads, television commercials, and telephone directory advertisements. Most of the ads were aimed at a mass of citizens who might find themselves looking for an attorney for such matters as personal injuries, bankruptcy, domestic relations, wills and probate, or drunken driving charges. In general, advertising was used more by younger lawyers trying to build their practices than by established practitioners, many of whom still looked askance at advertising. By 1998, the "attorneys" section of the Yellow Pages of the Portland telephone directory contained ninety pages, mostly featuring lawyer advertisements in various sizes and formats. A few aggressive lawyers combed police and hospital records and sent letters offering their services to injury victims. How to regulate advertising became a heated topic among bar members. By the end of 1978, the bar had approved disciplinary rules declaring that advertisements were not to be "false, fraudulent, misleading or deceptive."[23] However, twenty years after the *Bates* decision, advertising and the professional regulation of it remain troublesome for the Oregon State Bar, which struggled to devise rules that respect a lawyer's freedom of speech while maintaining professional ethical standards.

At the same time the *Bates* case was pending in the United States Supreme Court, the Oregon Supreme Court was considering another case of special interest to lawyers. This one involved the confidentiality of bar disciplinary records. The issue arose when a Salem journalist went to Marion County Circuit Court seeking to obtain disciplinary records of a newly elected member of the Oregon Court of Appeals, Jason Lee. Lee, of Salem, in

1974 challenged Jacob Tanzer, a Portland lawyer who had an impressive record as a lawyer and public administrator when Governor Tom McCall appointed him in 1973 to a new seat on the expanded Oregon Court of Appeals. Tanzer had served as a Multnomah County deputy district attorney and assistant state attorney general before being named administrator of the state Department of Human Resources in 1972. Among his achievements, Tanzer successfully represented the state in *Apodaca v. Oregon*,[24] the 1972 United States Supreme Court case that affirmed the Oregon system of allowing juries to return convictions by eleven-to-one or ten-to-two in felony cases other than murder.

Lee ran a low-budget campaign, composed in part of small advertisements that indirectly impugned Tanzer's integrity. Tanzer had overwhelming support from the state's legal community, but it wasn't quite enough. Lee prevailed by fewer than 2,000 votes out of more than 470,000 votes cast in the statewide race. Tanzer's backers quickly sued in Marion County Circuit Court, claiming that Lee's advertisements contained a false statement. The trial focused on an advertisement in which Lee said Tanzer, as an appeals judge, "decided that $72,000 should be paid from your hard earned TAX DOLLARS from attorney fees in a condemnation case." The ad said the firm made a $200 contribution to Tanzer's campaign two and a half months later. "(LEE accepts NO CONTRIBUTIONS)," the ad concluded.[25] Tanzer's backers argued that the trial court judge set the attorney fees in the condemnation case, not Tanzer and the Court of Appeals.

A jury ruled in Tanzer's favor and Lee's name was removed from the November ballot. The Oregon Supreme Court, however, in a four-to-three decision, reversed the judgment. The majority, citing the earlier elections case pitting Lee Johnson against Robert Y. Thornton, concluded that Lee's advertisement could be construed as accurate. The court said that it wasn't comfortable in the position of being a political censor. It returned Lee's name to its unopposed position on the general election ballot. Lee cruised to victory in November 1974, despite a substantial number of write-in votes for Tanzer.

Meanwhile, Russell Sadler, a free-lance journalist, had heard of alleged professional complaints against Lee stemming from a family dispute involving Lee's management of money given to his three children. Sadler demanded to see Lee's disciplinary files. Because the Oregon State Bar was a state agency by statute, Sadler contended that the records should be available under Oregon's public records laws. The bar, which had never allowed the public to inspect its disciplinary files, refused. When challenged in court, bar representatives said they feared that reputations of competent lawyers could be sullied by frivolous complaints. The state supreme court, ruling in June 1976, took the opposite view. "To strike down the Public Records Laws would give special treatment to attorneys and perhaps encourage public belief that a veil of secrecy is hiding professional misconduct," the court said in *Sadler v. Oregon State Bar*.[26]

Carl Neil, who had taken the Lloyd Center free-speech case to the United States Supreme Court, was the bar's president when the *Sadler* decision was issued. He reported that many lawyers feared an avalanche of publicity about misconduct allegations as aggressive news reporters nosed through bar disciplinary records. But the avalanche never hit. "Six months after the *Sadler* decision, it can now be seen that it has produced very little inconvenience to the bar office and minimal dissemination of information about disciplinary proceedings in which charges against an accused lawyer are baseless," Neil wrote in the *Bar Bulletin*.[27] Even before the open records ruling, the bar had opened its disciplinary trials to public view. The public disciplinary records and open trials combined to give Oregon the distinction of having a disciplinary system open to more public scrutiny than any other bar in the United States. As years went by, the Oregon system won acclaim from the American Bar Association and from public interest groups seeking access to disciplinary records in other states.[28]

Jason Lee, meanwhile, served on the court of appeals until his death in 1980. During his tenure he made an unsuccessful run for the Oregon Supreme Court and gained a reputation as the court's least proficient member.[29] Tanzer returned to the court of appeals in an uncontested election in 1976, and later served on the Oregon Supreme Court from 1980 to 1982.

Another structural change in legal practice in Oregon began in 1978, when the Oregon State Bar established its Professional Liability Fund (PLF) to provide mandatory malpractice insurance for all lawyers in private practice. Oregon lawyers had begun detecting difficulties in buying malpractice insurance in the late 1960s. At the same time that premiums were rising, some insurance carriers decided to leave the market. A bar committee chaired by Portland attorney Paul J. O'Halloren estimated that as many as a third of Oregon's lawyers carried no insurance at all. O'Halloren's committee drafted a novel insurance plan that would require participation by all lawyers in private practice. The plan was approved by lawyers attending the 1976 bar convention and by the 1977 Legislature.

The first board of directors of the new PLF included O'Halloren as chairman, Edwin J. Peterson as vice chairman, and Portland lawyers Walter H. Evans, Jr., and William L. Hallmark. The board hired Lester L. Rawls as the administrator of the fund. Rawls, who had worked as a branch manager for a Portland insurance company before graduating from law school in 1962, had served as the Oregon state insurance commissioner from 1972 to 1978. The new enterprise began insuring Oregon lawyers in July 1978. "The aim of the plan, from a public policy standpoint, is to provide some protection to the public from the professional negligence of lawyers," wrote Edwin J. Peterson. "The aim, from a lawyer's economic standpoint, is to guarantee availability of liability coverage."[30] The Professional Liability Fund was unique in the nation when it was adopted. The PLF's staff received inquiries from many states in later years, but more than twenty-five years after its creation, the PLF remains the only insurance program of its kind in the United States.

The latter half of the 1970s also marked the first attempt by a relatively new state regulatory agency, the Oregon Commission on Judicial Fitness and Disability, to remove a sitting judge from office. The controversy involved Multnomah County District Court Judge Shirley A. Field, who had been appointed to the bench in 1972 after an active career as a lawyer, state representative, and Republican party activist.

The Judicial Fitness Commission, as it came to be called, was created by voters in 1968, following a model established in California in 1960 and copied or modified by many states. After a second statewide vote in 1976, the commission was empowered to recommend censure, suspension, or removal of judges on grounds of incompetence, habitual drunkenness, the commission of a felony crime, or breach of ethical canons for the judiciary. Final action on Judicial Fitness Commission recommendations would be made by the Oregon Supreme Court. The nine-member commission, composed of three lawyers, three judges, and three nonlawyer citizens appointed by the governor, found little need in its early years to launch formal investigations.

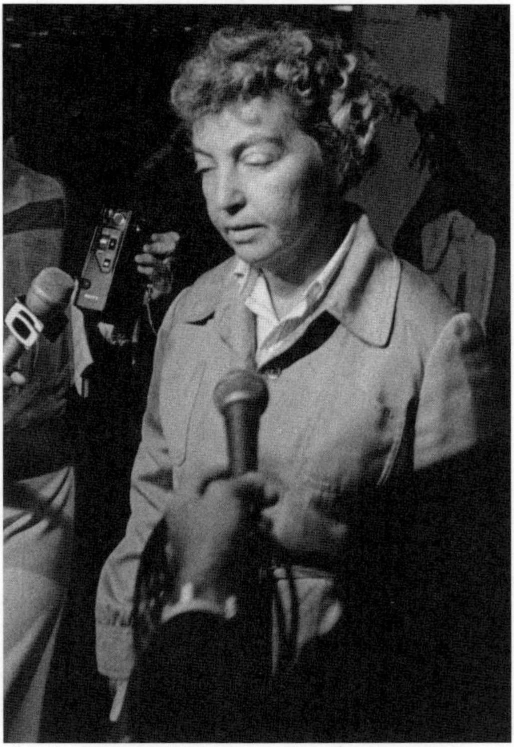

Courtesy of *The Oregonian*

Multnomah County District Judge Shirley Field was returning from a trip to Hawaii when news reporters questioned her about the recommendation that she be removed from the bench.

Judge Field had begun private practice in 1948 after graduating from Yale University School of Law. She won four terms as a state representative from Portland beginning in 1957, and served as a delegate to national Republican conventions in 1960, 1964, and 1968. In 1968 and 1970, Field waged aggressive but unsuccessful campaigns for seats on the Portland City Council. She had earned a reputation for a sharp mind and a sharp tongue when Governor Tom McCall appointed her to the district court bench in July 1972.

Lawyers appearing before Field in criminal misdemeanor cases quickly detected impatience by the judge. Many lawyers complained that she failed to honor the constitutionally protected rights of their clients. One defense lawyer recalled negotiating a plea bargain with the prosecutor, but Judge Field declined to hear the matter for another five days, which the client would have to spend waiting in jail. When the lawyer objected, Field replied, "Well… it couldn't happen to a nicer guy. I only wish I could put you in jail along with him. Unfortunately, we can't jail the attorney."[31] In one year alone, Judge Field amassed more than four hundred affidavits of prejudice filed by lawyers who thought they couldn't get fair treatment in her court. No other district judge received more than ten such affidavits in the same time span.

After five days of hearings, the Judicial Fitness Commission unanimously recommended, in September 1977, that Field be removed from office on the grounds that she had shown a willful failure to perform judicial duties and that her judicial performance was generally incompetent.[32] Among the commission members were Multnomah County Circuit Court Judge William Dale and Portland lawyers Clifford N. Carlsen and Donald Wilson. Judge Field did not testify before the commission, but in a deposition she admitted suffering from mental stress and undergoing psychiatric treatment. As sources of stress, Field listed pressure to keep up with the dockets and what she called "incessant scrutiny" from the Judicial Fitness Commission. The Oregon Supreme Court, in March 1978, agreed with the commission's recommendations. "While we recognize the pressures upon a trial judge in a busy metropolitan court, we believe Judge Field's inability to cope with her emotional problems after several attempts with professional help indicates that removal is a necessity," the court said.[33] Later, Field underwent surgery for a brain tumor. Although she never returned to legal practice, Field spent many years as a successful investor until her death in 1995.

Aside from Judge Field's problems, the middle and late 1970s saw major advances by women in Portland's legal system. For the first time, significant numbers of women began entering the profession. For example, only eleven women passed Oregon bar examinations in 1972, but that number rose to nearly fifty by 1975 and to more than seventy by 1977.[34] Women lawyers for the first time broke into the partnership ranks of large Portland firms and a Portland lawyer, Betty Roberts, became the first woman to sit on an Oregon appellate court.

Yet many women found it difficult to get a foot in the door. Carol Hewitt, who in January 1974 became the first woman partner at Lindsay, Nahstoll, Hart, Duncan, Dafoe & Krause, almost didn't get a job with the firm. After finishing second in her class at Willamette Law School, Hewitt served as the first woman law clerk for U.S. District Court Judge Gus Solomon. Although impressed by Hewitt in an interview, the Lindsay firm declined to hire her. But when Judge Solomon intervened on Hewitt's behalf in 1970, bluntly suggesting the time had come for women in the profession, the firm reconsidered.[35] The hard-working Hewitt quickly established herself as a tenacious business litigator, and earned her standing as partner in a mere three years. Between 1981 and 1989 Hewitt served as a member of the Oregon Investment Council, the state agency that supervises investments of all state funds. Hewitt served as chair of the council during her second four-year term. Her life and career were cut short by cancer in 1993 at age forty-seven.

In 1975 Velma Jeremiah became the first woman to be named a partner in Portland's largest law firm, then known as Davies, Biggs, Strayer, Stoel & Boley. Unlike Hewitt, who had gone straight through college and law school, Jeremiah had become a mother and worked at many jobs before tackling night classes at the Northwestern School of Law at age forty-two. When she finished law school in 1968, Jeremiah spent a full year applying for lawyer jobs while retaining her old position as executive secretary for Stimson Lumber Co. She found little encouragement. "Even though it was illegal, firms would tell you right to your face they didn't want to hire women," she recalled.[36] Jeremiah hadn't considered applying at the city's largest firm, which represented Stimson Lumber. Brian G. Booth and Frederick H. Torp, two partners in the Davies firm who had known Jeremiah while working on Stimson matters, encouraged her to apply.

Courtesy of *The Oregonian*

Velma Jeremiah.

Jeremiah in 1969 accepted a position as an associate lawyer that wasn't intended to lead to partner status. She worked on securities and estate planning and administration. "They found out a woman could work just as hard as a man," she said.[37] As time went by, the firm changed its position and, after Jeremiah's customary six-year tenure as an associate, the firm made her a partner in 1975. Jeremiah retired from practice in 1986 and developed a new interest. After taking a course on comedy, she began appearing on stage as a stand-up comic.

Other early women partners at Portland's major firms included Neva Campbell, who became a partner at Schwabe, Williamson & Wyatt in 1981, and Christie Helmer, who became a partner at Miller, Nash, Wiener, Hager & Carlsen the same year. Helmer in 1981 also became the first woman elected to the Oregon State Bar's board of governors.

Women attained another legal breakthrough in August 1977, when Portland attorney and legislator Betty Roberts was appointed to the Oregon Court of Appeals. Like Jeremiah, Roberts had entered the Northwestern College of Law in middle age, after having a family and working as a civics teacher at David Douglas High School. A Democrat, Roberts served in the Oregon House of Representatives from 1965 to 1969 and in the Oregon Senate until her appointment by Governor Bob Straub to the Oregon Court of Appeals. Among Roberts' legislative achievements was cosponsorship and passage in 1971 of the Oregon "bottle bill," which made the state one of the nation's leaders in mandating refunds on empty beer and soda containers.

Roberts held other political distinctions as well. She was the first woman ever to run for Oregon governor, finishing a close second behind Bob Straub in the May 1974 Democratic primary. Roberts also ran a second statewide race in November that same year, challenging U.S. Senator Bob Packwood. Former U.S. Senator Wayne Morse, who had been toppled by Packwood in 1968, won the Democratic primary in May, but he died during the summer. Roberts was chosen by her party to replace Morse as Packwood's challenger. It was short notice for another statewide race. Packwood prevailed over Roberts' spirited but less well-financed campaign.

Roberts' appointment to the court of appeals in 1977 was one of four additions made by Governor Straub after the legislature expanded the court from six to ten members. Two of the other new appointees also were Portland attorneys, George M. Joseph and John H. Buttler. Unlike Joseph, who had spent most of his career engaged in public law, Buttler had spent twenty-five years practicing business law with Hardy, Buttler, McEwen, Weiss & Newman, the firm originally started by the Cake brothers. Both

Buttler and Joseph retired from the court of appeals with identical tenure at the end of 1992.

Judge Roberts, meanwhile, left the court of appeals in 1982 to claim another distinction, that of first woman justice of the Oregon Supreme Court. This time her appointment was made by an old legislative foe, Republican Governor Victor Atiyeh. Roberts succeeded former Portland attorney Thomas H. Tongue, who had retired in February 1982. Roberts had announced an intention to run for the vacancy if Tongue did not seek reelection. Atiyeh responded that Roberts had earned the job based on her record at the court of appeals. "I have not picked a token," he said. As for selecting the first woman justice, Atiyeh added, "The day will come, I hope, when it is not as big a deal as it is now."[38]

During her tenure on the high court, Roberts became part of a majority that issued several rulings interpreting the civil-liberties guarantees of the 1859 Oregon Constitution, including free speech, weapons ownership, and protections against police searches and seizures, as being more expansive than similar guarantees in the federal Bill of Rights. Roberts retired from the Oregon Supreme Court in February 1986.

Courtesy of *The Oregonian*

Oregon Supreme Court Justice Betty Roberts, sworn in by Chief Justice Arno Denecke.

While Roberts was breaking new ground for women in the appellate courts, 1978 brought the first Multnomah County Circuit Court race contested solely by women. That year, Kathleen B. Nachtigal, a veteran practitioner of domestic relations and juvenile law, challenged Circuit Court Judge Elizabeth Welch, who had been appointed by Governor Bob Straub to fill the vacancy left by Judge Jean Lewis's retirement earlier the same year.

Nachtigal entered the race contending that Welch's background had been more political than legal. Although Welch had worked in the Multnomah County district attorney's office during two different stints, she had spent the three years before her appointment running the city's Office of Justice Programs under Mayor Neil Goldschmidt. Welch's professional background, however, played a much less significant role in the race than a statement she made to a newspaper reporter in a routine campaign article. Asked why she was a better choice for voters than Nachtigal, Welch answered, "You can put this under the 'arrogant' category if you wish, but I'm a lot smarter than (Mrs. Nachtigal) is."[39]

Unfortunately for Welch, many readers took her at her word and interpreted the statement as a sign of arrogance, and elected Nachtigal by a decisive margin. Welch returned to private practice for twelve years before her old city hall boss, Governor Neil Goldschmidt, appointed her to a seat on the Multnomah County District Court bench in January 1989. Her diligent handling of domestic relations cases prompted Governor Barbara Roberts to promote Welch to the circuit court in 1993, following the retirement of Judge Mercedes Deiz. As Welch was sworn in during the circuit court ceremony, one of the people applauding most loudly was Judge Nachtigal.

The 1970s also were critical years at Portland's largest law firm, which began the decade as Davies, Biggs, Strayer, Stoel & Boley. Several of the firm's lawyers represented Orbanco Financial Services, which in 1973 completed a hostile takeover of Security Bank of Oregon. The successful maneuver put the Davies, Biggs firm in the position of representing two major banking institutions, the older United States National Bank and Orbanco.

To avoid potential conflicts, partners Frederick Torp, Brian G. Booth, and Kenneth D. Stephens left the Davies, Biggs firm to create a new partnership in 1974 with Moe Tonkon, who was then in his forty-seventh year of practice in Portland. Tonkon and his longtime partner, Morris Galen, in 1972 had added a third partner and a former Davies, Biggs associate, Terry Baker, forming Tonkon, Galen & Baker.

Baker had been one of Oregon's greatest athletes, starring in football and basketball at Oregon State University. He ended his collegiate career by scoring the only touchdown on a ninety-nine-yard run in Oregon State's six-to-nothing victory over Villanova in the 1962 Liberty Bowl. "Like a James Bond in shoulder pads he called on himself to transmute imminent peril into triumph," *Sports Illustrated* magazine said of the touchdown run.[40] That single play would be remembered by Oregon sports fans for decades, much like Robert Mautz's "dead man" play in 1924. Baker won the Heisman Trophy as the nation's best college football player, and was named Sportsman of the Year by *Sports Illustrated.* Tonkon had encouraged Baker to attend law school during Baker's ensuing three-year career as a professional player with the Los Angeles Rams. In August 1974, Tonkon, Galen & Baker added new partners from the Davies, Biggs firm to form the firm that became known as Tonkon, Torp, Galen, Marmaduke & Booth. Don H. Marmaduke, a leading litigator who had left Davies, Biggs earlier, joined Tonkon's new firm to head the litigation section. The new partnership, which began with nine lawyers in 1974, grew to fifty-two lawyers by 1995.

The tumultuous decade of the 1970s drew to a close with a merger of two major Portland law firms that proved to be a harbinger for the 1980s. In September 1979, Davies, Biggs, Strayer, Stoel & Boley merged with the smaller firm of Rives, Bonyhadi & Smith to form Stoel, Rives, Boley, Fraser & Wyse. The combined office gave Portland its first law firm of more than 100 attorneys. The Rives firm, which brought twenty-seven lawyers to the merger, traced its roots to the early years of the century with its primary client, Pacific Power & Light Company (PP&L). John Laing had come to Portland from New York in 1910 representing Electric Bond & Share, a utility conglomerate that acquired several small electric utilities in Oregon and other states. Those utilities were merged into PP&L, and Laing served as the company's vice president and general counsel. Laing and Henry Gray, who joined Laing as house counsel, left the utility to open the independent firm of Laing & Gray in 1937, retaining PP&L as their chief client. George Rives, a San Francisco lawyer who specialized in law of regulated industries, did his first work for PP&L in 1958, and by 1963 came to Portland to join the firm that became Rives, Bonyhadi & Smith.

The merger provided diversification for the Rives firm, and offered an entry into the complex field of utilities and power generation for the Davies, Biggs firm. Since 1967, the city's largest firm, originally founded by Charles Carey, had been structuring its growing office around a variety of specialties, such as forest products, real estate, taxation, banking, securities, employee benefits, construction and design, and creditors' rights. As Thomas Stoel noted at the time, "In the past twenty years, a good many specialties have developed which were largely unknown twenty-five years ago."[41] Some of those specialties included employee benefit plans, occupational safety regulation, new real estate laws, and increased complexity in business regulation. The Rives firm, which had been housed in the Public Service Building along with PP&L's corporate headquarters, moved to the Georgia-Pacific Building, later known as the Standard Insurance Center, where Davies, Biggs had been quartered since that skyscraper's opening in 1970. With experienced lawyers in many specialties, the large firm took on the characteristics of a supermarket by providing a variety of legal services within the same office.

The supermarket analogy perhaps was most fitting for the Stoel firm, which for many years represented Fred Meyer as that pioneering Portland entrepreneur built an impressive chain of "one-stop shopping centers" bearing his name throughout the region. Meyer had a lengthy and close attorney-client relationship with Paul Boley, a partner in the Stoel firm, lasting until Meyer's death in 1978. Boley, who finished high school in The Dalles, had joined the firm in 1943 after finishing law school at Harvard University. Among several civic activities, Boley served as a trustee for Lewis and Clark College. Following the merger of Lewis and Clark with the Northwestern College of Law, the school's new law library was named in his honor.

At his death at age ninety-two in 1978, Fred Meyer held twenty-eight percent of the Fred Meyer, Inc. stock, valued at approximately $63 million. His estate plan, prepared under Boley's supervision, called for transfer of that stock to the newly created Fred Meyer Charitable Trust. At Meyer's insistence,[42] two of his long-standing business associates, Oran B. Robertson and Pauline Lawrence, were named as trustees in addition to their positions as directors of Fred Meyer, Inc. Another former close Meyer associate and trustee under the estate plan, Gerry Pratt, filed suit in Multnomah County Circuit Court seeking removal of Robertson and Lawrence on the grounds that they could not serve the potentially conflicting interests of both the trust and the corporation.

The case brought together several of Portland's leading trial lawyers for litigation that appeared destined to air long-standing personal grievances among Meyer's closest business associates. Wayne Hilliard, a partner with Dezendorf, Lubersky, Spears & Campbell, represented Oran Robertson after the Stoel, Rives firm withdrew from representing the estate. John D. Ryan, a leading personal injury lawyer whose father, Thomas G. Ryan, had been an assistant county prosecutor in the days of Judge Henry McGinn, joined Henry Carey, an aggressive business litigator who often challenged large institutions with class-action suits, in representing Pratt.

Other prominent lawyers lined up in the Fred Meyer estate case were Jack Kennedy, senior partner in the law firm of Kennedy, King & Zimmer, who earlier had helped save night law classes at Northwestern School of Law, representing Pauline Lawrence; and John R. Faust, Jr., who had joined

Schwabe, Williamson & Wyatt in 1979 after starting his career in the firm founded by the Cake brothers, representing the fourth trustee, Warne Nunn. Faust also had recently begun what proved to be a thirteen-year run as moderator of a popular Portland weekly public-affairs television program called Town Hall. Ironically, his predecessor on that show had been Gerry Pratt.

The lawyers battled sporadically before Circuit Court Judge James R. Ellis, but the dispute was resolved behind closed doors, where Kohlberg, Kravis & Roberts, a New York investment banking firm, was negotiating a leveraged buyout of Fred Meyer, Inc. The corporation ultimately agreed to sell all its stock for $55 a share, for a total of $420 million. The deal, finally consummated in 1982 with approval of Judge Ellis, netted more than $120 million for the charitable trust and ended any potential conflicts of interest between the trust and the corporation. Money from the sale roughly doubled the amount envisioned for the trust when Meyer died in 1978. Jerome Kohlberg, Jr., who actively pursued the purchase on behalf of the investment banking firm, had first learned about the Fred Meyer chain while working as a law clerk for U.S. District Court Judge Gus Solomon in 1952.

After the Fred Meyer, Inc., sale was completed, Judge Ellis was faced with awarding attorney fees to be paid by the charitable trust to the trustees' lawyers. Ellis ultimately awarded more than $800,000, with the largest share, $441,500, going to Henry Carey and John D. Ryan. Never bashful, the two lawyers had asked for $6.75 million, contending that they deserved a percentage of the increased value of the estate's stock from the outset of the proceedings until the final sale.

Although Ryan's ample oratorical skills fell short of convincing Judge Ellis on the Fred Meyer fee matter, his impromptu speaking abilities had left an indelible impression upon Oregon State Bar members a few years earlier. After two years of study, a bar committee recommended in 1977 that the bar create a formal system for recognizing lawyers as specialists in certain areas of the law. The plan appeared sure of passage until Ryan took the floor at the town-hall style meeting at the bar's annual convention in Seaside. His heartfelt speech favoring professional autonomy for lawyers single-handedly reversed the momentum and led to defeat of the specialization plan.[43] Though sentiment favoring specialties arose from time to time thereafter, the Oregon bar had taken no formal steps toward specialization in the twenty years after Ryan's speech.

CHAPTER SEVEN

Toward a New Century

The new decade was only a few weeks old when a ceremony unlike any other before it unfolded at the U.S. Courthouse in 1980. Chief Judge James M. Burns, speaking in person and by closed circuit television to an audience that packed the two largest courtrooms, welcomed three new judges to the U.S. District Court bench: James A. Redden, Helen Frye, and Owen M. Panner. As Burns noted, it was a day of firsts: the first time in Oregon that three federal judges were sworn in at the same time, the first time that two Oregon federal judicial positions had been created at once, and the first time that a woman had been chosen to serve on Oregon's federal bench.[1]

The three new judges were appointed by President Jimmy Carter. By selecting Panner, senior partner of the largest law firm in Bend and member of the Republican party, Carter added another historical first by making an Oregon appointment from across political party lines. Panner was reared in Oklahoma and came to central Oregon soon after graduating from the University of Oklahoma Law School in 1949. The soft-spoken Panner had built a reputation as an excellent trial attorney and legal counselor. Redden, who formerly had practiced law in Medford, served as state treasurer from 1972 to 1976 and as Oregon Attorney General from 1976 until his appointment to the federal bench. Redden made a run for governor in 1978, but lost in the Democratic primary to the eventual winner, Bob Straub. A man with a gentle, self-deprecating humor, Redden blamed his loss in part on his cam-

Courtesy of *The Oregonian*

U.S. District Court Judge Helen Frye.

paign lawn signs: the red background dissolved in Oregon's spring rains.

Frye, like many of Oregon's pioneering women lawyers, turned to the law after earlier career pursuits. She had been a teacher at South Eugene High School and had started a family before she enrolled in the University of Oregon Law School, where she graduated with top honors in 1966. Thomas E. Wurtz, a classmate of Frye's, recalled that she customarily went home in the middle of the afternoon during law school. "I thought she probably would be studying at home," Wurtz related. "But of course, it turned out she was caring for her family and she did not have to do any more studying after she got home."[2] Frye practiced with a Eugene firm for five years before Governor Tom McCall appointed her in 1971 to a seat on the Lane County Circuit Court, a position she held until the federal appointment.

Perhaps the big ceremony for the three new judges in U.S. District Court was an omen: as tumultuous as the 1970s were for Portland's legal community, the 1980s would bring another round of changes affecting the judiciary and nearly every kind of legal practice. It proved to be a decade of economic instability for much of the Portland legal community, as an economic downturn in the business world, particularly in timber, coincided with a growing influx of new law school graduates. The decade saw the first interstate mergers of major law firms and numerous mergers among smaller firms as law offices of all sizes looked for new approaches to keep a competitive edge and to provide better service to clients.

One of the key administrative changes in Portland's legal community occurred in January 1981, when Michael D. Schrunk, son of former mayor Terry Schrunk, took office as district attorney, succeeding Harl H. Haas. Michael Schrunk had worked as a deputy district attorney in the office from 1970 to 1977. As a young deputy, Schrunk quickly earned the nickname of "Mr. District Attorney" for his quiet professionalism. He tried approximately two hundred jury trials during those seven years, ranging from drunken driving cases to multiple homicides. Schrunk left the office for private practice in 1977, and in early 1980 filed to run for the district attorney seat being vacated by Haas. No opponent was willing to challenge him. Before taking office in 1981, Schrunk served as a special prosecutor to convict Gary Gortmaker, a fifteen-year veteran Marion County district attorney, of theft and official misconduct involving office funds in that county. Schrunk held the office of

Courtesy of *The Oregonian*

Michael D. Schrunk.

Multnomah County district attorney longer than any district attorney before him. He won his first three terms without opposition, drew a token challenge while winning his fourth in 1992, and ran unopposed again in 1996. Among his accomplishments, Schrunk bolstered the prosecution of domestic violence and child sexual abuse cases, and helped create a regional task force of state, local, and federal agents to crack down on major drug dealers. Working with Judge Haas, who returned to public life in 1984 by winning a Multnomah County Circuit Court seat after four years in private practice, Schrunk also helped develop an innovative drug-treatment diversion program for defendants charged with possession of small amounts of illegal drugs for personal use.

The early 1980s brought several new faces to the Multnomah County bench—many of them women. County voters for the first time began showing a strong disposition favoring female judicial candidates. In 1982, Nely Johnson and Dorothy Baker won two new seats created by the legislature to help Multnomah County District Court meet the demands of its growing urban population. After larger fields were narrowed in the primary election, both Baker and Johnson won general-election victories against male candidates for the bench. The soft-spoken Johnson, a native of Romania whose family left that Communist-ruled country when she was fourteen years old, had worked as a public defender and in private civil practice. Baker had been a Multnomah County deputy district attorney before opening her own office to practice domestic relations law.

Two years after the election victories by Johnson and Baker, Kristena A. LaMar cleared yet another elective hurdle by becoming the first woman to defeat an incumbent male judge at the polls. LaMar, who had worked for three years as a Multnomah County Juvenile Court referee, challenged William E. Hurley, who had been appointed to a circuit court vacancy by Governor Vic Atiyeh in 1983. Hurley was an experienced trial lawyer with the firm of Bernard, Hurley, Crawford & Kneeland. But Hurley, like Judge

Elizabeth Welch six years earlier, had little time before the 1984 election to establish a reputation as judge. When LaMar challenged him in the primary election, Hurley found that he didn't like campaigning. He did little in the race but buy a few billboard advertisements. LaMar, meanwhile, made numerous public appearances and canvassed neighborhoods. Her victory reversed the roles of that first race in Multnomah County pitting man against woman back in 1926—when challenger Fred Olson defeated the newly appointed Mary Jane Spurlin. In 1987, LaMar began serving as a full-time settlement judge, holding pretrial meetings with civil litigants to encourage settlements before trial. She took over offices formerly used by county government officials and became the first full-time judge in the courthouse whose work did not require a courtroom.

Meanwhile, fundamental structural changes started taking effect in both the state and the Portland court systems in the early 1980s. One of the most significant began in January 1983, when the state government for the first time took over administrative and budget authority for all district and circuit courts. Legislation approved in 1981 put the Chief Justice of the Oregon Supreme Court in charge of the entire state court system. The first to undertake that burden was Berkeley Lent, a Portland lawyer and veteran state legislator who had worked his way through Reed College and Willamette Law School on the docks and in sawmills. After entering practice in 1950, Lent concentrated on workers' compensation and personal injury cases. During his fourteen-year stint as a legislator, beginning in 1957, Lent introduced expanded coverage for injured workers and fathered a tort claim law that allowed injured parties to file lawsuits against state agents who caused injuries. Lent in 1971 was appointed by Governor Tom McCall to a vacancy on the Multnomah County Circuit Court bench, leaving his law firm of Lent, York, Paulson & Bullock. Lent won a seat on the state supreme court at the polls in 1976, and advanced to chief justice in 1982 after Justice Arno Denecke retired.

As chief justice, Lent supervised the early months of a bumpy transition to the new statewide court system. Difficulties included creating a uniform personnel system for 1,100 court employees across the state, implementing a new statewide judicial computer system, and troubleshooting problems as they surfaced in the various counties. After seven months, Lent stepped aside. "I found that I could not perform the duties required of the chief justice as administrator of the trial courts and still keep up with my judicial work in a way that satisfied me," he said.[3] Lent remained as an associate justice until retiring in 1988.

His successor as chief justice was another Portland lawyer, Edwin J. Peterson. Peterson had been appointed to the top state court in 1979 after twenty-two years in private practice, all with the Portland firm of Tooze, Kerr, Peterson, Marshall & Shenker. Peterson served as president of the Multnomah Bar Association in 1972, followed by three years on the Oregon State Bar's board of governors. Aside from being an experienced business trial lawyer, Peterson was a talented pianist who often played at the annual Oregon State Bar tent shows in the 1950s and early 1960s. Faced with problems in the new statewide judicial system, Peterson realized that the title of chief justice wasn't considered a plum. "I won by default," Peterson said.

Courtesy of *The Oregonian*

Oregon Chief Justice Edwin J. Peterson.

"Some members of the court think I am a damn fool for wanting the job."[4] Soon after his election by the supreme court as chief justice, Peterson announced a new goal: speeding up the state's court system.

Court delay wasn't considered a major problem in Multnomah County at the time. In fact, a study by the National Center for State Courts between 1976 and 1983 rated the Portland courts as "consistently fast" compared to many other urban court systems.[5] Still, Peterson set a goal of resolving civil cases within twelve months after they were filed. It was a startling aim compared to the county's existing average of about eighteen months.

Chief Justice Peterson and Multnomah County Presiding Judge Donald H. Londer, who succeeded Charles Crookham as presiding judge in 1986, kept up their efforts to speed the civil dockets. Londer, who fought as an amateur boxer in his youth, was a Multnomah County deputy sheriff when he started attending the Northwestern College of Law. After graduating in 1964, Londer worked with Nels Peterson practicing personal injury law for five years before opening his own office with another Peterson associate,

Courtesy of *The Oregonian*

Multnomah County Presiding Judge Donald H. Londer.

Sanford Kowitt. Londer was appointed to the district court bench in 1976, and was promoted to circuit court in 1983 following the retirement of Judge Alan F. Davis. Londer, who was tenacious about denying requests for trial delays without serious reasons, reported that plaintiffs' lawyers and defense attorneys gradually found that the accelerated pace paid economic dividends in their practices. By the time Peterson stepped down as chief justice in 1991, cases routinely were coming to trial in fewer than twelve months. Londer in 1996 surpassed a decade as presiding Multnomah County Circuit Court judge, holding that office until his death from cancer in 1998, longer than any other judge in county history.

The push to speed up Multnomah County dockets coincided with another important change in the way business was being handled at the courthouse. Beginning in 1982, Multnomah County Circuit Court, acting on recommendations from Judge Robert E. Jones, began an experiment with arbitration of civil cases in which the amount in dispute was under $15,000. Parties who consented could try their cases before an arbitrator instead of a judge or jury. Litigants who were unhappy with the arbitrator's ruling could appeal and have a full trial on the merits in court. Jones, who was appointed to the bench in 1979 by Governor Victor Atiyeh, had been a leading medical malpractice defense lawyer and had risen to senior partner in twenty-five years with the firm of Jones, Lang, Klein, Wolf & Smith. As a judge, Jones continued his commitment to improving the trial bar by teaching trial practice at the Northwestern School of Law, holding lunch sessions with young litigators, and publishing a monthly list of trial tips in the *Multnomah Lawyer*, a publication of the Multnomah Bar Association. After a decade, the arbitration program in Multnomah County was deemed a success. Nearly two thousand cases per year were being diverted to arbitration. The average hearing lasted only two to three hours and the final results were accepted by the litigants in more than ninety percent of the cases.[6]

In late 1982, Multnomah County also began requiring parties in domestic relations cases to meet with a mediator in an attempt to reach agreement in child-custody disputes, short of contested hearings in court. The mandatory mediation played a key role in helping to reduce the average time between filing a marital dissolution petition and the court hearing from over thirteen months in 1982 to seven months a decade later.

While the state and county court systems were undergoing substantial administrative changes in the mid-1980s, a social movement unlike any other in Oregon provided a new challenge to the state judiciary. It began quietly enough when followers of a spiritual guru from India, Bhagwan Shree Rajneesh, bought the 64,000-acre Big Muddy Ranch near Antelope in June 1981. His supporters, called Rajneeshees, paid $5.75 million for the arid, mostly vacant cattle ranch. Rajneesh, displaying a penchant for elegant jewelry and Rolls Royce automobiles, arrived two months later. Rajneesh ostensibly never talked about worldly affairs, and expressed his spiritual views to a small inner circle headed by a woman named Ma Anand Sheela. Sheela held an unlimited power of attorney for Rajneesh and maintained dictatorial power over his followers and their plans to build a commune in Oregon for Rajneeshees from all over the world.

During the next four years, affluent Rajneeshees pumped millions of dollars into the Big Muddy, hoping to turn it quickly into a self-supporting spiritual commune. The rude aggressiveness of Sheela and her ambitious plans, however, led to dozens of courtroom dramas in Portland, Hood River, and The Dalles spanning almost five years. In the beginning, the legal actions were all civil suits. Defamation suits flew back and forth between Sheela and central Oregon citizens who spoke against her or the Rajneeshees; municipal law disputes arose when Rajneeshees took political control of the tiny town of Antelope and later formed their own city, Rajneeshpuram, on 2,000 acres within the ranch; and land-use arguments surfaced over Rajneeshee development plans and state regulations. In the end, however, the final scenes were played out in criminal courts, where

Rajneesh, Sheela, and several other Rajneeshees were charged and convicted of a wide variety of crimes in state and federal courts. The offenses included sham marriages to circumvent immigration laws, arson at the Wasco County Planning Department, widespread eavesdropping with electronic bugging devices at dozens of sites within Rajneeshpuram, and the poisoning of 750 restaurant patrons with salmonella typhimurium bacteria in The Dalles. The poisoning episode presumably was a test to see if Rajneeshee leaders could keep other citizens away from the polls in the November 1984 election, in which commune leaders hoped to elect two of the three members to the Wasco County governing board. Sheela hoped to win the election with help from 3,000 homeless people imported to the commune to vote with the Rajneeshees. The election scheme collapsed, however, when state officials cracked down on enforcing voter-registration qualifications, and Sheela dropped the election-rigging plan. As *The Oregonian* concluded when the Rajneesh dramas had run their course, "If it was all true, events on the ranch in recent years had made Rajneeshpuram a nest of crime unparalleled in Oregon history."[7]

Although many Oregonians were suspicious about the legality of Sheela's conduct, all the criminal charges were still over the horizon when Portland lawyer Garry P. McMurry forced Rajneesh out of his self-imposed silence in August 1984. The reason was a $1 million defamation suit filed by McMurry on behalf of an Antelope woman, Donna Smith Quick, who had spoken against the Rajneeshees after they took political control of that small town. Sheela, in a letter to the *Rajneesh Times* newspaper, had described Quick and several other residents as racists, bigots, and thugs because of their opposition to some Rajneeshee activities. McMurry included Rajneesh as a defendant because Sheela was acting as his personal secretary. Swami Prem Niren, a skillful, former southern California business litigator who led Rajneesh's legal defense, insisted that Rajneesh would not testify in the case. He contended that forcing Rajneesh to testify would violate his religious rights and expose him to possible personal injury because of the bhagwan's allegedly serious allergy and back difficulties. McMurry's strategy posed a hidden legal problem for Rajneesh, however: by refusing to testify, Rajneesh risked being held in contempt of court and having his visa revoked. The decision was made by Multnomah County Circuit Court Judge Clifford B. Olsen, who had eastern Oregon roots himself. After graduating from Willamette University Law School in 1949, Olsen's first job was as Grant County district attorney in John Day. The county was so small that the prosecutor's job was a half-time position, which allowed the young lawyer to start a civil practice as well. Olsen moved to Portland in 1957 and practiced civil law until his appointment to the bench in 1968. As a veteran judge, Olsen wasn't intimidated by Rajneesh's refusal to testify. He held out the possibility of arresting Rajneesh if the guru failed to honor McMurry's subpoena.

Concerned about the contempt threat, Niren ultimately agreed to make Rajneesh available for questioning in a deposition videotaped in Rajneeshpuram. The deposition was taken on a Sunday and played to the jury in Olsen's courtroom the next day. As it turned out, Rajneesh's testi-

Courtesy of *The Oregonian*

Bhagwan Shree Rajneesh, with his chief lawyer, Swami Prem Niren, behind the Rajneesh's left shoulder.

mony had little bearing on the evidence in the defamation trial. His appearance did nothing more than reinforce the rude abrasiveness Sheela had already established as chief spokeswoman for Rajneesh's followers.

"I will only say the truth because I am incapable of lying," Rajneesh said when he was asked to take the oath to tell the truth. He agreed to take an oath on a book of his own religious writings "just to play the game," he said. "If it were the Bible, I would have refused immediately," he said, adding that the same would apply for the Koran or any other holy book "full of lies." During his 90-minute appearance, Rajneesh castigated the world's major religions as being full of lies and went out of his way to criticize McMurry, who was questioning him. "I have never come across such a stupid person in my entire life," he said at one point. Rajneesh insisted he knew nothing about the defamation case or Sheela's letter that prompted it. As McMurry persisted, Rajneesh interrupted, "I have told you again and again. Are you deaf?"[8]

Although Rajneesh and his followers had been creating controversy in Oregon for three years, the Donna Smith Quick trial was the first time that a jury had been asked to resolve a dispute involving the religious sect. Judge Olsen, in an earlier trial without a jury, had awarded $75,000 in defamation damages to another central Oregon resident, Rosemary McGreer, who had been attacked in print by Sheela in the same letter involving Quick. Many lawyers, including Niren, wondered whether the unpopular sect could get a fair trial before a jury. In the silver-haired McMurry, the Rajneeshees faced a veteran, skilled litigator who had prior experience, including a continuing battle with another alternative religion. McMurry, who had been a law partner with Senator Bob Packwood early in Packwood's legal career, had won a $2.1 million fraud judgment against the Church of Scientology in Multnomah County Circuit Court in 1979 on behalf of a former Scientologist, only to have the judgment set aside by the Oregon Court of Appeals. That retrial was pending when the Rajneeshee case arose. Niren, although eleven years younger than McMurry, brought impressive credentials, too. Ironically, he had been born in Tigard but had moved to southern California as a young child. Before becoming a Rajneeshee in 1981 and taking on his new name, Philip J. Toelkes had worked for two big California law firms, the latter being the influential Manatt, Phelps, Rothenberg & Tunney firm in Los Angeles, where he earned a reputation as a tenacious corporate litigator.

Unlike Sheela, Niren displayed a calm demeanor in his public appearances. In the Quick trial he contended that the Rajneeshees were "the most vilified minority in recent Oregon history," and urged jurors to respect their free-speech rights.[9] He also insisted that Quick had not been injured by the things Sheela had written about her. Indeed, Quick had received a standing ovation at one large public gathering she attended after Sheela's letter of criticism had been printed. After the two-week trial, jurors voted ten-to-two in rejecting Quick's defamation claim. "As a native Oregonian, as a lawyer and as a civil libertarian, I am so pleased all the people who said we could not get a fair trial in this case were wrong," Niren said afterward.[10]

However, Niren's surprise victory proved to be the last significant one for the Rajneeshees. Sheela was starting to feel mounting pressure from rivals within the sect. Her concern for her own standing was an element in the widespread eavesdropping scheme she approved and for the attempted killing of a perceived rival by using poison in a syringe. Niren, who had become dissatisfied with Sheela early in 1985, spent several months driving a tractor on the ranch instead of representing the sect in court. Fearing criminal indictments, Sheela and several of her supporters suddenly left Rajneeshpuram in 1985 and fled to Germany. Rajneesh invited law enforcement officers to investigate Sheela's behavior, but he also knew that a federal investigation was continuing into his immigration status. Perhaps having been tipped off about a secret federal indictment, Rajneesh, too, made a surprise departure a month after Sheela fled. A private jet took off from

Rajneeshpuram headed for the Bahamas, but Rajneesh was arrested when his plane landed for refueling in North Carolina.

Within days, Rajneesh was back in Portland, where U.S. District Court Judge Edward Leavy set bail at $500,000 on an indictment accusing Rajneesh of thirty-two counts of immigration offenses. The guru's supporters quickly raised the bail, allowing Rajneesh to leave custody. He was back in Judge Leavy's courtroom a few days later, however. Protected in court by nine security guards, Rajneesh pleaded guilty to two immigration fraud counts and a fine of $400,000, to be kept from the bail. Under the negotiated plea agreement approved by U.S. attorney Charles Turner, Rajneesh was spared further incarceration, provided that he left the United States forever. "I never want to return again," he told Judge Leavy, in a voice free of his earlier braggadocio.[11] Some of his supporters hoped to keep their commune alive, but it was Niren, the highest-ranking member remaining in the Rajneeshee organization, who announced that the commune would be closed and the property sold. Ironically, less than a month after Rajneesh's forced departure from the United States, U.S. District Court Judge Helen Frye annulled the incorporation of Rajneeshpuram on the ground that religious control of all municipal affairs violated the separation of church and state as mandated by the First Amendment of the United States Constitution. The challenge had been filed in 1983 by the Oregon Department of Justice under Attorney General Dave Frohnmayer. Niren and other Rajneeshee lawyers had battled aggressively against the suit, but the outcome was moot by the time the final ruling was issued.

Justice was slower in coming for Sheela than for the guru. In July 1986, she was extradited from Germany to face federal and state charges in Oregon. Represented by Portland defense attorney Stephen Houze, a former member of the Multnomah County Public Defender's office who had gone into private practice, Sheela reached a plea bargain with both state and federal authorities. In a single day she pleaded guilty to federal immigration, conspiracy, and wiretapping charges before Judge Leavy in U.S. District Court. She then pleaded guilty to state charges, including arson and attempted murder, before Wasco County Circuit Court Judge John Jelderks. Jelderks had heard seemingly countless motions and arguments in Rajneeshee-related cases since the sect's arrival in central Oregon, and he came to Portland for the brief state court hearing with Sheela. The plea agreement called for a term of four-and-a-half years in prison but, under federal parole regulations in effect at the time, Sheela was released from federal custody in December 1988 and was quickly deported to West Germany.

Her release proved to be too speedy. Although the Rajneeshees quickly faded from public consciousness, the investigation wasn't over. In 1990, a new federal indictment accused Sheela and seven others of attempting to kill U.S. attorney Turner. Turner had been a career deputy U.S. attorney before being appointed by President Reagan in 1982 to the top position in the office, which he held for the next eight years. The plot against Turner dated back to the summer of 1985, when Sheela feared the likelihood of federal immigration charges arising from some of several hundred sham marriages she had arranged in order to gain permanent residence for foreign-born Rajneeshees. The plot called for Turner to be lured into helping a young, disguised Rajneeshee woman with a flat tire, whereupon he would be shot. The plan was never carried out, although some of the defendants bought guns and charted Turner's route from his home to the U.S. Courthouse.

Three defendants pleaded guilty to the conspiracy charges. Ten years after the commune's collapse, two more defendants were tried and convicted in the courtroom of U.S. District Court Judge Malcolm Marsh. President Ronald Reagan in 1987 had nominated Marsh to succeed Judge Edward Leavy, who had been promoted to the Ninth Circuit Court of Appeals. Although born in Portland, Marsh spent much of his childhood in McMinnville. After serving in the U.S. Army, he graduated from the

University of Oregon Law School in 1954 and spent thirty years at Salem's largest law firm, Clark, Marsh, Lindauer & McClinton, where he defended product liability and medical malpractice cases. The defendants in the conspiracy to kill Turner remained silent throughout the trial and sentencing hearing, leaving uncontested the government's contentions about the death plot. Sheela and two others, however, were still at large. Sheela remarried and settled in Switzerland, where she was immune from extradition. Rajneesh died in 1990 in India after several unsuccessful attempts to relocate himself with portions of his entourage in other countries. Oregonians quickly forgot about Rajneesh and his band of acolytes after the guru left the state. Turner, the subject of the death plot, gave an inkling of the intensity of the state's feelings when he heard the news of Rajneesh's death in 1990. "No person has ever had a greater effect on Oregonians than Rajneesh," he said, "and that includes such historical figures as Mark Hatfield, Tom McCall and Wayne Morse. As opposed to their efforts on behalf of Oregonians, his was a legacy of crime and corruption, fraud and deceit."[12]

Sheela's final state court appearance was one of the first high-profile cases to be resolved in the new mezzanine courtrooms of the Multnomah County Justice Center, an innovative sixteen-story building completed in 1983 at a cost of $53.5 million. The impressive triangular-tower structure provided a new headquarters for the Portland Police Bureau in its top six stories, a 476-bed high-security jail known as the Multnomah County Detention Center on five floors in the middle, and four courtrooms on a mezzanine. The ground floor included the jail lobby, two eating establishments, and several small shops at street level to help the building blend into the city's urban core. The impetus for the new building came from construction of the Interstate-205 freeway in East Portland, the route of which forced demolition of the county's old Rocky Butte Jail. The federal government paid for the jail portion of the Justice Center, and the city, county, and state governments chipped in to add the additional space and functions.

Portland lawyer Lyndon (Tuck) Wilson coordinated planning and construction of the building, a complex job given the number of government jurisdictions involved. Technically, the building was listed as a condominium in county real estate records because of its unusual joint ownership. Wilson went on to manage construction of the Portland Convention Center and the West Side light rail transit line, tasks that also required careful handling of numerous government agencies.

The new detention center jail became involved in complex litigation as soon as it opened, when a U.S. District Court case involving inmate crowding and conditions at the old Rocky Butte Jail expanded to take in the new jail. Although the old jail had been hailed as being at the forefront of jail construction in the early 1950s, thirty years later the complex of basalt buildings and steel bars seemed more reminiscent of the Middle Ages. Portland lawyer Jerome LaBarre first filed the suit in 1980, on behalf of jail inmates who had objections about crowding, lack of exercise, and other treatment. "It was like the expanding theory of the universe," LaBarre said after the case was finally settled almost a decade later. "Issues were resolved and new ones were added."[13] Along the way, U.S. District Judge James A. Redden held two high-ranking county officials, County Executive Dennis Buchanan and Sheriff Fred Pearce, in contempt for continuing to operate the new jail above its design capacity. Redden imposed no sanctions, however. The case finally settled, with the county agreeing not to house more than the 476 inmates that the detention center was designed to accommodate. As many as 700 inmates had been held in the building soon after its opening. To comply with the ruling, Pearce devised a rating system for determining which inmates posed the greatest threat of violence to the community. When the jail capacity reached its peak, inmates scoring the lowest on the matrix were released and told when to report back to court. County voters in 1987 and 1989 approved funds for the 210-bed medium-security Inverness Jail, located in a warehouse district in outer Northeast Portland, which took some pressure off the detention center. To reduce transport of inmates among buildings, the courts adopted television and telephone technology to allow inmates to make their first court appearances on criminal charges by video from Inverness Jail and the Justice Center courtrooms.

The four courtrooms on the Justice Center mezzanine began handling a high volume of initial court appearances, pleas, and sentencings in routine criminal cases. One courtroom was designed for high-security trials, complete with a jury room, but it was seldom used for that purpose. Defense lawyers feared that the mere location of a trial adjacent to the jail would prejudice jurors against criminal defendants. As a result, the Justice Center was more than a dozen years old before it saw its first jury trial, which was held in 1996 for an assailant who held hostages and wounded two victims with a gun while taking over a downtown stock-brokerage office. Another quirk to the mezzanine courtrooms resulted from a construction budget so tight that it did not allow for separate hallways for judges. Judges using two of the Justice Center courtrooms must enter through the sally port used by jail inmates. Judges quickly learned that leaving the bench too quickly at the close of a hearing could leave them locked into the same tiny cubicle with a defendant they had just sentenced. Designers of the new U.S. District Courthouse made sure that no such event would happen there; the federal project included money for construction of completely separate doors and hallways so the judges would be protected from incidental exposure to the public or litigants.

The legal community celebrated another grand opening not long after the Justice Center's when the Oregon State Bar finished its $1.9 million, 40,000 square foot home in Lake Oswego in December 1986. It was the first time since the creation of the integrated bar in 1935 that its headquarters were not in or near downtown Portland. The bar had about 1,800 members when its first office opened in the Yeon Building in 1935. The office moved to the Pittock Block in 1949 and then to a former insurance office at 808

Southwest Fifteenth Avenue in 1964. The bar's last Portland home was a 15,000-square foot building with the patriotic address of 1776 S.W. Madison Street, which the bar acquired from the Union Oil Company in 1974. By 1982, however, with the bar's membership nearing 10,000, the Madison Street building also had become too small. A long-range planning committee, chaired by Ronald E. Bailey, a partner in Bullivant, Houser, Bailey, Pendergrass & Hoffman, PC, concluded that new construction made more sense than trying to expand the Madison Street building. Completion of the new building took less than six months. There was strong sentiment among lawyers in eastern and southern Oregon for a location that would be more central to all bar members. The Lake Oswego location wasn't much of a compromise, but it knocked a few minutes off the commute for lawyers coming up Interstate-5 from the south. The new site was less convenient for downtown Portland lawyers, but it offered the consolation of free parking.

While administrative changes and new facilities were altering the face of practice at the courthouse, economic pressures and regional opportunities in the 1980s changed the faces of many major Portland law firms. Large firms in Seattle and Portland realized that many of their clients undertook business in Oregon and Washington, and some throughout the Pacific Rim. Schwabe Williamson & Wyatt, the Portland firm whose heritage dated back to Ralph Wilbur in 1892, started a trend by opening a Seattle office in 1981. That office merged twice, in 1986 and 1992, resulting in a Seattle office known as Schwabe Williamson Furguson & Burdell. Miller, Nash, Yerke & Weiner opened a branch in Seattle in 1985, deciding to build its own practice in the Puget Sound region instead of merging with a Seattle firm. The early 1980s were busy ones for the Miller, Nash firm for another reason, too. U.S. National Bank, which finished building a new forty-one story office tower in downtown Portland just as Oregon's economy headed into a recession, wanted its outside counsel to relocate in the new building. The Miller, Nash firm, which had represented rival First Interstate Bank for sixteen years, agreed to switch clients and move from the Georgia-Pacific Building after U.S. Bank's existing counsel, Stoel, Rives, Boley, Fraser & Wyse, decided not to move. Stoel Rives remained in the Georgia-Pacific Building, which was renamed later as the Standard Insurance Center.

While Portland firms were casting their eyes toward Seattle, Seattle firms began expanding into Portland for the same reasons. Preston, Thorgrimson, Shidler, Gates & Ellis, a firm with roots dating back to 1883, opened a Portland office in 1982, followed by Perkins Coie, Seattle's biggest law firm, in 1983, and by Bogle & Gates PLLC in 1986. The Portland branches of these Seattle firms grew slowly but steadily. By 1995, Perkins Coie had thirty lawyers in Portland, making it the city's twelfth-largest firm. Bogle & Gates PLLC and Preston Gates & Ellis LLP were ranked fourteenth and sixteenth in the same compilation, with twenty-six and twenty-five lawyers, respectively.[14] Other large Portland firms soon negotiated mergers with Seattle firms. In 1987, Stoel, Rives, Boley, Fraser & Wyse, whose original founder, Charles H. Carey, began practice in 1883, merged with the Seattle firm of Jones, Grey & Bayley, creating Stoel Rives Boley Jones & Grey and retaining its position as Portland's largest law firm with more than 200 lawyers. Three years later, the Portland firm of Ragen, Tremaine, Kreiger, Schmeer & Neill, which included 57 lawyers, merged with the 175 lawyers in Seattle's Davis, Wright & Jones, creating Davis Wright Tremaine LLP.

The Portland portion of Davis Wright Tremaine was itself the result of the merger of three smaller Portland firms. The eldest was known as Black, Kendall & Tremaine, which dated back to Albert Ridgway in 1911, and which later was headed by George Black, Jr. This firm merged in 1985 with Ragen, Roberts, O'Scannlain, Robertson & Neill, which had come together in 1979 as a combination of Ragen, Roberts & O'Scannlain and Martin, Robertson, Neill, Uffelman & Anderson. The merger created one of the most cumbersome names in Portland history for telephone receptionists—

Ragen, Roberts, Tremaine, Krieger, Schmeer, O'Scannlain & Neill. The Davis Wright Tremaine name simplified matters when it evolved in 1990.

A few months later, the Portland office of Spears, Lubersky, Bledsoe, Anderson, Young & Hilliard, which had grown from the founding law office of William D. Fenton to a staff of 88 lawyers, merged with the 150-lawyer Seattle firm of Lane, Powell, Moss & Miller, creating Lane Powell Spears Lubersky LLP. These new mega-firms took advantage of a revision in the legal ethics code in 1984 that allowed the names of deceased or retired partners to remain in firm names. This ended the long-standing former practice of changing firms's names as deaths and retirements occurred.

In 1995, Stoel Rives Boley Jones & Grey simplified matters further by reducing its formal name to Stoel Rives LLP. Steve Kenyon, the firm's managing partner, said the shortened name reflected common usage in markets served by the firm. It also made life easier for telephone receptionists, who were gently teased in a *New York Times* article about the difficulty of using long firm names. The article said some callers to Stoel Rives Boley Jones & Grey "have been known to hear something akin to 'Story's Bowling Alley.'"[15]

The office that became Davis Wright Tremaine lost one of its senior partners when President Reagan nominated Diarmuid F. O'Scannlain for a seat on the Ninth Circuit Court of Appeals in 1986. O'Scannlain, a native of New York City, had settled in Portland in 1965 after he and his wife, Maura, who had grown up in Tacoma, Washington, decided to reside on the West Coast. After a brief stint in private practice, O'Scannlain served as an assistant state attorney general, where he attended staff meetings of Governor Tom McCall. McCall appointed O'Scannlain as public utility commissioner in 1971, a position he held for nineteen months before McCall named him head of the state Department of Environmental Quality.

Having been exposed to a steady dose of politics in his work, O'Scannlain in 1974 ran for Congress as a Republican. He was defeated in a hard-fought campaign and vowed he would never run for office again. He returned to private practice, where he worked on energy, environmental, and regulatory law, and in 1980 he worked on energy matters for President Ronald Reagan's transition team. When he took the bench in December 1986, O'Scannlain became the eighth Oregon lawyer to be confirmed on the Ninth Circuit Court of Appeals since its creation in 1892.

O'Scannlain, who was known for his quick wit around the office, didn't leave his sense of humor behind when he took the bench. It showed up from time to time in his opinions, such as in the case where his court affirmed the power of federal officials to allow frozen chickens to be labeled as "fresh" under federal administrative law. "We affirm this absurdity by holding, quite properly, that the California legislature is federally pre-empted from requiring that frozen chickens be labeled 'frozen,'" he wrote. "Lewis Carroll's Humpty Dumpty may well be speaking for the federal bureaucracy when he says, 'When I use a word, it means just what I choose it to mean—neither more nor less.' Let us hope that Alice's world can be confined to the Wonderland within the Washington Beltway."[16]

Another Portland lawyer with remarkable writing ability, Phillip Margolin, achieved a national reputation as an author of fictional murder mysteries in the 1980s and 1990s. Margolin, who practiced criminal defense in state and federal court for many years, started writing fiction at home on weekend mornings while his children watched television cartoons. His third novel, *Gone But Not Forgotten*, achieved national best-seller lists in 1993, allowing Margolin to suspend his law practice to write fiction full-time. His first novel, *Heartstone*, originally published with only modest success in 1978, was reissued in 1995 as a paperback and it, too, made the best-seller lists. Margolin's second novel, *The Last Innocent Man*, was made into a television movie filmed at the Multnomah County Courthouse in 1986. Margolin and a few other courthouse denizens played bit parts in the movie. Circuit Court Judge Kimberly C. Frankel's brief appearance introduced her to the repetition and tedium of film-making. "It's going to help my patience," she said after her three-hour filming session. "Almost nothing in the real courtroom takes as long as this takes."[17] One of Margolin's favorite plotting techniques involved plunging his fictional lawyers into quagmires of legal ethics. His success at the bookstores made him the most widely read Portland lawyer-author since C.E.S. Wood and his *Heavenly Discourse*.

While consolidation of major firms was the major trend throughout the Pacific Northwest in the last two decades of the century, some of Portland's largest law offices continued to provide the seeds for new and fast-growing firms. In 1982, Stephen T. Janik, a partner at the Stoel Rives firm who concentrated on land-use law and real estate law, established a partnership with Robb Ball, Jack Orchard, and Ken Novack to form Ball, Janik & Novack. Ball and Orchard had been members of O'Connell, Goyak & Ball, and Novack was president of Summit Properties, a major real estate development firm. Another key member of the new firm was Jacob Tanzer, who resigned from the Oregon Supreme Court that year to enter private practice. Ball Janik LLP was noted originally for its real estate expertise, but the firm quickly spread into other areas, including government relations, taxation, litigation, estate planning, and debtor-creditor law. The firm grew quickly and by 1995 had more than forty lawyers, making it the ninth largest firm in Portland.

Another fast-growing firm sprang to life in 1992, when several litigators from Schwabe Williamson & Wyatt left to form Hoffman, Hart & Wagner. The new firm concentrated on insurance defense litigation. John Hart, who had worked with Bruce Spaulding late in Spaulding's career, had already established himself as one of the state's leading lawyers in representing doctors accused of malpractice. Mark Wagner maintained a rigorous pace in defending a broad range of insurance claims, and Michael D. Hoffman defended doctors and insurance companies in both Oregon and Washington. Within a few years, the new firm had grown to forty lawyers, making it the tenth largest in Portland.

Continuous growth wasn't the rule for all major Portland firms, however. Some firms split apart. The largest such split occurred in 1990 at Lindsay, Hart, Neil & Weigler, the city's fifth largest firm, which traced its roots back to the 1930s and Gunther Krause. Between 1985 and 1990, the fast-growing Lindsay, Hart firm had climbed from sixty lawyers to nearly ninety. Internal divisions arose over issues such compensation, management, differing practice areas, and opposing views on firm growth. In 1990, fourteen lawyers stayed with Lindsay, Hart, Neil & Weigler, and most of the others went with the new firm of Ater Wynne Hewitt Dodson & Skerritt, LLP.

A more gradual implosion occurred at the smaller but older firm of Rankin, McMurry, VavRosky & Doherty, which in 1985 celebrated its centennial as a firm with fifteen lawyers. One of its original founders, Joseph N. Teal, had been an insistent proponent of public docks in Portland, and his ultimate success helped start the firm's long tradition of practice in municipal law. In 1986, Gary P. McMurry, who had lost the 1984 civil defamation trial against the Rajneeshees, won a huge verdict in his second trial against the Church of Scientology. Jurors returned an award of $39 million in punitive damages favoring McMurry's client, but Circuit Court Judge Donald H. Londer declared a mistrial instead of signing a judgment order. McMurry later settled the case for an undisclosed sum, but he also left the firm to work as a sole practitioner. Four other partners left to start smaller firms and, in 1993, Howard N. Rankin, who had been with the office for forty-five years, left to join Ater Wynne Hewitt Dodson & Skerritt, LLP. Rankin, a former Oregon State Bar president and adjunct law professor, said he needed to work with a larger staff in his field of municipal bonds and finance. Peter R. Mersereau and James P. Shannon, the only remaining partners from the Rankin, McMurry, VavRosky & Doherty firm of 1985, continued the firm's tradition in municipal law.

The late 1980s also were a time of transition at the United States

Courthouse. Judge Gus J. Solomon died in 1987 at age eighty, with more than thirty-seven years of service as a federal trial judge, surpassing the prior record of thirty-five years set by the district's first judge, Matthew Deady. The courthouse was renamed in Solomon's honor in 1989. "He stood for things rather basic; for decency, for trustworthiness, for honesty, for telling the truth, for standing up for things that make a difference," Governor Neil Goldschmidt said during the courthouse-renaming ceremony.[18] Solomon used to enjoy telling a joke about how he handled his toughest decisions. "I would ask myself how God would decide it, and then I would rule the same way. Then when I was reversed by the Court of Appeals, I knew where they were coming from."[19]

Solomon was an intimidating figure, however, for many lawyers who appeared in his court. Early in his career as a judge he would give impromptu quizzes at ceremonies admitting lawyers to federal practice, grilling them on federal procedural rules. He thought quickly and reacted quickly, earning a reputation as "fastest gavel in the west."[20] He was merciless on lawyers who wasted time or who were ill-prepared. An incident related by one of Solomon's contemporaries, Chester E. McCarty, was typical of Solomon's attitude toward judicial efficiency. "Each lawyer said he would need three weeks to try his side of the case," McCarty recalled from a visit to Solomon's court. "Gus asked them what the issues were. After they told him, he said, 'We don't need more than two days to try that.' And they didn't."[21]

Another distinguishing trait was Solomon's love of clear language, and his disdain for big words when simpler ones would suffice. "Never dictate anything that calls for clear thinking," he once advised. "Write everything in longhand. If you dictate you are likely to get into the habit of using words of many syllables like 'formulated' or 'constituted.' If you write in longhand you are likely to get into a habit of using words of one syllable like 'made' or 'was.'"[22] Stephen Gillers, who clerked for Solomon in 1968 and went on to become a law professor at New York University, recalled how Solomon's quest for speed slowed down for language. "He and I would spend hours on Saturdays or even Sundays reviewing drafts of opinions, debating structure, word choices, syntax, you name it... Several times we'd spend a half an hour on a single word. I have never since worked with anyone who cares as much about language as he did."[23]

After the addition of Judge Malcolm Marsh to the federal bench in 1987, Oregon's two Republican senators, Mark Hatfield and Bob Packwood, recommended that President George Bush nominate Oregon Supreme Court Justice Robert E. Jones to succeed James M. Burns. Jones had spent nineteen years as a Multnomah County Circuit Court judge and nearly seven years on the state supreme court. He also had strong conservative political credentials as a Republican member of the Oregon House of Representatives early in his career. However, an opinion he wrote in a 1987 Oregon Supreme Court case temporarily stalled his confirmation. The case was *State v. Henry*, in which the state's high court relied on the free-speech provision of the 1859 Oregon Constitution to strike down a state criminal statute against obscenity. Using the state Bill of Rights to provide more expansive personal freedoms than were permitted under the U.S. Constitution was an idea that Oregon political reformer William S. U'Ren had advocated early in the century. But U'Ren's concept never drew much interest on the state supreme court until the appointment of Hans Linde, a former University of Oregon Law School professor, in 1977. Linde contended that state constitutions could give citizens wider freedoms than the federal Bill of Rights if there was evidence to support such conclusions either from the legislative history of a state constitution or from accepted social history of the era. Linde, with support from several other Oregon Supreme Court justices, including, at different times, Jacob Tanzer, Betty Roberts, Berkeley Lent, Edwin Peterson, and Robert E. Jones, found sufficient historical support to expand constitutional liberties beyond federal protection on matters such as free speech, the right to bear arms, and separation of church and state. One of the legal tools they relied on was Charles Carey's *History of the Oregon Constitution*, which remained the single best history of the state constitutional convention chaired by Judge Deady in 1857.

The subtleties of state constitutional interpretation were lost, apparently, on conservative forces in the White House, who feared that Jones was a liberal who used his position as a supreme court justice to create social policy instead of interpreting law. Hatfield and Packwood continued their support for Jones, as did Governor Neil Goldschmidt and Oregon Attorney General Dave Frohnmayer. Conservatives who were concerned about the *Henry* case ultimately referred it to Robert Bork, a conservative legal scholar whose nomination for the U.S. Supreme Court by President Reagan had been torpedoed in a messy confirmation debate between liberals and conservatives in the U.S. Senate. Bork agreed that the *Henry* ruling was not an activist decision and that it was appropriate based on Oregon's legal and historical precedents. Jones ultimately was confirmed and sworn into office in May 1990, more than a year after he was first recommended for the seat.

Multnomah County Circuit Court Judge Ancer L. Haggerty became the next Portland lawyer—and first African-American—to take a seat on the U.S. District Court bench following his nomination by President Bill Clinton in 1993. Haggerty, a former University of Oregon lineman who played on the 1964 Sun Bowl team, served as a Marine in the Vietnam War. He suffered shrapnel wounds and returned from his year-long tour as the most highly decorated African-American officer in the war. After earning his law degree in San Francisco, Haggerty started his career in the Metropolitan Public Defender office, and later became partner at Schwabe Williamson & Wyatt. Governor Neil Goldschmidt appointed him to the Multnomah County District Court in 1989 and a year later elevated him to fill a vacancy in circuit court.

Although Haggerty's tenure was relatively brief as a circuit court judge, he presided over two of the most unusual civil trials of the era. The first put him at the center of a case that brought the largest contingent of security police ever to patrol the Multnomah County Courthouse and included bodyguards for all the participants. Police snipers crouched at the corners of the courthouse roof and eighty officers combed the building in October 1990 when Tom Metzger, a white supremacist leader from southern California, went to trial on civil conspiracy charges arising from the fatal beating of an Ethiopian national, Mulegeta Seraw, by three of Metzger's followers in 1988. The assailants were sent to prison as a result of negotiations on criminal charges. Portland attorney Elden M. Rosenthal, teaming up with Morris Dees of the Southern Poverty Law Center in Montgomery, Alabama, contended that agents sent to Portland by Metzger to stir racial hatred incited the fatal attack. The lawyers hoped that a substantial civil judgment would shut down Metzger's operations, known as the White Aryan Nation.

Police feared that the trial and its heavy national publicity would attract white supremacists to Portland for a showdown. The confrontation never materialized. After a week-long trial, jurors set damages at $12.5 million, and Metzger ultimately lost his home and office when attorneys represent-

Courtesy of *The Oregonian*

Multnomah County Circuit Judge Ancer L. Haggerty, presiding over the Metzger trial.

ing Seraw's estate executed on the judgment. Like other participants in the trial, Judge Haggerty was given 24-hour police protection. He was escorted to and from the courthouse by two bodyguards dressed in fatigues and wielding assault weapons.

Judge Haggerty's second unusual trial arose from the mysterious death of Portland lawyer Cheryl Keeton, an associate in the office of Garvey Schubert & Barer, whose body was found in September 1986 in a van that rolled into Highway 26 just west of Portland. The vehicle was not hit in traffic; Keeton had died of twenty-one blows to her head. Suspicions quickly focused on her estranged husband, Bradly Cunningham, with whom Keeton was engaged in bitter divorce proceedings. However, Washington County investigators contended they couldn't find enough evidence to charge Cunningham. Ultimately, members of Keeton's law firm hired Portland attorney Michael Shinn to bring a civil wrongful death suit against Cunningham, who had moved to Texas where he tried to build a commercial real-estate empire. Cunningham never responded to the suit. Judge Haggerty entered a default judgment in favor of Keeton's estate in 1991 and impaneled a jury to determine damages. Shinn then put on the evidence he had amassed against Cunningham, which suggested that Cunningham had fatally beaten Keeton and then rolled her van down a hill into the freeway, hoping to disguise the cause of death. Jurors set damages at $81.7 million, just as Shinn had recommended. The collapse of Cunningham's real estate ventures left him broke, but Keeton's estate managed to collect a few hundred thousand dollars for the benefit of her children from assets owed to Cunningham from business litigation in Texas.

As a result of circumstantial evidence that Shinn gleaned from divorce proceedings between Keeton and Cunningham, Washington County officials subsequently indicted Cunningham for murder and returned him to Oregon. Cunningham attempted to defend himself at the trial after his court-appointed counsel declared their intention to offer an insanity defense. Cunningham's attempt at defending himself ended with a speedy jury verdict of guilty. He was sentenced to life in prison in 1995, nine years after the homicide.

In addition to adding judges to federal court, Portland lawyers in the 1980s and 1990s sent new faces to Oregon's appellate courts and other elective offices in Salem. Multnomah County Circuit Court Judge R. William Riggs, a ten-year veteran of the court, won election to the Oregon Court of Appeals in 1988; no one signed up to run against him for a seat being vacated by a retiring judge. Given that Riggs had no opposition, Chief Justice Edwin J. Peterson assigned him to begin appellate duties nine months before his elective term began to help the court of appeals with its backlog of cases. Riggs had been appointed to a domestic relations seat on the Multnomah County Circuit Court in 1978 by Governor Bob Straub in an era when domestic relations judges and probate judges were restricted to those duties by state statute. Judge Riggs helped convince the state legislature in 1981 to give full jurisdiction to all circuit court judges, allowing domestic relations judges to handle criminal and other civil matters as well.

Susan P. Graber, a litigation partner in the Stoel Rives firm, followed Judge Riggs to the court of appeals in 1988 by appointment of Governor Neil Goldschmidt. She served only two years before Goldschmidt promoted her to the Oregon Supreme Court, where she became the second woman and the second-youngest judge to serve on the state's top court. Justice Graber quickly became one of the most productive members of the court in the quantity of opinions issued.

Two more Portland lawyers ascended to the Oregon Supreme Court in the seven years after Graber. By coincidence, both had practiced together as partners in the Portland firm of Kulongoski, Durham, Drummonds & Columbo. Robert Durham and Ted Kulongoski both started their legal careers in Lane County, where Kulongoski spent eight years serving as a state legislator while making unsuccessful runs for the United States Senate in

1980 and for governor in 1982. By the mid 1980s, both attorneys had moved to Portland where they represented organized labor. Durham, who also served as a volunteer attorney for the ACLU, was appointed to the Oregon Court of Appeals by Governor Barbara Roberts in 1991 after illness forced the resignation of Judge Jonathan Newman. Roberts promoted Durham to the supreme court three years later to fill a vacancy created by the retirement of Chief Justice Edwin J. Peterson. Kulongoski, meanwhile, served as state insurance commissioner during Governor Neil Goldschmidt's administration and in 1992 won election as Oregon attorney general. In 1996, Kulongoski won election to the Oregon Supreme Court when Justice Richard L. Unis chose not to seek re-election.

Two attorneys who started their careers in the Lindsay, Hart, Neil & Weigler firm, Jack Landau and Rick Haselton, were appointed to the Oregon Court of Appeals by Governor Barbara Roberts in 1993 and 1994, respectively. Landau worked for four years as an assistant state attorney general before his appointment, and Haselton worked as a sole practitioner and in a smaller firm concentrating on appellate law before his appointment. Rex Armstrong, an associate in the Portland office of Bogle & Gates, PLLC, won a seat on the Oregon Court of Appeals at the polls in 1994, filling a seat being vacated by a retirement. Armstrong had been a volunteer for the American Civil Liberties Union and successfully represented the defendant in the *State v. Henry* state constitutional case that slowed confirmation of U.S. District Court Judge Robert E. Jones. Hardy Myers, a Stoel Rives partner who had served three terms as speaker of the Oregon House of Representatives in the early 1980s, was elected state attorney general in 1996.

Portland's growing contingent of women lawyers continued to make professional advances during the closing decades of the century. Elizabeth Perris, a partner in the firm of McMenamin, Joseph, Babener, Greene & Perris, and later in Greene & Perris, became a judge of the U.S. Bankruptcy

Court in Portland in 1984. A frequent speaker and writer on bankruptcy topics, Judge Perris soon began handling many of the largest and most complex bankruptcy cases. Janice M. Stewart, a partner in McEwen, Gisvold, Rankin & Stewart— the firm that dated back to the Cake brothers and 1886—became the first woman U.S. magistrate in Portland in 1993. Stewart succeeded George Juba, who had served as the Oregon's district's first full-time magistrate since 1971. Stewart worked as a litigator in private practice and spent part of her time working with the Oregon State Bar's Professional Liability Fund defending lawyers accused of professional negligence. Stewart joined Magistrates John Jelderks, a former Wasco County Circuit Court judge who had proved his evenhandedness during dozens of hearings involving Rajneeshees in the mid 1980s, and Donald Ashmanskas, a former Washington County Circuit Court judge known for his self-effacing sense of humor as well as his legal knowledge.

Perhaps the most dramatic advancement by a woman occurred in 1994, when Kristine Olson, a former assistant U.S. attorney who had been forced to resign from that office in 1984, was appointed by President Clinton to serve as the first woman U.S. Attorney for Oregon. Olson was a Yale Law School graduate who was hired by U.S. attorney Sid Lezak in 1974. Olson came under fire from Lezak's successor, Charles Turner, for two matters in the early 1980s. One involved grand jury proceedings of a minority activist accused of possessing an illegal machine gun. Olson had doubts about the accuracy of the allegation, and a federal grand jury to which she presented evidence did not return an indictment. In another matter, Olson served on a Portland City Club committee that studied prostitution in Portland and recommended that prostitution be legalized in zoned areas of the city. Turner contended that the report embarrassed the U.S. attorney's office and that Olson had not cleared her participation on the committee in accord with an office policy.

After resigning in 1984, Olson became an assistant dean of the

Northwestern School of Law at Lewis and Clark College, where she cultivated an interest in Native American cultures and laws aimed at preserving Native American artifacts and burial grounds. She was working at the law school when, after Turner's resignation in 1993, she was appointed to succeed him as the head of the thirty-nine lawyer U.S. attorney's office.

The growing strength of women in the profession led to the creation of a new statewide organization, Oregon Women Lawyers, in 1989. Katherine O'Neil, who had worked in two of Portland's older law firms before starting a firm of her own, Graff & O'Neil, chaired a Multnomah Bar Association committee on the status of women in 1987 and 1988. Many women continued meeting at O'Neil's home to discuss barriers facing women and minorities in the profession. The group decided to join with a few county groups of women lawyers scattered around Oregon, such as Queen's Bench in Portland, to form a statewide organization. "We were very diverse in background," O'Neil once said, "but we absolutely coalesced on one point: to have an organization that would advance women and minorities in the legal profession."[24]

As women advanced in the profession, domestic problems led to public trouble for some prominent men. Two Multnomah County judges saw their personal lives became topics for the Judicial Fitness Commission and the Oregon Supreme Court, with markedly different results. The first incident occurred in February 1981, when Multnomah County Circuit Court Judge Phillip J. Roth slapped his wife, Alison Blake Ramsey, who was a deputy district attorney, and used a fish mallet to break the window of a car driven by a man with her. Roth, who won his court seat by election in 1964, often showed a flair for the dramatic. He once had himself rolled into the courtroom on a hospital gurney to preside over a trial while he was suffering from a bad back. He married Ramsey, his second wife, in a courthouse ceremony on Valentine's Day 1978.

The two were estranged, however, when Ramsey was being driven to her apartment by Mark Allen, a prominent Portland theatrical producer-director. Roth's inappropriate behavior led to the issuance of two misdemeanor charges against him, but both were dismissed under civil compromise rules that allow minor charges to be dismissed as a result of negotiated financial settlements. The Judicial Fitness Commission concluded that the matter had no bearing on Roth's judicial performance, but nevertheless recommended a public censure. The supreme court quickly agreed, noting that Roth's conduct included criminal behavior.[25] Roth issued a brief statement afterward: "The judicial robe covers many things and in my case it covers the heart of a man. The episode that produced all this anxiety and turmoil in myself and others was one that was sure to rouse the fury of any man, although I should have found some extraordinary means of patrolling myself."[26] Roth remained on the bench until retiring at the end of his fifth term in January 1995.

The next disciplinary action involving a judge occurred ten years later, and was more bizarre yet. Although it had nothing to do with his judicial performance, the case led to removal from the bench for District Court Judge Robert L. Kirkman. Kirkman had been a temporary judge at various times between 1977 and his formal appointment to the bench in December 1984. The Judicial Fitness Commission learned in 1990 that Kirkman was still legally married to his first wife in 1987 when he took

Courtesy of *The Oregonian*

Multnomah County District Judge Robert L. Kirkman, listening to testimony before the Oregon Judicial Fitness Commission.

out a marriage license stating that he was divorced and married a second woman. In 1984, Kirkman had shown his prospective second wife a phony divorce decree purportedly signed by a Clackamas County judge. Although Kirkman did not admit signing the decree, the Judicial Fitness Commission concluded that he had forged it. The commission unanimously concluded that Kirkman had breached several disciplinary rules, including conduct constituting a crime, although the matter was too old for prosecution. Kirkman resigned from the bench before the Oregon Supreme Court acted on the Judicial Fitness Commission recommendation. The supreme court doubtless would have provided him no relief anyway; it quickly disbarred Kirkman when the bar's disciplinary recommendation arrived at the court in 1992.[27]

Kirkman's disgrace soon was overshadowed by another. It started quietly on an overcast January day in 1991 when Jack Kennedy, a leading domestic relations lawyer and senior partner of the firm of Kennedy, King & Zimmer, strode down a Multnomah County Courthouse hallway with his client, U.S. Senator Bob Packwood, to the courtroom of Circuit Court Judge Kathleen B. Nachtigal. Packwood's divorce from his wife of twenty-four years, Georgie, seemed largely indistinguishable from any other dissolution of a long-term marriage. The only issues before Judge Nachtigal were the amount of alimony to be paid by the senator to support his former wife and a division of the Packwoods' marital assets. The two-day hearing, however, proved to be the first public step in the gradual unraveling of Senator Packwood's career that ultimately ended with his resignation from the Senate on October 1, 1995.

Packwood's divorce had been largely forgotten by late 1992, when he narrowly won a fifth term by defeating U.S. Representative Les AuCoin in a bitter campaign. The *Washington Post* had been prepared to report shortly before the election that it had located several women, including some former Packwood staff members, who said that Packwood had inappropriately kissed them or had continued to urge them to have sex with him despite their rejections. Packwood stalled the *Post's* publication of the revelations until after the election by flatly denying the allegations and then promising to supply the newspaper with additional facts—presumably about the sexual lives of the women making the allegations. After the article was published, Packwood declared that he had a drinking problem, admitted some of the incidents described by the women, and said he couldn't recall others. "I just didn't get it," he said of the women's rejections of his sexual advances. "My actions were just plain wrong and there is not better word for it," he said at a press conference in December 1992.[28]

For almost three more years, however, Packwood's attitude continued to vacillate between apologies to and attacks on the accusers. The Senate Ethics Committee launched an investigation that lasted more than two of those years, and it heard private testimony from seventeen women who complained of Packwood's inappropriate sexual behavior. Packwood had a right to confront the women in public testimony, but he waived that right before the Ethics Committee. Another aspect of the investigation proved to be even more damning. In examining Packwood's divorce case, the committee found that Packwood had solicited or encouraged two businessmen and three lobbyists to offer jobs to Georgie Packwood, which would have had the effect of reducing Packwood's obligation for spousal support after the divorce. In Judge Nachtigal's courtroom, Georgie Packwood had testified about her suspicions that suggestions she received about jobs had been prompted by her estranged husband. As the committee pursued its investigation, it learned that Packwood had kept a personal diary throughout his tenure as a senator. Ultimately, the committee obtained the diaries, which were laden with accounts of Packwood's sexual exploits with staff members, including accounts of sexual intercourse in his Senate offices. Portions of the diaries mentioned his discussions with lobbyists and political friends about finding work for his former wife, and about supposedly "independent" campaign contributions that were being funneled by political action groups into his 1992 re-election campaign. Worse yet for Packwood, the Ethics Committee found some forty instances in which the senator had changed portions of the diaries that he had turned over to the committee.

The accuracy of incidents contained in the diaries was open to question, however. And Packwood attacked his own credibility during his private testimony before the Ethics Committee. "Sometimes it's accurate. Sometimes it's inaccurate," he testified of his diary. "Sometimes it's fact. Sometimes it's fiction. It is not a reliable document."[29] He contended that he had changed portions of the diaries to save embarrassment to others, in case the documents were leaked to the press. The Ethics Committee was not impressed, however. In a six-to-nothing decision that caught Packwood by surprise, the panel in September 1995 called for his removal from office. Committee members characterized the diary-tampering as "reprehensible and contemptuous."[30] Packwood responded aggressively. Although he had waived the right to confront witnesses against him in the private Ethics Committee hearing, he claimed that his rights were violated by never having a chance to cross-examine his accusers. But within days, Packwood realized that trying to hold his job was untenable. If he were removed by vote of the Senate, he would forfeit his pension. If he resigned, however, his pension was protected. And, as testimony had revealed during his divorce case before Judge Nachtigal, Packwood had few assets to his name aside from his healthy federal pension. He resigned effective October 1, 1995.

After waiting the one year required by law, Packwood set up shop in Washington, D.C., as a lobbyist and consultant. Packwood's departure from the Senate mirrored that of John H. Mitchell at the start of the twentieth century: two Portland lawyers ending their lengthy political careers in disgrace in the U.S. Senate.

Construction had already begun on the new federal courthouse that would bear the name of Packwood's long-time Senate associate, Mark

Hatfield, when the Multnomah County auditor, Gary Blackmer, issued a report urging construction of a new Multnomah County courthouse. "The courthouse has been patched, modified, retrofitted and jury-rigged to prolong its service life to more than 80 years," his report said. "After 80 years of intensive use, the facility is functionally and operationally obsolete."[31] It was a sad description for the building championed by Lionel Webster, the building that once was the largest courthouse on the West Coast and one of the largest buildings in Portland. Yet it was accurate. The building, constructed with eleven courtrooms, had been remodeled repeatedly to accommodate a circuit and district court bench of almost three dozen judges. In addition to the problem of shortage of space, modern practices involving security and handling of criminal defendants had turned the Multnomah County Courthouse into a relic. The auditor estimated the costs of building a new courthouse at $120 million.

County commissioners quickly rejected any speedy action on the auditor's recommendation. The amount of money was staggering for a local government hard-pressed to provide jails and other basic services. Someday it would take another Lionel Webster, or perhaps the equivalent of several Lionel Websters, to figure out where and how to build Multnomah County's third courthouse. It would be a challenge for a new century, and perhaps for a new generation of Portland lawyers.

Appendix

Multnomah County District Attorneys

T.S. Brandon, 1855-58
W.G. Lanford, 1858-60
David Douthitt, 1860
William W. Page, 1861
William Carey Johnson, 1862-64
E.W. Hodgkinson, 1864-66
Marion F. Mulkey, 1866-68
Addison C. Gibbs, 1868-72
George H. Durham, 1872-76
Raleigh Stott, 1876-78
John F. Caples, 1878-84
John M. Gearin, 1884-86
Henry McGinn, 1886-90
Thomas G. Stevens, 1890-92
Wilson T. Hume, 1892-96
Charles F. Lord, 1896-98
Russell E. Sewall, 1898-1900
George E. Chamberlain, 1900-02
John M. Manning, 1902-07
George J. Cameron, 1908-12
Walter H. Evans, 1912-21
Stanley Myers, 1921-30
Lotus L. Langley, 1931-34
James R. Bain, 1935-45
Thomas B. Handley, 1945-46
John B. McCourt, 1946-54
William M. Langley, 1955-57
F. Leo Smith, 1957-58
Charles E. Raymond, 1959-62
Chester Pecore, 1962
George Van Hoomissen, 1962-70
Desmond Connall, 1970-72
Harl Haas, 1973-81
Michael D. Schrunk 1981-

U.S. District Court Judges

Matthew Deady, 1859-93
Charles B. Bellinger, 1893-1905
Charles E. Wolverton, 1905-26
Robert S. Bean, 1909-31
John McNary, 1927-36
James Alger Fee, 1931-54
Claude McColloch, 1937-58
Gus J. Solomon, 1949-86
William J. East, 1955-85
John F. Kilkenny, 1959-69
Robert C. Belloni, 1967-
Alfred T. Goodwin, 1969-71
Otto R. Skopil, 1972-
James M. Burns, 1972-
Owen M. Panner, 1980-
James A. Redden, 1980-
Helen J. Frye, 1980-
Edward Leavy, 1984-87
Malcolm F. Marsh, 1987-
Robert E. Jones, 1990-
Michael R. Hogan, 1991-
Ancer L. Haggerty, 1994-
Ann Aiken, 1998-
Garr (Mike) King, 1998-

Full-time U.S. Magistrates

George Juba, 1971-1993
Edward Leavy, 1976-1984
Michael R. Hogan, 1980-91
William M. Dale, 1984-92
John Jelderks, 1991-
Donald Ashmanskas, 1992-
Janice M. Stewart, 1993-

Judges of the Oregon Territorial Supreme Court

Orville Pratt, 1849-53
William Strong, 1850-53
Thomas Nelson, 1851-53
Matthew Deady, 1853-59
Cyrus Olney, 1853-57
George H. Williams, 1853-59

Oregon Supreme Court judges assigned to Multmomah County, 1859 to 1878:

Aaron E. Wait, 1859-60
William W. Page, 1862
Erasmus D. Shattuck, 1862-1867, 1874-78
W.W. Upton, 1867-74

Judges of Multnomah County Circuit Court, created 1878:

Charles Bellinger, 1878-80
Raleigh S. Stott, 1880-84
Seneca Smith, 1884-86
Loyal B. Stearns, 1885-98
Erasmus D. Shattuck, 1886-98
Michael G. Munley, 1892-94
Hartwell Hurley, 1893-95
Thomas A. Stephens, 1894-97
Henry E. McGinn, 1895; 1911-17
Alfred F. Sears Jr., 1896-1907
Melvin George, 1897-1907
John B. Cleland, 1898-1910
Arthur L. Frazer, 1898-1907
Calvin U. Gantenbein, 1906-13; 1915-19
Robert G. Morrow, 1906-31
Earl C. Bronaugh, 1907-10
Thomas O'Day, 1907-09
William N. Gatens, 1909-22
John P. Kavanaugh, 1910, 1922
Thomas J. Cleeton, 1913-14
George Davis, 1913-17
Robert Tucker, 1916-44
George W. Stapleton, 1917-24
George Tazwell, 1919-42
John McCourt, 1919-20
Walter Evans, 1921-31
George Rossman, 1922-27
Louis P. Hewitt, 1923-45
Ashby Dickson, 1925-26; 1943-55
John H. Stevenson, 1925-30
William Ekwall, 1927-35
Jacob Kanzler, 1927-40
Clarence Gilbert, 1929-37
Hall S. Lusk, 1930-37
James Crawford, 1931-62
James P. Stapleton, 1931-41
John P. Winter, 1935-42
Alfred P. Dobson, 1937-59
Donald E. Long, 1937-43; 1949-55; 1957-63
Martin W. Hawkins, 1940-59
Charles Redding, 1941-71
Fred W. Bronn, 1943-46
Walter Tooze, 1943-50
Franklin C. Howell, 1944
James R. Bain, 1945-61
Frank J. Lonergan, 1945-61
MacCormac Snow, 1950-53
Virgil H. Langtry, 1951-69
Eugene K. Oppenheimer, 1951-64
Lowell Mundorff, 1953-55
Carl Dahl, 1955-73
William Dickson, 1955-72
Paul R. Harris, 1955-67
Alfred T. Sulmonetti, 1955-78
John J. Murchison, 1959-85
Arno Denecke, 1959-62
Alan F. Davis, 1959-83
Herbert M. Schwab, 1959-67
Jean L. Lewis, 1961-78
Dean F. Bryson, 1961-70
Richard J. Burke, 1963-79
Chares S. Crookham, 1963-88
Robert E. Jones, 1963-82

Harlow F. Lenon, 1965-81
Phillip J. Roth, 1965-95
James M. Burns, 1966-72
William M. Dale, 1967-84
Pat E. Dooley, 1969-84
Clifford B. Olsen, 1969-88
John C. Beatty Jr., 1970-85
Berkeley Lent, 1971-77
James R. Ellis, 1972-
William S. McLennan, 1972-90
Mercedes F. Deiz, 1973-92
George A. Van Hoomissen, 1973-80
Richard L. Unis, 1977-90
R. William Riggs, 1978-88
Elizabeth Welch, 1978; 1993-
Irving M. Steinbock, 1978-92
Kathleen B. Nachtigal, 1979-93
Robert P. Jones, 1979-
Philip T. Abraham, 1981-95
Stephen B . Herrell, 1981-
Robert W. Redding, 1982-
Lee Johnson, 1983-95
Donald H. Londer, 1983-
William E. Hurley, 1984
Kristena A. LaMar, 1984-
William C. Snouffer, 1984-
Harl H. Haas, 1983-
Stephen L. Gallagher, Jr., 1985-
Stephen S. Walker, 1989-95
Kimberly C. Frankel, 1989-
Linda L. Bergman, 1989-
Ancer L. Haggerty, 1990-94
Nely L. Johnson, 1990-
Joseph F. Ceniceros, 1991-
Garry L. Kahn, 1992-93
Ellen F. Rosenblum, 1993-
Marshall L. Amiton, 1994-
Anna J. Brown, 1994-
Janice M. Wilson, 1994-
Frank L. Bearden, 1995-
Julie E. Frantz, 1996-
William J. Keys, 1996-
Roosevelt Robinson, 1996-

Judges of Multnomah County District Court, created 1913:

J.W. Bell, 1913-1923
Jos. H. Jones, 1913-1920
Arthur C. Dayton, 1913-20
Richard Deich, 1921-28
Mary Jane Spurlin, 1926
Martin W. Hawkins, 1921-27
A.C. Dickson, 1924
J.Hunt Hendrickson, 1928-49
John A. Mears, 1928-40
Fred L. Olson, 1927-50
George N. Woodley, 1930-42
Lowell Mundorff, 1941-43
John Cahalin, 1943-50
Robert Mears, 1944-52
Frank E. Day, 1949-51
Ray D. Shoemaker, 1951-70
John F. Gantenbein, 1951-75
Richard J. Burke, 1951-63
Carl D. Etling, 1961-73
William C. Beers, 1962-82
George Juba, 1969-71
James R. Ellis, 1969-72
Mercedes F. Deiz, 1970-72
William L. Richardson, 1972-76
Aaron Brown Jr., 1972-95
Phillip M. Bagley, 1972-76
Richard L. Unis, 1972-76
Robert W. Redding, 1973-81
Anthony L. Casciato, 1972-92
Philip T. Abraham, 1972-81
Richard L. Unis, 1972-77
Edmund Jordan, 1972-76
Shirley Field, 1972-78
Irving M. Steinbock, 1973-78
Donald H. Londer, 1975-83
Thomas L. Moultrie, 1976-
William C. Snouffer, 1976-78, 1980-84
Edwin York, 1977-1979
Joseph F. Ceniceros, 1978-91
Kimberly C. Frankel, 1978-88

Stephen S. Walker, 1978-88
Frank L. Bearden, 1979-95
Linda L. Bergman, 1980-89
Stephen L. Gallagher Jr., 1981-84
Charles B. Guinasso, 1982-
Nely L. Johnson, 1983-90
Robert L. Kirkman, 1985-91
Marshall L. Amiton, 1985-93
Ancer L. Haggerty, 1989-90
Ellen F. Rosenblum, 1989-93
Elizabeth Welch, 1989-93
Michael H. Marcus, 1990-
Janice Wilson, 1991-94
Roosevelt Robinson, 1991-96
Anna J. Brown, 1992-94
Dale R. Koch, 1993-
David Gernant, 1993-
Douglas G. Beckman, 1993-
Paula J. Kurshner, 1994-
Merri Souther Wyatt, 1994-
Julie E. Frantz, 1994-1996
Michael Loy, 1995-
Jean Kerr Maurer, 1996-
Henry Kantor, 1995-
John A. Wittmayer, 1996-
Clifford L. Freeman, 1996-

Judges of Portland Municipal Court, created 1870:

D. C. Lewis, 1871
O.N. Denny, 1887-75
W.H. Adams, 1878-79
C.B. Stearns, 1880-82
S.A. Moreland, 1883-85
Ralph H. Dement, 1885-88
A. H. Tanner, 1889-90
Charles H. Carey, 1891-94
B. M. Smith, 1894-95
Frank D. Hennessy, 1898-1900
George J. Cameron, 1901; 1905-08
Henry W. Hogue, 1902-04
John Van Zante, 1909
Frank S. Bennett, 1910
George Tazwell, 1911-13
John H. Stevenson, 1914-15; 1917
Arthur Langguth, 1916
George Rossman, 1917-22
William A. Ekwall, 1922-26
F.W. Stadter, 1926-33
M.H. Tomlinson, 1928-33
Donald E. Long, 1934-36
Julius Cohn, 1937-42
Jacob J. Quillan, 1943-61
Alfred E. Wheelock, 1943-44
J.B. Seabrook, 1950
John J. Murchison, 1951-59
Raymond Bagley, 1953-71
Joseph J. Labadie, 1960-69
Edmund A. Jordan, 1964-71
Aaron Brown Jr., 1969-71
Anthony L. Casciato, 1971
Philip T. Abraham, 1964-71
Edmund A. Jordan, 1964-71
Richard L. Unis, 1967-71
William L. Richardson, 1971

U.S. Attorneys, Oregon Territory

Amory Holbrook, 1849-53
B.F. Harding, 1853-54
W.H. Farrar, 1854-59

U.S. Attorneys, District of Oregon

A.J. Thayer, 1859-62
Erasmus D. Shattuck, 1862-63
E.W. McGraw, 1863-65
Joseph N. Dolph, 1865-68
J.C. Cartwright, 1868-72
Addison C. Gibbs, 1872-73
Rufus Mallory, 1873-82
J.F. Watson 1882-86
Lewis L. McArthur, 1886-90
Franklin P. Mays, 1890-93

Daniel R. Murphy, 1894-98
John H. Hall, 1898-1904
Francis J. Heney, 1905
William C. Bristol, 1905-08
John McCourt, 1908-1913
Clarence L. Reames, 1913-18
Bert E. Haney, 1918-19
Lester W. Humphreys, 1919-23
John S. Coke, 1923-25
George Neuner, 1925-33
Carl C. Donaugh, 1933-46
Henry L. Hess, 1946-54
Clarence E. Lucky, 1954-61
Sidney Lezak, 1961-82
Charles Turner, 1982-90
Kristine Olson , 1994-

Portland City Attorneys
(City attorney created by municipal charter amendment, 1864)

Joseph N. Dolph, 1865-66
W.W. Upton, 1867
D. Freidenrich, 1868
W.F. Trimble, 1869
Cyrus A. Dolph, 1870-71
C.A. Ball, 1872
M.F. Mulkey, 1873-74
Addison C. Gibbs, 1875
John M. Gearin, 1876-77
J.C. Moreland, 1878-82
S.W. Rice, 1883
R.M. Dement, 1884
Albert H. Tanner, 1885-87
W.H. Adams, 1887-1892
W.T. Muir, 1892
J.V. Beach, 1893
R.R. Giltner, 1894-95
William M. Cake, 1896-97
J.M. Long, 1898-1901
L.A. McNary, 1902-06
J.P. Kavanaugh, 1907-10
Frank S. Grant, 1911-13; 1921-38
W.P. LaRouche, 1914-20
L.E. Latourette, 1939-47
Alexander G. Brown,1947-68
Marian C. Rushing, 1969-73
Clifford N. Carlsen, 1973
John Osburn, 1974-77
Christopher Thomas, 1977-85
Jeffrey Rodgers, 1985-

Notes

INTRODUCTION

1. *Oregon Journal*, Nov. 29, 1908.
2. William L. Prosser, *Law of Torts*, (St. Paul, Minn.: West Publishing Co., 1971) p. xi.

CHAPTER ONE – *Pioneer Days*

1. *The Oregonian*, 6 July 1993.
2. For this calculation and other incidents of Portland's earliest days, see Eugene Snyder, *Early Portland: Stump-Town Triumphant* (Portland: Binfords & Mort, 1970).
3. For a fuller account of the Cayuse trial, see Ronald B. Lansing, *Juggernaut: The Whitman Massacre Trial* (Pasadena, Calif.: Ninth Judicial Circuit Historical Society, 1993).
4. Donald C. Johnson, "Politics, Personalities and Policies of the Oregon Territorial Supreme Court, 1849-59," *Environmental Law* 4 (1973) p. 11
5. See Sidney Teiser, "First Associate Justice of the Oregon Territory: O. C. Pratt," *Oregon Historical Quarterly* 49 (1948): 171.
6. *History of the Bench and Bar of Oregon* (Portland: Historical Publishing Co, 1910) 35.
7. Ibid., p. 37.
8. Johnson, "Politics, Personalities," p. 64.
9. Harry E. Pratt, "22 Letters of David Logan, Pioneer Oregon Lawyer," *Oregon Historical Quarterly* 44 (1943):258.
10. *The Oregonian*, 28 March 1874.
11. *O'Kelly v. Territory of Oregon*, 1 Or 51 (1853).
12. *Josiah Parrish v. Thomas Stevens*, 1 Or 62 (1853).
13. *Lownsdale v. Parrish*, 62 U.S. 90 (1838).
14. *James P. O. Lownsdale v. City of Portland*, 1 Or 397 (1861).
15. Pratt, "22 Letters of David Logan," 254.
16. Ibid.
17. Ibid.
18. Oregon City *Spectator*, 26 July 1853.
19. *Vandolf v. Otis*, 1 Or 153 (1854).
20. *History of the Bench and Bar of Oregon*, 26.
21. William L. Brewster, *75th Annual Report*, Library Association of Portland, 1938.
22. William J. Hawkins, *The Grand Era of Cast Iron Architecture in Portland*, (Portland: Binfords, 1976) p. 36
23. Ibid.
24. Matthew Deady, *Pharisee Among Philistines: The Diary of Matthew Deady*, 1871-72 (Portland: Oregon Historical Society, 1975), 278.

25. Charles A. Carey, *General History of Oregon* (Portland: Binfords & Mort, 1971), 764.
26. Deady, *Pharisee Among Philistines*, 19.
27. *The Oregonian*, 28 March 1874.
28. *Supreme Court Rules*, 2 Or 15, 1865.

CHAPTER TWO – *Building Legal Institutions*

1. *The Oregonian*, 17 April 1910.
2. *The Oregonian*, 12 Sept. 1883.
3. *Portland Directory* (S. J. McCormick, 1880).
4. *Portland City Directory* (R. L. Polk & Co., 1890).
5. Erskine Wood, *Life of Charles Erskine Scott Wood, a Renaissance Man*, limited edition,1978, p.21.
6. Merrill D. Beal, *"I Will Fight No More Forever"; Chief Joseph and the Nez Perce War*; (Seattle: University of Washington Press, 1963).
7. *The Oregonian*, 23 Sept. 1888.
8. *Holladay v. Holladay*, 13 Or 523 (1886).
9. *The Oregonian*, 27 July 1900.
10. Harry E. Pratt, "22 Letters of David Logan, Pioneer Oregon Lawyer," 44 (1943): 258.
11. *The Oregonian* 27 July 1900.
12. *Pennoyer v. Neff*, 95 U.S. 714 (1877).
13. FC 10085, 17 Fed Cas. 1292.
14. George S. Turnbull, *Governors of Oregon* (Portland: Binfords & Mort, 1959) p. 50.
15. Deady, *Pharisee Among Philistines*, p. xxvi.
16. Nancie Fadeley, "The Early Days," *Oregon State Bar Bulletin*, (Dec. 1990), 5.
17. *In re Leonard's Application to Be Admitted as an Attorney*, 12 Or 93 (1885).
18. Helen F. Althaus, "Women with the West in Their Eyes," *Oregon State Bar Bulletin* (July 1976).
19. Joseph Gaston, *Portland, Oregon: Its History and Builders* (S. J. Clarke Publishing Co., 1911) p. 562
20. Minutes, Multnomah Law Library, 1893.
21. Oregon Bar Association, First Annual Meeting, 1891.
22. Oswald West, "Reminiscences and Anecdotes: Mostly About Politics," *Oregon Historical Quarterly*, 51(1950): 97.
23. Ibid., p. 100.

CHAPTER THREE – *The Progressive Era*

1. Frederick V. Holman, *Roses at Portland, Oregon*, Portland Rose Society, 1902.
2. E. Kimbark MacColl, *The Shaping of a City* (Portland, Georgian Press, 1967) 253.
3. Russell G. Hendricks, "Election of Sen. Chamberlain, the People's Choice," *Oregon Historical Quarterly* 53 (1952): 63.

4. *Kadderly v. City of Portland*, 44 Or 118 (1903).
5. Lincoln Steffens, *Upbuilders*, (Seattle: University of Washington Press, 1968; original publication date, 1909) 326.
6. *Ex Parte Tanner*, 49 Or 31 (1907).
7. *Oregon Journal*, 4 June 1912.
8. *Oregon Voter*, 1 Oct. 1921, p. 29.
9. Ibid.
10. *The Oregonian*, 27 July 1905.
11. Oswald West, "Reminiscences and Anecdotes," *Oregon Historical Quarterly* 51 (1950) 97.
12. *Proceedings, Oregon State Bar Association*, 1910, p. 180.
13. *Muller v. Oregon*, 208 U.S. 412 (1908).
14. Ibid.
15. Ronald Collins, "Looking Back on *Muller v. Oregon, American Bar Association Journal*, 69 (1983): 294.
16. 243 U.S. 629 (1917).
17. 243 U.S. 426 (1917).
18. Lewis J. Paper, *Brandeis* (Inglewood Cliffs, N.J.: Prentice-Hall Inc., 1983) 166.
19. Oregon Bar Association, 19 November 1913.
20. *Oregon Journal*, 24 Dec. 1916.
21. Hall S. Lusk, "On Judge Henry E. McGinn," *Oregon Historical Quarterly*, 73 (1972): 269.
22. *Edwards v.* Mt. *Hood Construction Col*, 64 Or 314 (1913).
23. *Frederick and Nelson v. Bard*, 74 Or 457 (1915).
24. 112 Or 713 (1928).
25. *The Oregonian*, 31 Dec. 1908.
26. *State v. Finch*, 54 Or 482 (1909).
27. *The Oregonian*, 12 Nov. 1909.
28. *Oregon Journal*, 28 Jan. 1914.
29. *The Oregonian*, 14 July 1917.
30. *The Oregonian*, 16 Dec. 1956.
31. Broussard, Albert S., "McCants Stewart: The Struggles of a Black Attorney in the Urban West," *Oregon Historical Quarterly* 89(1988):157.
32. *Oregon Journal*, 13 Sept. 1918.
33. Committee on Legal Education and Admission to the Bar, Oregon Bar Association, 1913.
34. *City of Portland v. Southern Pacific Co.*, 177 F 958 (1910).
35. *Southern Pacific Co. v. City of Portland*, 227 U.S. 559 (1913).
36. *Report of Public Docks*, Portland Chamber of Commerce Transportation Committee, 1910.
37. Ibid.
38. *Oregon Journal*, 29 March 1914.
39. See Cowan, Geoffrey, *The People v. Clarence Darrow* (New York: Times Books,

1993) pp. 132-28, 158-60, 204-08.
40. *City of Portland v. Rave et al.*, unpublished opinion, Municipal Court of Portland, 1916.
41. *Equi v. United States*, 261 F. 53 (1919).
42. Erskine Wood, *Life of Charles Erskine Scott Wood*, 158.

CHAPTER FOUR – *Between the Wars*
1. *U.S. v. Albers*, 263 F 27 (1920).
2. Lawrence J. Saalfield, *Forces of Prejudice in Oregon, 1920-1925* (Portland: Archdiocesan Historical Commission, 1984) 32.
3. *Society of Sisters v. Pierce*, 296 F 928 (1924).
4. 268 U.S. 510 (1925).
5. Oregon Constitution, Article VII (Amended), Section 3.
6. Testimony, U.S. Senate Judiciary Committee, 29 Jan. 1926.
7. *Oregon Journal*, 14 Feb. 1926.
8. *The Oregonian*, 2 April 1926.
9. *The Oregonian*, Oct. 31, 1950.
10. Related to author by Kathleen Beaufait, Salem.
11. *The Oregonian*, 14 April 1961.
12. Pamphlet, *The Truth About Rand*, Multnomah County Library.
13. Portland *Telegram*, 28 Sept. 1928.
14. *State ex rel. Joseph v. Mannix*, 133 Or 329 (1930).
15. *The Oregonian*, 27 May 1930.
16. Ibid.
17. "In Memoriam," *The Advocate*, Northwestern School of Law at Lewis and Clark College, Autumn 1991.
18. *The Oregonian*, 25 March 1979.
19. *The Oregonian*, 31 March 1937.
20. *Oregon Journal*, 16 May 1964.
21. *In re Portland Electric Power Co.*, 97 F Supp 857 (1951).
22. "Fifty Years On," *The Advocate*, Northwestern School of Law at Lewis and Clark College, Fall 1987.
23. Nels Peterson, *An Autobiography*, unpublished.
24. "Fifty Years On," op. cit.
25. *State v. Lessard*, Multnomah County Circuit Court 103670 (1932).
26. *State v. Lessard*, 146 Or 9 (1934).
27. 15 *Oregon Law Review* 1 (year).
28. *The Oregonian*, 11 Oct. 1961.
29. Application form, reprinted in E. Kimbark MacColl, *The Growth of a City* (Portland: Georgian Press 1979), 477.
30. *State v. DeJonge*, 152 Or 315 (1935).
31. 299 U.S. 353 (1937).
32. *Ekwall v. Stadelman*, 146 Or 439 (1934).

33. *The Oregonian*, 6 Feb 1964

CHAPTER FIVE – *Post-War Growth*

1. *Miller, Nash, Wiener, Hager & Carlsen: Its History, 1873-1973*, unpublished, 1986.
2. *U.S. v. Yasui*, 48 F. Supp. 40 (1942).
3. *The Oregonian*, 19 Nov. 1942.
4. Ibid.
5. 320 U.S. 81 (1943).
6. 320 U.S. 115 (1943).
7. *Namba v. McCourt*, 185 Or 579 (1949).
8. Samuel B. Horovitz, "NACCA and its Objectives," NACCA *Law Journal*, 10 (1952): 5.
9. *The Oregonian*, 5 May 1950.
10. *The Oregonian*, 12 June 1950.
11. *U.S. v. 298 Cases, etc., Ski Slide Brand Asparagus*, 88 F. Supp. 450 (1949).
12. Paul Pitzer, "Dorothy McCullough Lee: Success and Failure of Dottie-Do-Good," *Oregon Historical Quarterly*, 91(1990): 5.
13. Ibid.
14. *The Oregonian*, 20 Feb. 1981.
15. *State v. Smith*, Multnomah County Circuit Court C33156 (1955) affidavit of Bruce Spaulding.
16. *The Oregonian*, 2 Nov. 1955.
17. *Oregon Journal*, 28 Oct. 1955.
18. *The Oregonian*, 5 Nov. 1955.
19. *The Oregonian*, 11 Aug 1956.
20. *State v. Langley*, 214 Or. 445 (1958).
21. *In re William Langley*, 217 Or. 45 (1959).
22. *The Oregonian*, 27 June 1957.
23. *The Oregonian*, 28 June 1957.
24. *In re Jolles*, 235 Or. 262 (1963).
25. Multnomah Bar Association, Multnomah Law Library Committee, 1960.
26. Related to author by Herbert Anderson, 1992.
27. *Harrington v. Multnomah County Law Library*, Multnomah County Circuit Court 280830 (1962).
28. *Pioneers*, Advance Sheet, Oregon Women Lawyers (Spring 1990).
29. Helen F. Althaus, speech to Queen's Bench, Portland (July 9, 1991).
30. 302 F. Supp. 899 (1969).
31. *The Oregonian*, 14 Nov. 1970.
32. *The Oregonian*, 2 Dec. 1962.
33. *The Oregonian*, 26 Oct. 1968.
34. Ibid.
35. *Thornton v. Johnson*, 253 Or. 342 (1969).

CHAPTER SIX – A *Decade of Tumult*

1. *Oregon Journal*, 18 Nov. 1969.
2. Ibid.
3. *Tanner v. Lloyd Corp.*, 30 F. Supp. 128 (1970).
4. 446 F. 2d 545 (1971).
5. 407 U.S. 551 (1972).
6. *Lloyd Corp. v. Whiffen*, 315 Or. 500 (1993).
7. *The Oregonian*, 28 May 1979.
8. 254 Or. 584 (1969).
9. Related to author by Philip T. Abraham.
10. *The Oregonian*, 20 Dec. 1969.
11. *The Oregonian*, 14 Feb. 1979.
12. Related to author by Robert McKee.
13. *Oregon Journal*, 22 Nov. 1979.
14. *Stevenson v. Holzman*, 254 Or. 94 (1969).
15. *The Oregonian*, 30 July 1972.
16. *Amalgamated Transit v. Yerkovich*, 24 Or. App. 221 (1976).
17. *The Oregonian*, 8 Feb. 1990.
18. *The Oregonian*, 9 May 1974.
19. 421 U.S. 773 (1975).
20. Courtesy Stoel Rives.
21. *Oregon Bar Association Second Annual Meeting* (1892) 17.
22. 433 U.S. 350 (1976).
23. Oregon Code of Professional Responsibility, DR 2-101.
24. 406 U.S. 404 (1972).
25. *Committee to Retain Judge Tanzer v. Lee*, 270 Or. 215 (1974).
26. 275 Or. 279 (1976).
27. Carl Neil, "Report to the Membership," *Oregon State Bar Bulletin* (March 1978) 6.
28. Mary Collins, "Top Secret: Lawyers on Trial," *Washington Journalism Review*, (Jan./Feb. 1992) 37.
29. *Oregon Journal*, 4 March 1976.
30. "Oregon State Bar Liability Fund First in Nation," *Oregon State Bar Bulletin* (March 1978) 6.
31. *In re Field*, 281 Or. 623 (1978).
32. *The Oregonian*, 20 Sept. 1977.
33. *In re Field*, 281 Or. 623 (1978).
34. Helen F. Althaus, speech to Queen's Bench (July 9, 1991).
35. Suzie Boss, "Our Woman on Wall Street," *Northwest Magazine*, (Sept. 10, 1989).
36. Interview with author.
37. Ibid.
38. *The Oregonian*, 18 Dec. 1981.

39. *The Oregonian*, 22 Oct. 1978.
40. "Sportsman of the Year," *Sports Illustrated* (Jan. 7, 1963) 7.
41. *The Oregonian*, 8 Sept. 1979.
42. *Oregon Journal*, 17 June 1981.
43. *Oregon Journal*, 30 Sept. 1977.

CHAPTER SEVEN – *Toward a New Century*

1. Investiture ceremony, U.S. Courthouse, Portland (March 24, 1980).
2. Ibid.
3. *The Oregonian*, 2 July 1983.
4. Ibid.
5. *Implementing Delay Reduction and Delay Prevention Programs in Urban Trial Courts*, National Center for State Courts (September, 1985).
6. Kristena A. LaMar, letter to Senate Judiciary Committee (March 25, 1993).
7. *The Oregonian*, 30 Dec. 1985.
8. *The Oregonian*, 20 Aug. 1984.
9. *The Oregonian*, 23 Aug. 1984.
10. *The Oregonian*, 24 Aug. 1984.
11. *The Oregonian*, 15 Nov. 1985.
12. *The Oregonian*, 20 Jan. 1990.
13. *The Oregonian*, 5 Sept. 1990.
14. *Business Journal*, 24 Nov. 1995.
15. *New York Times*, 14 Oct. 1994.
16. *National Broiler Council v. Voss*, 44 F. 3d 740 (1994).
17. *The Oregonian*, 3 Dec. 1983.
18. *Proceedings in Renaming the United States Courthouse in Honor of Gus J. Solomon*, 49 F.Sup. LXXX (1989).
19. Heard by the author in Judge Solomon's court, 1986. A similar account from a former law clerk is in *The Oregonian*, Feb. 16, 1987.
20. *The Oregonian*, Dec. 3, 1983.
21. *The Oregonian*, 17 Feb. 1987.
22. *Oregon Journal*, 27 Oct. 1979.
23. 749 F. Supp. XCV (1989).
24. *Advance Sheet*, newsletter of Oregon Women Lawyers (fall 1993).
25. *In re Conduct of Roth*, 293 Or. 179 (1982).
26. *The Oregonian*, 3 June 1982.
27. *In re Conduct of Kirkman*, 313 Or. 131 (1992).
28. *The Oregonian*, 11 Dec. 1992.
29. *The Oregonian*, 8 Sept. 1995.
30. Ibid.
31. *The Oregonian*, 28 Dec. 1995.

Index

ABOUT THE AUTHOR

Fred Leeson has been a daily newspaper journalist in Portland for 26 years, including 13 years writing about Multnomah County courts and Oregon appellate courts. He is a graduate of Stanford University (1971) and the Northwestern School of Law at Lewis & Clark College (1982). He is an inactive member of the Oregon State Bar. His newspaper work has won national honors from the Society of Professional Journalists and the American Bar Association. Leeson resides with his family, two cats and several guitars (none of which he can play as well as he wishes) in Northeast Portland.

COLOPHON

The interior text of *Rose City Justice* is set in Goudy typeface. This type was created by Frederick Goudy for the University of California Press in 1938. It is an inviting and easy to read face. The block display typeface is Broadband and the display script is ITC Isadora. The rosette that appears throughout the book is based on an architectural element. While working on this book, it was a pleasure to look to the grace, tenacity, and thorniness of the rose as a symbol of our city and its legal system.

This book is printed on 70 lb. Valorem Natural, a recycled paper.

Production of this book was achieved through the thoughtful expertise and cooperation of the following:

Editing: Mary Oberst, Oregon State Bar

Book design and layout: Cathy Ingram, Oregon State Bar

Indexing: Jean Brownell

Printing: Publishers Press — Salt Lake City, Utah

Humor: Bob McMenamin